D1567971

Society in Action

Piotr Sztompka

Society in Action

The Theory of
Social Becoming

The University of Chicago Press

HM
101
S989
1991

Piotr Sztompka is professor of sociology at the Jagiellonian
University in Kraków, Poland, and visiting professor in the
Department of Sociology, University of California.

The University of Chicago Press, Chicago 60637
Polity Press, Cambridge
© 1991 by Piotr Sztompka
All rights reserved. Published 1991
Printed in Great Britain
00 99 98 97 96 95 94 93 92 91   5 4 3 2 1

Library of Congress Cataloging-in-Publication Data
Sztompka, Piotr.
    Society in action: the theory of social becoming/Piotr
Sztompka.
        p.   cm.
    Includes bibliographical references and index.
    ISBN 0-226-78815-6
    1. Social change.   2. Social action.   3. Social movements.
I. Title.
HM101.S989   1991
303.4—dc20   91-9542
                                                    CIP

This book is printed on acid-free paper.

3 3001 00765 9385

The being of structures consists in their coming to be, that is, their being 'under construction'.

Jean Piaget, *Structuralism*

Society is never given in a ready-made shape, but is permanently in the process of becoming.

Paweł Rybicki, *The Structure of the Social World*

Contents

vii

Contents

Preface

This book has a double genealogy: intellectual and personal. One lineage is located in the realm of thought. I attempt to provide a reconstruction, synthesis and continuation of two theoretical orientations which, to my mind, represent the most important achievements of the last decade: the theory of agency and historical sociology. But the theoretical discourse is never autonomous and self-contained. It is just the reverse, always an imaginative reinterpretation of reality, as perceived or lived by the theorist. Hence the theory of social becoming presented in this book has also another lineage, perhaps less obvious, since it is hidden at the level of personal experience.

It is an indirect, abstract, theoretically reworked testimony to a most fascinating historical period, a time of deep, fundamental transformations of the social world in the direction of freedom, justice, pluralism and democracy. Of course, I have in mind the social, political and economic changes in the societies of Eastern Europe from the birth of the Solidarity movement in Poland in the summer of 1980 to the last dramatic spasm of totalitarian tyranny in Romania in the winter of 1989. A system which has left such a deep imprint on the destiny of the world in the twentieth century seems to be passing away. Instead of the typical end-of-century malaise and decadence, we are entering the 1990s in a spirit of hope.

Being a Pole and living in Poland, my personal biography could not but cross with this eventful historical process. Not that I claim any credit for the victories attained. I have never been a 'political animal', and my actual contribution has been small. But whether I liked it or not, I was immersed in history-making on a grand scale, witnessing it, observing, feeling,

ix

rejoicing. And I was trying to account for it with the means provided by my professional training, using my theoretical imagination.

The theory of social becoming was probably already born in that summer of 1980 when, together with most Poles, I felt the exhilaration of action, mobilization and struggle, the reawakening of the national soul and its yearning for freedom, the sudden reaffirmation of social bonds and individual dignity, the sudden growth of comradeship and solidarity. Then my idealistic hypotheses about 'people's power' and the strength of social movements (Sztompka 1982) were brutally tested in the winter of 1981, when the darkness of martial law fell over my country, and for several months I could see society virtually paralysed. But before long, the desire for freedom started to stir again. To be sure, the rhythm of events slowed down, but the persistent, underground, less spectacular but eventually more fruitful pressure for change continued for years (Sztompka 1988 [1984]). Matched with a growing affirmation of renewal among political elites and the sudden release of foreign constraints that came with 'the man of the decade' and his *perestroika*, a peaceful Polish revolution took place in the summer of 1989 and established the first non-communist government in Eastern Europe.

While I was engaged in writing this book, the dominoes were falling, and the 'autumn of nations of 1989' became reality. With amazement, excitement and hope I saw the Hungarian communists voting themselves out of power, East Germans dancing on the ruins of the Berlin Wall, the Bulgarians parting with dogmatic orthodoxy and Czechoslovakian crowds carrying the leading dissident to the presidential palace. As I was completing the manuscript, the Romanian people were sacrificing their lives to oust the last Stalinist tyrant.

Writing about social becoming I was witnessing social becoming in its most spectacular and dramatic form. And I saw it work against all the odds. No wonder that there is a strong undercurrent of romantic optimism below all my highly abstract and theoretical argumentation. I am sorry that optimism is so unfashionable in sociological theory nowadays, drowned in postmodernist malaise, disenchantment and boredom. Unashamedly against the current, I wish to bring optimism back into sociology, though not in the form of faith in providence with its admonition 'pray and obey', nor in the form of developmentalist eschatology with its prescription 'wait and see'; nor in the shape of systemic or functionalist models with their directive 'adapt and conform'. The theory of social becoming entails a different message.

It asserts the idea of emancipation, of the betterment of human society, of the realization of fundamental values. At the same time it rejects any hint of the necessity or inevitability of this process. So, while I believe in progress, I do not believe that it occurs automatically. Just the reverse it

Preface

ultimately and entirely depends on what people think, want and do. History can be better: the point is to make it so. Antonio Gramsci, one of my intellectual masters, grasps this peculiarity of the human condition with precision: 'In reality one can "scientifically" foresee only the struggle, which cannot but be the results of opposing forces in continuous movement . . . In reality one can "foresee" to the extent that one acts, to the extent that one applies a voluntary effort and therefore contributes concretely to creating the result "foreseen" ' (Gramsci 1971: 438). He is right: what will happen depends on what people will make happen. The theory of social becoming is founded on this insight and attempts to unravel the mechanism through which human creativeness operates. Hence, its message is fully activistic: 'hope and fight'. My optimism is founded on the fact, that I have seen human masses hoping and fighting – and in reality making history for the better.

There is a tradition of ending prefaces with words of gratitude. My intellectual debts are fully acknowledged in the bibliography. Without the 200 or so authors mentioned there, this study would not have been possible. Probably too it would never have been written without the excitement of these exceptional times. Therefore I dedicate the book to all those courageous, committed and determined men and women who have made recent European history move forward, and given it such an unprecedented pace and such an inspiring direction.

Piotr Sztompka, Kraków

Part I

The background

1

Toward a theoretical reorientation

Finally, a true paradigm?

For two decades now,[1] sociology has been waiting in vain for a new paradigm. A vigorous debate about the theoretical crisis has been engaging the leading theorists, theoretical fashions have come and gone only to give way to a recognition of 'permanent crisis' as the normal condition of the discipline, 'theoretical pluralism' as the normal state of sociological theory, and 'disciplined eclecticism' (Merton 1976: 142) as the only viable policy for theoretically informed research.

But in the shadow of those meta-theoretical disputes, the actual sociological theorizing has been undergoing a slow but persistent reorientation. Underlying the unsuccessful attempts to decree a new paradigm from above, a paradigmatic shift has been occurring *de facto* from below in current theoretical practice. The traditional emphasis on social totalities, systems *sui generis*, with specific structures and characteristic modes of operation – the typical pattern for the masters of the nineteenth century as well as for modern structural-functionalists, system-theorists and orthodox Marxists – has been replaced by a focus on the ultimate constituents of society: human individuals and their actions.

With such a shift of attention, the images of both social structures and individual actors have radically changed. The social structures have lost their unchallenged status as givens determining (constraining or facilitating) human conduct, and have come to be viewed as products, results (mostly unintended, and even unrecognized) of individual efforts. Accordingly the long reign of 'homo sociologicus', viewed as fully shaped,

moulded by structural pressures, faithfully fulfilling structural requirements or playing structurally imposed roles, has given way to the
ascendancy of 'homo creator', an autonomous agent, actively shaping,
moulding his own world, including the structural conditions of his
existence. The dominant themes of structural determinism and 'social
mould theory' have been replaced by the themes of agential determinism
and structural emergence. Clearly the lines of causation assumed to
operate in the social realm have been reversed too: no longer from
structures to action, but rather from action to structures.

Such a radical change of perspective has brought inevitable dangers.
Reaction to the earlier one-sidedness, to the absolutization of structures,
easily led to the opposite bias, the absolutization of actions. The
pendulum swung to the opposite extreme. 'Society' was reduced to the
minutiae of everyday life, individual behaviour, interpersonal contacts,
interactions, transactions, conversations. The new subjectivism of
radical microsociology, ethnomethodology and conversational analysis
seized the theoretical imagination. The result was certainly refreshing,
insightful, often brilliant – but strangely impoverished, again missing
important dimensions of the social world.[2] The 'first sociology' – to
paraphrase Allan Dawe (1970, 1978) – was replaced by the 'second
sociology', but remained equally biased, although in the opposite direction. Sooner or later the need for a 'third sociology' was bound to be felt,
fusing the two instead of counterpoising them, combining the wisdom of
both rather than ignoring half their message.

In fact, the problem of bridging the levels of totalities and individualities, of linking structures and actions, and of overcoming the
macro – micro divide was posed with new vigour in the 1980s, emerging
as the central task of sociological theory for the end of the twentieth
century.[3] Recent times have seen wide-ranging efforts to build a
synthetic, multidimensional theory of society, facing up with modern
tools to the old challenge defined by the founding fathers of the discipline
in their intuitive notions of 'complication supérieure' (Comte), or
'dialectics of social life' (Marx). Two lines of theoretical development
seem to converge on this goal. One is the evolving theory of agency,
another runs under the rather misleading name of 'historical sociology'.[4]
The theory of agency studies the active, constructive side of social life,
but with due recognition of the structural framework within which human
conduct takes place. Historical sociology, by reintroducing the dimension
of time, provides the causal mechanism through which agential creativeness and structural influences actually merge in the flow of the historical
process.

I combine these efforts by introducing a concept of social becoming
which attempts to find the middle ground between the rigid determinism

of reified totalities and the unbridled voluntarism of free individuals.[5] The theory of social becoming (SB) draws from both streams of recent theoretical thought – the theories of agency and of 'historical sociology' – trying to combine their insights in a comprehensive, synthetic model. To the extent that each of those theoretical developments has already had synthetizing ambitions – linking actors and structures, or micro and macro level – the theory of social becoming is attempting a sort of meta-synthesis, or a synthesis of syntheses. Its distinctive feature is the realistic, ontological mood of theorizing. The merging of individuals and social wholes, actors and structures, is achieved neither by mutual reduction, nor by conceptual 'conflation' (Archer 1988: xii–xiv) but rather by positing a third, intermediate domain of reality where the flow of social life in fact occurs. This is the properly social world where individualities and totalities are treated as two sides, analytic aspects distinguishable only in thought. This specific social world is inhabited by a new brand of human being – 'homo historicus' and 'homo creator', rather than 'homo sociologicus'. The creativeness and constraint are treated as two facets, analytic dimensions of human nature, separable only in imagination. The real, not merely conceptual, synthesis of those analytical aspects – individualities and totalities, creativeness and constraints – is due to the historical, processual nature of social life, to its ontological embeddedness in time.

These are the main claims, and this book is a systematic exposition of the theory of social becoming. Whether it can contribute something to the new unfolding lineage of sociological theory remains to be seen.

Using masters

It is characteristic of every new sociological theory that it invokes the classics, the founding fathers of the discipline, as witnesses to the validity of its claims. Linking contemporary debate with the classical roots is a common method of gaining legitimacy for modern statements. But the intellectual links are never simple. Quite often the connection is mediated by later developments within a specific school or orientation; the followers, and even the epigoni, provide the immediate background, with the actual masters standing further back.

The proponents of the 'new theoretical movement' seek their intellectual roots in various directions. Among the theorists of agency, those who move toward a synthesis of action and structure from the structural side invoke the functionalism of Talcott Parsons and his lifelong project of combining the theory of action with the theory of social systems. Indirectly, via Parsons, they reach back to Max Weber and Emile Durkheim, two intellectual forefathers whose opposite approaches seem to be responsible for the internal tension of the Parsonian opus. This line of ancestry is clearly recognizable in modern neo-functionalism (e.g. Alexander 1985, Alexander 1988a). Another group, working under the label of 'morphogenesis', finds its roots in the general systems theory, and indirectly in the organicism of Spencer, Durkheim, Pareto (e.g. Buckley 1967, Archer 1985, 1988).

Quite different traditions inform those contemporary theorists who move toward a synthesis from the side of action. Some resort to the phenomenology of Schutz (indirectly to Husserl), others to linguistic philosophy (Wittgenstein), ethnomethodology (Garfinkel) or symbolic interactionism (Mead and Blumer). This seems characteristic for the so-called 'structuration theory' (Giddens 1984), as well as for 'radical micro-sociology' (Collins 1981). Others find inspiration in exchange theory and network analysis, and indirectly in the distant founding father of both, Georg Simmel. There are also some who start from the theories of collective behaviour, and via them reach back to old French masters, Gabriel Tarde and Gustave Le Bon.

The other branch of the 'new theoretical movement' – historical sociology, finds obvious intellectual affinities with those among the masters who took history most seriously: Max Weber, Alexis de Tocqueville and Karl Marx.[6] At least some part of their work was strongly anchored in detailed historical studies, and the dynamics of social processes always formed their central preoccupation. That is precisely what modern historical sociology is about (Abrams 1982, Skockpol 1984, Lloyd 1988).

Even this brief and partial survey demonstrates clearly what rich and heterogeneous sources underlie two recent attempts to synthesize action and structure: the theories of agency and historical sociology. The idea of social becoming, to be developed in this book, attempts to go one step beyond both of them. Therefore it has to find its own intellectual ancestry. Which of the masters could provide the foundation on which a theory of social becoming should base itself, with its claim to link agency and history, to merge the streams of agential theory and historical sociology, to produce a synthesis of syntheses? My answer is: Karl Marx. Or more precisely, some themes in Marx's work which underlie the important trend within later Marxism known as the 'activist' interpretation. The most eminent exponents of this trend are Antonio Gramsci and Gyorgy Lukács. They will be treated as intellectual conduits linking Marxian theory with the evolving theory of social becoming. Thus I shall consciously use the heuristic inspiration of Marx, Gramsci and Lukács to construct a theory which will inevitably depart a considerable distance from their work, revise it in many ways, and even reject some of its tenets.

In its final effect, SB will be no more 'Marxist' than modern theories of agency are Durkheimian, or those of historical sociology are Weberian.

The justification for the choice of the Marx–Gramsci–Lukács lineage as the foundation for the theory of social becoming can be provided only when our construction is completed. The rest of the book can be read as an extended argument for the fruitfulness of the choice. But even now, at the outset, it is encouraging to note that I am not alone in acknowledging Marx as the fertile heuristic source for the area of theoretical work we are entering. One of the undisputed leaders of the new theory of agency, Anthony Giddens, observes, 'Marx's writings still represent the most significant single fund of ideas that can be drawn upon in seeking to illuminate problems of agency and structure' (1979: 53).

I am going to follow this lead and start on my way with a tentative reconstruction and explication of the ideas of agency and history as they appear, mostly in implicit form, in the works of Marx, especially as read and revised by Gramsci and Lukács. In this attempt there are distinct dangers due to the fact that we are reading Marx with the benefit of theoretical hindsight, in terms of the frameworks derived from later theories, including the most recent developments. Two dangers were noticed long ago by Robert Merton. One was labelled 'adumbrationism', meaning the imputation of insights and ideas absent from the original work and identifying superficially analogous formulations, which at the earlier time had no real impact, and probably an entirely different sense (Merton 1967: 13). Another, opposite, danger was called 'obliteration by incorporation', which meant ignoring or hiding the early sources of recent ideas under claims of novelty or originality (Merton 1979: 9). Both problems are most relevant for the historian of ideas whose goal is the faithful reproduction, the truthful rendering of classical thought. They would trouble me very much indeed if my question were what Marx really meant.

But my focus is different, as in this book I take on a different role, that of a systematic theorist rather than of a historian of sociology. My goal is to contribute, in however small a measure, to the modern theory of social dynamics, and Marx serves only as a source of heuristic insights, intuitions, models and hypotheses, a sort of springboard for contemporary theoretical efforts. His work is used rather than worshipped, applied rather than digested. I believe with Plamenatz that 'The importance of a man's ideas consists in more than what he has succeeded in doing with them; it consists also in what can be done with them' (Plamenatz 1975: 11).

Such an approach justifies, I believe, treating Marx's work in a more liberal, loose and selective manner, as a treasury of models, concepts, hypotheses, from which one can pick out this or that valuable piece. Neither preserving the detailed context – intellectual, situational or personal – in which the ideas were formulated, nor rendering their literal meaning is the main preoccupation. In defence of this loose treatment of Marx's heritage I would cite a contemporary historian of ideas:

> Unless absolute historical accuracy is the only criterion, such strategies are entirely valid. Sometimes it is more appropriate (and useful) to bring into relief the values and implications of 'what X apparently said or suggested' rather than to attempt to divine, through laborious, and often futile, attention to historical detail, 'what X really meant'. The worth of a theory need not be confined to what its author saw in it or intended by it – or to the specific problems that occupied his intention. (Femia 1987: 20)

In this spirit of liberal and inventive reinterpretation I shall face the problem which troubles most students of Marx: namely a certain dualism (or, if you will, internal contradiction) in his thought. Leszek Kołakowski counterposes the 'romantic, Promethean, Faustian theme' with the 'deterministic, rationalist theme' (1976: 418–26). Alvin Gouldner distinguishes 'critical Marxism' and 'academic Marxism' (1972, 1974). Jerzy Topolski speaks about 'determinist' and 'activist' interpretations of historical materialism (1974, 1978). Jeffrey Alexander singles out 'instrumentalist collectivism' as the leitmotif of Marx's systematic, scientific work, and 'voluntarist individualism' as a residual theme appearing in his ideological and political contributions (1982b). Of course the age-old debate about the 'young Marx' versus the 'mature Marx' attempts to correlate such analytical inconsistencies with biographical periods. Then, depending on the philosophical, theoretical or ideological predilections of a given author we find strikingly different portraits of a 'true Marx', and completely divergent developments of Marxism in the hands of followers or epigoni.

I do not take sides in this debate, because I think the debate itself utterly misguided and in urgent need of being superseded. I shall try to show that it ignores, from one side or the other, the inherent duality and multidimensionality of Marxian ontology, and the synthetic, dialectic ambition of his method. In my view, the divergent, opposite interpretations and readings of Marx are not due to inconsistency in the original work, but are instead pre-synthetic, non-dialectic approaches on the part of his followers and interpreters. For the theory of social becoming it will be crucial to recover the synthetic, middle-of-the-road quality of 'activist Marxism'. It will also be important to reconstruct those sides or dimensions of the Marxian image of society which have been relatively neglected in the prevailing interpretations. From the point of view of a theory of social becoming it is obvious that *some* parts of Marx's work will be more relevant than others as a heuristic source; namely those in which he himself focuses on the active, creative side of social and historical processes, on the mechanisms of social emergence, on 'making history', on social and historical 'praxis'. Whatever the place assigned to such themes in Marx's sociological system, whatever the evaluation of their significance (for some they would be 'residual'), no student of Marx can deny that they keep appearing time and again in his writings. They have to regain their rightful place, and this must be done by means of explication and clearer definition.[7] But we have to guard against going too far; neither side of the complex social reality can be separated from the other. Only by reintegrating individuals and their actions with social wholes and historical processes, in the spirit of the original Marxian project, can a strong classical foundation be laid for my own theoretical effort.

I select this synthetic and 'activist' face of Marx, as mediated by the 'activist' tradition in Marxism, as a source of ideas and insights for developing a theory of social becoming. In the process I shall elaborate that tradition, try to enrich it, and thus inevitably go far beyond Marx and Marxism.

Setting the path

The strategy of theory construction is obviously dependent on the assumed image of a theory. To plan our procedure for building SB, we have to imagine what such a theory would look like when worked out. In formal terms, it requires stating what is meant here by a theory, and in substantive terms, what kind of questions are expected to be resolved by its propositions.

After discovering more than twenty different concepts of a theory in sociological literature (Sztompka 1979) – I long ago abandoned any hope of a strict, precise and universally acceptable definition. Instead I propose a loose characterization of this specific product of sociological enterprise by means of two criteria: functional and structural. What purpose does a theory serve and what is its use? It should provide some understanding of social phenomena and processes by unravelling the hidden mechanisms of their operation and the underlying forces moving them. In other words, it should answer questions about how and why they occur. That means providing an explanation, but the explanatory function of a theory is treated much more liberally than in the natural sciences.[8] Any kind of enlightenment concerning the deep mechanisms and forces of social reality qualifies, provided it is empirically grounded and internally coherent.

What is the structure of a sociological theory so conceived? What does it consist of? Usually, one can distinguish three levels of theoretical structure. The topmost is made of meta-theoretical assumptions or presuppositions of various kinds, the most important of which specify basic ontological commitments about the inherent nature of social reality: human individuals, society and history. The intermediate level consists of a conceptual model of social reality (or some relevant fragment of it). It provides an overall picture of the 'anatomy' and 'physiology' of the domain studied, and singles out its components, their interrelations, and some core principle of their movement and change. Finally, at the lower level, the model is filled out with flesh of an empirical, contingent variety. The types of phenomena representing the components of the model are distinguished, the networks of their interlinkages described, the modes of processes embodying the mechanism of the model specified. In other words, concepts are turned into variables, and the model generates empirical hypotheses which can be tested by social reality.

Once formulated, a theory starts to live its own life and enters that same world which it also purports to explain. Conceived by some people, thoroughly learnt, vaguely perceived, or intuitively grasped by others, it becomes a component of social consciousness, helping to shape the shared *Weltanschauung*. Thus, every theory about society has, at least potentially, ideological implications for society. Once it becomes widely accepted, these implications become actual, so that by invading social consciousness, a theory can also influence social practice, not only the thoughts people entertain but also the actions they take. In this way a theory *about* society may produce changes *in* society. It has pragmatic implications, often profound. Both kinds of implications – ideological and pragmatic – should be recognized and taken into account in the process of theory construction. One has to be aware of what follows from the theoretical constructs for the society one is trying to understand.

The foregoing conception of a sociological theory and its place within social reality dictates the course of my efforts in building the theory of social becoming, and therefore determines the outline of this book. In chapter 2 I shall report in more detail on the recent debate about human agency and the historical process. Various strands of the theory of agency and historical sociology will be treated as an intellectual context out of which SB is emerging, which it joins, and to which it attempts to contribute. Then in chapter 3 I shall give an account of the deep 'context of discovery'; the main heuristic source from which I draw both the core concept of social becoming and some other crucial notions of the theory. That is, as I said, the activist interpretation of Marxian thought, as enriched by the insights of Gramsci and Lukács. A sketch of such an interpretation will be given, and then Marx and the Marxists will depart for good, leaving me alone with the job of elaborating further, and occasionally replacing, their hints and guesses.

The main theory construction will occupy Part II of the book, and will proceed in three steps. In chapter 4 the ontological foundations of a theory will be laid, by defining my stand on five ontological questions crucial, I believe, to every sociological theory. They are: What is a social whole? What is a historical process? What is a human individual? What is the human role in society and history? What is the place of discourse about society in society? Faithful to my earlier choice of middle-of-the road, synthetic solutions to 'sociological dilemmas' (Sztompka 1979), I shall present the ontological premises of SB in conscious opposition to the extreme, one-sided assumptions commonly encountered in social and sociological thought.

In chapter 5 the conceptual model of social becoming will be slowly elaborated by means of a series of approximations. I shall start from the simplest, and most abstract image, progressively complicating and enriching it in several steps. To the static matrix of social components (structure, agents, actors, actions etc.) the level of agency and praxis will be added, and integrated with other levels by the introduction of the dimensions of time and history. Then two environments of the sociohistorical process – nature and social consciousness – will appear in the picture. In turn, the ultimate moving force of social operation and historical change will be located in the universal traits of the human condition and human nature. Finally the reflexive impact of the model on its own functioning will be acknowledged and found responsible for the baffling fact that the mechanism of social becoming is changing itself, undergoing 'mutations' in the course of history. As can be seen, the construction of the model is guided by the same leading principle as before, the attempt to supersede one-sided biases and to represent the social world in its true complexity and multidimensionality.

In chapter 6 we leave purely conceptual considerations, and the model is filled out with flesh. All components are studied in their actual, empirical variety. Social structure is analysed into its four dimensions: ideal, normative, interactional and distributive; various types of individual and corporate agents are distinguished; the multiple determinants of agency and praxis are singled out; and the modalities of the whole process of social becoming are described. Finally the possibility of blocked or distorted social becoming is recognized, and various pathologies of social transformation are singled out. In this way the theory is brought down to earth, as close as possible, but not so close as to lose the character of theory.

This ends the exposition of the theory of social becoming and we pass on to its applications and implications. In Part III of book two social processes, relatively well described in the literature of sociology, are selected and subsumed under SB, as special illustrative cases. One process is selected because of its particularly significant agents, the social movements. The theory of social movements as bearers of 'double morphogenesis' (Sztompka 1988) is recalled as the embodiment of the same 'theoretical logic' as SB. Another illustration, the social revolution, is selected because of the particularly salient, spectacular form in which social becoming occurs here. The theory of revolution is taken to account for the peak experience of social becoming, but otherwise it fits neatly into the general framework of SB developed earlier.

At the end of the book, the theory of social becoming will demonstrate its additional, reflexive strength. It will be claimed that SB feeds back into social processes, encouraging and facilitating them in the direction described by the theory. Thus, it appears as a self-fulfilling theory, itself contributing to the becoming of human society. Its emancipatory and creative potential is the final argument for its adoption.

2

The evolving focus on agency

In search of agency

Probably since the dawn of human reflection people have been searching for the ultimate causes of events, the driving motors of phenomena and processes, the forces responsible for their fate. Inevitably it became one of the perennial, leading themes of social thought, and, much later, of sociological science. Here it was defined as the quest for the underlying, moving springs of social dynamics, of the operation and transformation of society. In this long evolution of human thought agency has been gradually *secularized*, *humanized* and *socialized*.

At the beginning it was placed outside the human and social world, in the domain of the supernatural. Whether in the guise of animistic forces, of personified deities, single gods or metaphysical providence, agency was always operating from without, shaping and controlling individual and collective life, human biographies and social histories.

In the next stage agency was brought down to earth, located in the slowly unravelled natural forces of various sorts. Human society, its functioning and change were believed to be direct products of natural determination – physical, chemical, biological, climatic, geographic, even astronomical. Agency became secularized. It was still outside humanity and society, but somehow closer.

It took more time before agential powers were ascribed to human beings, but even then not to all. Agency was located in Great Men: prophets, heroes, leaders, commanders, discoverers, inventors, geniuses. They were the movers of society, but their charismatic capacities were not

13

from society; rather they were inborn, genetically inherited and individually developed. Agency became humanized, but not yet socialized.[1]

With the birth of sociology, a surprising twist occurred; agency became socialized, but once again dehumanized. It was located firmly within society, but society itself was conceived in organic terms, as a self-regulating and self-transforming whole. The metaphor of an organism used to describe the functioning of society, and the metaphor of growth applied to its development, had the same implication: agency was treated as a power inherent in the social organism, its specific, but unanalysed, taken-for-granted *élan vital*, necessarily manifesting itself in social life and in directional, irreversible social change. This 'sociological fallacy' (Nisbet 1970: 203), an original sin of our discipline, haunted sociology for long years. It underlay all varieties of evolutionism and developmentalism, with their visions of history occurring somewhere above human heads; it became one of the most obvious weaknesses of orthodox functionalism, or mechanistic system theory, presenting us with strange models of society without people. The critics demanded, 'Let us get men back in, and let us put some blood in them' (Homans 1971: 113). In due time those calls were heeded, and agency finally found its proper place: in the actions of social agents. It became humanized and socialized at the same time.

Great Men (and, as the times changed, also Great Women) returned as agents, but their exceptional powers were treated as the emanation of society rather than an inborn quality. They were seen as embodiments, crystallizers of structural tensions, social moods, historical traditions. They were the leaders but, paradoxically, only because they knew how to follow those they led. Their conduct took the form of 'representative activities': 'carried out on behalf of people, in order to keep futures open for them' (Dahrendorf 1980: 18), or the exercise of 'meta-power', that is shaping the social contexts for others: 'power to structure social relationships, to alter the "type of game" the actors play, or to manipulate or change the distribution of resources or the conditions governing interaction or exchanges among the actors involved' (Baumgartner et al. 1976: 225).

Then a process parallel to what Weber called 'the routinization of charisma' occurred in sociological thinking about agency. The seat of it moved from personal endowment to social roles, and particularly those roles which have the inherent agential prerogatives of introducing and enforcing changes by regulating the conduct of others (ordering, legislating, taking administrative decisions etc.). The problem of the legitimacy of offices and their incumbents came to the fore.

But perhaps the most crucial step was taken when the idea of agency was extended downward, to all people and not only the elect few, to all social roles and not only powerful offices. It was recognized that obviously *each* individual has only a minuscule say in social change, but at the same time social change must be treated as a composite result of what *all* individuals do. Distributively each has a minor, practically invisible agential power, but collectively they are all-powerful. Two neighbouring disciplines come to the aid of sociology at this theoretical juncture. The metaphor of the market, borrowed from economics, helped the understanding of how the 'invisible hand' emerges out of multiple and dispersed decisions taken by innumerable producers, consumers, buyers and sellers. A metaphor borrowed from linguistics helped understanding of how in everyday practices people create, recreate and change their own society, just as in everyday talk they produce, reproduce and modify their language. The notion of unintended, latent effects of human action (Merton 1976 [1936]) became crucial, as social change was seen as the aggregated, and historically accumulated result of what all societal members do for their own private reasons and egoistic purposes.

At least in modern society, however, it has to be recognized that not all social change is unintended, and not all people act in isolation. The notion of intended, planned change and the concept of collective, group action supplement the image of spontaneous change brought about by individuals. With this agency finds its final embodiment: collective, or corporate agents. Some of them are seen as acting from above, enacting changes. They are governments, legislatures, corporations, administrative bodies etc. Others are acting from below, gradually inducing change. These are associations, pressure groups, lobbies, social movements. Their complex interplay makes up the political stage of contemporary societies, and their intended outcomes cross with the dispersed everyday activities of individual actors, performed on the stage of ordinary life. Thus, individuals and collectivities together shape the twisting course of human history.

We have traced the wanderings of the idea of agency through the labyrinth of social and sociological thought. At the entrance it was entirely superhuman and extrasocial. At the exit it appears as fully human and fully social, in the two forms of *individual actors* and *collective agents*. Recent sociological theory focuses on both, attempting to unravel the secrets of their operation and the mechanisms through which they produce and reproduce social reality. Let us follow this route in more detail.

The background

Paradoxes of human experience

To understand the functioning of agency a good starting point is to consider some fundamental ontological traits of human (i.e. social) existence. The striking feature of the human condition is its dual, contradictory, inherently split character. We are torn between opposing tensions. This is witnessed by common experience as well as in all discursive forms of human consciousness (philosophy, literature, art etc.), which typically emphasize two main oppositions.

One is the opposition of autonomy and constraint (or in other words, freedom and dependence, individuality and participation, uniqueness and membership, subjectivity and reification). All our life we feel the oppressive presence of what Ralf Dahrendorf calls the 'vexatious fact of society', we feel bound by norms, rules, traditions, expectations and requirements, and occassionally hit our heads against the hard wall of social sanctions:

> We obey laws, go to the polls, marry, attend schools and universities, have an occupation, and are members of a church; we look after our children, lift our hats to our superiors, defer to our elders, speak to different people in different tongues, feel that we belong here and are strangers there. We cannot walk a step or speak a sentence without there intervening between us and the world a third element, one that ties us to the world and at the same time mediates between these two concrete abstractions: society. (Dahrendorf 1968: 22–3)

But at the same time we perceive ourselves as persons, unique individuals with identity, integrity, independence, freedom. We profess some level of control over our actions, feel responsible for our decisions, experience pride, guilt and shame. The 'facticity' of the outside world, 'the way in which society is experienced by individuals as a fact-like system, external, given, coercive' clashes with the individual capacity for 'making and re-making it through their own imagination, communication and action' (Abrams 1982: 2). This is a 'two-sided world', 'a world of which we are both the creators and the creatures, both makers and prisoners; a world which our actions construct and a world that powerfully constrains us' (p. 2). This leads to ambivalent, and constantly alternating self-definitions as 'puppet-masters' or 'marionettes': 'It is part and parcel of daily experience to feel both free and enchained, capable of shaping our own future and yet confronted by towering, seemingly impersonal, constraints' (Archer 1988: x).

In modern sociological idiom, this is referred to as the dilemma of structure and action. The emphasis on one or the other aspect of this 'experiential bivalence' (Archer 1988: x) produces two alternative models of society, to be found in various social theories. Those who focus on social constraints, and individual dependence opt for the structural model whose classical archetype is the Durkheimian approach. Those who focus on individual freedom and treat structures as loose and flexible opt for the action-model. This would be close to the Weberian approach.

The second universal human experience has to do with the opposition of persistence and change (or in other words, stability and movement, repetition and novelty). On the one hand we perceive the continuity and 'sameness' of our world, even for long stretches of time. We live in the same houses, walk through the same neighbourhoods, work in the same factories, curse the same governments, look at the same programmes on television. On the other hand we also face – to paraphrase Dahrendorf – the ever-present 'vexatious fact of history'. We follow customs that originated long ago, live in towns planned and built by our ancestors, imagine the future post-industrial civilization, listen to Bach and read Shakespeare, feel a pang of nostalgia remembering our own youth, and an undefined fright in anticipation of our death. From time to time, in those rare moments when history or biography suddenly accelerate, whether because of a social revolution or a personal crisis, we clearly see the movement and transition. Sociologists refer to this duality as the opposition of continuity and transformation. The emphasis on one or the other pole produces the alternative models of society to be found in social theories. Those who treat society as stable, permanent, continuous, opt for the static model; those who focus on change, discontinuity, novelty, opt for the dynamic model.[2]

Those two oppositions – of structure and action, and of continuity and transformation – founded in the ontological dualities of the human world, define the problematic field of sociological theory. They may be treated as two cross-cutting Cartesian axes organizing the area of theoretical work. Before sociological theory was able to raise itself above this maze and recognize both dualities as irreducible, as basic and indispensable traits of society, requiring a multidimensional, synthetic approach, it was vainly pursuing one-sided solutions, splitting the ontological unity of opposites at the conceptual level and producing distorted, inadequate models. Vacillating between the poles of theoretical space, modern sociological theory was in fact replicating in a shorter time-span the whole story of classical sociological theory from the middle of the nineteenth century.

The swing of the theoretical pendulum

For many years after the Second World War, the focus was clearly on the structural side. With 'Durkheim's Problem' taken to its logical limit,

society was seen as a self-regulating system, and individuals as its emanations, representatives, epiphenomena. Structural constraints (system requirements, needs, prerequisites) were treated as determining human
conduct. Fully internalized structural imperatives (values, norms), were
seen as the main human motivations, making people behave in ways
functional for the system. In other words there was a perfect fit between
the structure of the social system and the personality of its components,
human actors. 'The imperialism of the object' (Giddens 1984: 2), of the
reified social wholes, was matched with 'the oversocialized conception of
man' (Wrong 1961), treated as a perfect, obedient replica of the system.
With some important variations, this model was typical for the whole
structural-functional school, dominating Western sociology up to the end
of the 1960s.

In the wake of the critique of structural-functionalism, the pendulum
swung to the opposite extreme. Taking up 'Weber's Problem' and pushing
it to the limit, sociologists moved the focus to the individual side. Human
action instead of social structures becomes the main object of research.
The dissection of its subtle, meaningful, symbolic components, the
analysis of intimate, everyday interactions, the reconstruction of the
processes through which individuals construct their subjective 'life-
worlds' – almost entirely these replace any interest in structures. Sociologists attempt to expose 'the endemic fragility and brittleness of social
reality, its "merely" conversational groundings, its negotiability, perpetual and irreparable *underdetermination*' (Bauman 1989: 129). With
the rise of the 'new humanism', the 'new subjectivism', hermeneutics and
interpretation, we enter the era of 'the imperialism of the subject'
(Giddens 1984: 2). In spite of important differences, this is the common
emphasis of such schools as symbolic interactionism, ethnomethodology,
phenomenological sociology, dramaturgical sociology, radical micro-
sociology etc. The rightful call to bring people back into sociological
theory (Homans 1971) ended, paradoxically in a sociological theory
without society, concerned exclusively with individual people and their
actions.

> Previous emphasis on structurally determined constraints to interaction
> gives way to a new concern with the process in which ostensibly 'solid'
> realities are construed and re-construed in the course of interaction . . . The
> overall outcome of such revisions is a vision of fluid, changeable social
> setting, kept in motion by interaction of plurality of autonomous and
> uncoordinated agents. (Bauman 1989: 142)

A corresponding swing of the pendulum may be observed along the
second axis of theoretical space, from static to dynamic models. Both

narrow empiricism and the 'grand theory' of the functionalist sort, dominating in the fifties and sixties entailed a presentist perspective, a neglect of change, except perhaps for the internal compensatory reactions producing the restoration of the *status quo*. The utopian quality of a social system – as pointed out by numerous critics – was its strange timelessness: 'The system is the same however often we look at it. Children are born and socialized and allocated until they die; new children are born, and the same happens all over again. What a peaceful, what an idyllic world the system is!' (Dahrendorf 1968: 117). This static bias of structural-functional models was not accidental; it was a logical implication of its fundamental idea of consensus, harmony or equilibrium. As long as society was conceived in such terms, there was no way to accommodate immanent, internally generated change.

It is not surprising that the correction of the static bias was started by the conflict theory of society, with its emphasis on dissensus, disequilibrium, strains and tensions. Attacking structural functionalism, one of the earliest critics proclaimed:

> A Galilean reformulation is required; we must realize that all units of social organization are continuously changing unless some force intervenes to arrest this change . . . Moreover, change is ubiquitous not only in time but also in space; that is to say, every part of every society is constantly changing, and it is impossible to distinguish between 'change within' and 'change of', between 'microscopic' and 'macroscopic' change. (Dahrendorf 1968: 126)[3]

The focus on incessant change was also quite congenial for various theories of the 'new subjectivist' block. The area of individual action, everyday conduct, communication, 'discourse' was obviously full of contingency, fragility, fluidity, movement. And most of the symbolic father-figures of this orientation (Mead, Husserl, Wittgenstein, Gadamer) strongly advocated a processual, dynamic perspective. Sociologists embrace 'the image of society in the state of a constant Brownian movement, a society construed ever anew out of the flexible stuff of personal interaction, a society without tough structure or firm developmental tendency' (Bauman 1989: 133). Unfortunately from the valid recognition of change, it was only a small step to the invalid absolutization of change. This step was taken by the fashion of the eighties, the theory of postmodernism, or postmodernist sociology. 'The urge for change became the glorification of change. Change was seen as a value in itself . . . In all cultural forms, change, far from being the tool of modernity for achieving the goal of progress, has become an end in itself . . . There begins a period of no progress and no history, a period of "postculture"' (Mongardini 1990).

19

The background

The simultaneous shift of focus along two axes of problematic space – away from structure toward action and away from continuity toward change – has produced the domination of individualistic and dynamic sociology. What were the reasons for such a complete reorientation? As usual, they are to be sought in two directions. On the one hand, in the purely intellectual area, the internal development of the structural-functional school, or more generally of structural determinism, has led to the paradigm crisis (Kuhn 1970), the exhaustion of further potential for elaboration, the proliferation of insoluble puzzles, and a growing awareness of empirical inadequacy. Critical reaction led to the study of individual conduct and social change. On the other hand, perhaps more importantly, the social and political transformations of the world in the late sixties and seventies, dramatically modified the very subject matter of sociological science. The diagnosis of the new, emerging shape of human society at the end of the twentieth century would lead us far beyond the scope of this book, and certainly exceed my competence. Let me therefore merely venture some general observations.

The oppressive, rigid 'facticity' of structures – political, economic, stratificational – was undermined by the growing activism of the masses, partly as an expression of accumulated grievances and deprivations, partly as a defence against the by-products of expanding modernity (ecological destruction, nuclear threat, moral decay etc.). Mobilization from below took the form of extensive social movements (both 'old', class-based, and 'new', cutting across traditional alliances), and growing aspirations for participation, autonomy, self-management or simply freedom, were strongly articulated in the political process. Even in totalitarian societies people were raising their heads and asserting independence, often successfully initiating the transition to democracy. Sociological theory had to recognize that individuals and their actions did count, and sometimes quite decisively, even against the most repressive structures. At the same time the changes in social consciousness, the prevailing *Weltanschauung*, led to the growing affirmation of much more loose, open, flexible structures. Even though recent revelations about 'the end of history' (Fukuyama 1989) are clearly the case of a perverse, counter-utopian utopia,[4] one point is certainly true: there is a worldwide ideological and political trend toward liberal democracy, with its ideas of pluralism, participation, representation and legitimacy growing in salience and acceptance. Hence, social (economic, political, cultural) structures are seen more and more as liberating rather than repressive, enabling rather than constraining, opening rather than restricting the pool of human options and 'life chances' (Dahrendorf 1979). Sociological theory could not but respond to this spreading climate by affirming individual autonomy and relaxing grip of structures.

The turn away from the idea of an immutable, stable and persistent social system was brought about by the breakdown of postwar prosperity and harmony in the West, even in the sixties. Economic recession, international conflicts, the eruption of ethnic, racial, intergenerational and class antagonisms caught the imagination of the masses. The uncertainties of today encourage idealizations of yesterday as well as dreams about tomorrow – both optimistic and catastrophic. The salience given by the mass-media to 'newsworthy' social and political turmoils occurring even in the most remote regions of the world adds to the feeling that nothing is eternal. People start to perceive their world as changing, sometimes even shaking and collapsing. The new mode of social consciousness, which Giddens describes as 'historicity', spreads out: 'Consciousness of history as a progression of change, rather than as the constant re-enactment of tradition, and the availability of "exemplars" located differentially in time or space for current processes of transformation, basically alter the overall conditions of social reproduction in the contemporary societies' (1979: 222). At the same time, the breakdown of modernizing efforts and acute crises in the underdeveloped countries of the Third World, as well as the ever more obvious failure of planned social transformations in the countries of 'real socialism', put into doubt the developmental schemes typical for neo-evolutionism, theory of modernization or theory of socio-economic formations. Real societies refuse to be squeezed into Procrustean beds; they do not fit the postulated 'stages of growth', or 'phases of modernization', or 'sequences of formations'. The unilinear accounts have to crumble in the face of multidirectional and multidimensional, cross-cutting and overlapping, often haphazard and chaotic episodes of change.[5] 'The theory of change embodied in both the classical theory of social evolution and the contemporary theories of neo-evolutionism and functionalism are singularly without merit when it comes to our understanding of the nature of change, the conditions under which change takes place, and the effects of change upon social behavior' (Nisbet 1969: 270). Under the pressure of changing realities and a growing awareness of change in popular consciousness, sociological theory could not but turn to the study of change. But the momentum of this theoretical reorientation easily carried it beyond reasonable balance, toward the one-sided absolutization of change and complete neglect of persistence and continuation.

Toward a synthetic framework

This brings us to the last decade and 'the new theoretical movement' (Alexander 1988b), marked most clearly by the attempt at theoretical

21

synthesis. More and more sociologists focus on the linkage, rather than the opposed one-sided traditions. Some try to link and reconcile earlier theories, their assumptions, concepts and hypotheses. They work at the meta-theoretical level, since their subject matter is existing theory. Others look straight at the social world and try to grasp its ontological duality, multidimensionality and inherent dialectics. They work at the theoretical level proper, since their subject matter is existing society. Sometimes, both kinds of work are carried out by the same persons. Both attempts are complementary; the reinterpretation and revision of theories adds to the reconceptualization of society, and vice versa.

Of course the winds of the new integrative doctrine were felt much earlier. Occasionally we hear calls for integration, synthesis, the golden mean, or the *via media* from as early as the 1960s, and there are several meta-theoretical efforts in this direction.[6] But apart from meta-theoretical declarations, there are two deeper symptoms of this synthetic persuasion slowly gaining ground in modern sociological theory. One is the almost obsessive theme of 'paradoxes', 'ironies', 'dualisms', or 'dualities' – covered also by the idea of 'dialectics' in its neutral, non-ideological sense. Schneider gives the sweeping overview of this theme. He traces the 'dialectical bias' in the entire history of sociological thought, but concedes that 'dialectical perspectives continue on into contemporary sociology', 'having been involved in some of the most fundamental insights in sociology' (1971: 668–9). Several more concrete concepts which express the dialectic theme are distinguished: unintended consequences, 'heterogony of ends' (displacement of goals), 'cunning of reason', sudden reversals of evolutionary trends, circular processes, paradoxical effects, the coalescence of opposites etc. He ventures a hint that dialectic may well reveal 'some very potent "logic" or "grammar" of social life' (p. 677). If we look at the work of other modern sociologists we shall find good illustrations of Schneider's points. Let us take just two examples.

R. K. Merton has a penchant for uncovering paradoxes in human life. The most familiar of these is perhaps the one situated in the theory of anomie: 'the structure of society and culture, ordinarily thought of as operating to produce patterned behavior in rough accord with social norms could, under designated conditions, operate to produce deviant behavior (both aberrant and nonconforming)' (1964: 231). Elsewhere Merton maintains that 'the very elements which conduce toward efficiency in general produce inefficiency in specific instances' (1968: 254). Another paradox is discovered in bureaucratic structures where 'activities originally conceived as instrumental are transmuted into self-contained practices, lacking further objectives' (pp. 187–8), or more precisely when 'the organizational means become transformed into ends-in-themselves and displace the principal goals of the organization' (1976: 102). In the theory of propaganda we find the famous 'boomerang effect': 'Under certain conditions . . . people respond to propaganda in a fashion opposite to that intended by the author' (Merton and Kendall 1944: 1). The list of paradoxes could be extended.[7]

The same leitmotif pervades Peter M. Blau's work. He focuses on paradoxes, dilemmas, opposing factors: 'There is a dialectic in social life, for it is governed by many contradictory forces' (1964: 336). The main pattern responsible for the incessant dynamics of society is described as follows: 'Although there is a strain toward reciprocity in social relations and a strain toward equilibrium in social structures, the same forces that restore balance or equilibrium in one respect are imbalancing or disequilibrating forces in others, which means that the very processes of adjustment create imbalances requiring further adjustments' (p. 7). I add two examples of the innumerable paradoxes or dilemmas that result: 'The effective achievement of collective goals requires organizations with committed and loyal members, but attachments to organizations preclude the mobility necessary for individuals to safeguard their investments and receive a fair return in turn' (p. 167); 'The very outstanding qualities that make an individual differentially attractive as an associate also raise fears of dependence that inhibit easy sociability and thus make him unattractive as a sociable companion' (p. 316).

The concern with 'dialectics' in all its forms is the first symptom of the implicit pull toward synthesis, toward a multidimensional view of society which would combine opposites, merge levels, resolve dilemmas and reject one-sided biases. Another symptom is the career of certain mediating concepts, which are multidimensional by their very nature, referring neither to human individuals nor to super-individual wholes, but rather conveying some fusion of both levels. In the history of sociology this category of concepts may be illustrated by such ideas as 'représentations collectives' (Durkheim), 'class consciousness' (Marx), 'hegemony' (Gramsci), 'praxis' (Lukács) etc. In modern sociology one may find such fashionable and influential notions as 'habitus' (Bourdieu), 'historicity' (Touraine), 'figurations' (Elias), 'mobilization' (Etzioni), 'anomie' (Merton), 'duality of structure' (Giddens), 'agency' (Archer) – and many others. It is not easy to say what exactly the referents of these concepts are, what kind of objects are described, because clearly they are neither people nor systems. This very difficulty is a signal that the traditional dichotomies of the individual and society, as well as of the social static and social dynamics, are intuitively felt to be insufficient.

It is only recently that the attempts to replace them with new syntheses have come to the fore as the leading preoccupation of theoretical work. Contemporary observers are unanimous: 'Throughout the centers of Western sociology – in Britain and France, in Germany and the United

States – synthetic rather than polemical theorizing now is the order of the day' (Alexander 1988b: 77); 'A wide range of synthetic efforts are under way in contemporary sociological theory . . . The consensus in sociological theory is . . . on the need to create new theories through a variety of synthetic efforts' (Ritzer 1989: 36–7); 'Today we can recognize that theoretical syntheses are emerging, sifting out what is valuable and closing off paths that have proved to be fruitless' (Giddens 1987: viii).

Both dichotomies – rephrased in modern idiom as the oppositions of structure versus action and continuity versus change – inspire theoretical syntheses of their own. One important line of theoretical development is the *theory of agency*, taking up the first opposition (of structure and action) as its main preoccupation. This theory has been evolving for more than two decades, starting with Walter Buckley's early concept of morphogenesis (1967), through Amitai Etzioni's vision of the 'active society' (1968a), Alain Touraine's account of 'self-production of society' (1977), Michel Crozier and Erhard Friedberg's image of 'actors – systems interdependence' (1982), Anthony Giddens's 'structuration theory' (Giddens 1979, 1981, 1984), Tom Burns and Helena Flam's 'rule-systems theory' (1987), up to the new, much enriched variety of 'morphogenetic perspective' in the works of Margaret Archer (Archer 1985, 1986, 1988, 1989).

As a result of this multilinear but to some extent cumulative intellectual trend, social reality began to be seen with a sort of *agential coefficient*. I propose to define this concept, summarizing the legacy of the theories of agency as a set of six ontological assumptions: first, that society is a process, undergoing constant change; second, that change is mostly endogenous, taking the form of self-transformation; third, that the ultimate motor of change is the agential power of human individuals or social collectivities; fourth, that the direction, goals and speed of change are contestable among multiple agents, and become the area of conflict and struggle; fifth, that action occurs in the context of encountered structures, which it shapes in turn, resulting in the dual quality of structures (as both shaping and shaped), and the dual quality of actors (as both producers and products); and sixth, that the interchange of action and structure occurs in time, by means of alternating phases of agential creativeness and structural determination.

The evolving theory of agency has become recognized as the central area of sociological theorizing. It is acknowledged not only by its co-founders who claim that 'The problem of structure and agency has rightly come to be seen as the basic issue in modern social theory' (Archer 1988: ix), but also by more detached observers who are ready to admit that 'the scope and intensity of this search for linkage is without precedent in the history of sociology' (Alexander 1988b: 287), and that it 'promises to be a significant area of theoretical advance for some time to come' (Collins 1986: 1350).

Another line of crucial theoretical development is the so-called 'historical sociology', focusing on the second opposition (of continuity and change). Its modern rise to prominence[8] is associated with the names of such scholars as: Norbert Elias (1978, 1982, 1987), Philip Abrams (1982), Charles Tilly (1981, 1984a), Michael Mann (1986), Theda Skockpol (1979, 1984) and Christopher Lloyd (1988). As the result of an evolving emphasis on the historical dimension, social reality is perceived ever more often with a sort of *historical coefficient*. I propose to use this name for a set of six ontological assumptions emerging as a common foundation of historical sociology.

First, it is assumed that social reality is not a steady state but, rather, a dynamic process: it occurs rather than exists, and is composed of events rather than objects. Time is an immanent, internal factor of social life. What happens, how it happens, why it happens, what results it brings about – all is taken to depend essentially on the time when it happens, the location in the processual sequence, the place in the rhythm of events characteristic for a given process. Not only the properties and traits of phenomena, but also their regularities ('laws') are treated as time-dependent; in various phases of the process different mechanisms of events are held to obtain.

Second, it is claimed that social change is a confluence of multiple processes with various vectors, partly overlapping, partly convergent and partly divergent, mutually supportive or destructive. The state of society is always a concrete intersection of those differentiated, hetergeneous and multidirectional processes.

Third, society itself undergoing change is perceived not as an entity, object or system, but rather as a fluid network of relations, pervaded by tension as well as by harmony, by conflict as well as by cooperation.

Fourth, the sequence of events within each of the social processes is treated as cumulative. Each phase of the process is seen as an accumulated outcome, effect, crystallization, point of arrival of all preceding phases, and at the same time the germ, embedded potential and point of departure for the succeeding process. At each historical moment there opens up a determinate field of opportunities, possibilities and options for the future course of the process, significantly delimited by its whole past course.

Fifth, the social process is seen as constructed, created by human agents – individual or collective – through their actions. Behind every phase of the social process there are people, collectivities, groups, social movements, associations etc. whose actions have brought it about. Every phase of the social process provides a pool of opportunities, resources, facilities – one is tempted to say 'raw materials' – for the people taking

25

up the construction of social reality.

Sixth, it is recognized that people do not construct society 'as they please', but only in given structural conditions inherited from the past, i.e. constructed for them by their predecessors, in their turn similarly structurally constrained. It follows that there is a dialectic of actions and structures, in which actions are partly determined by earlier structures, and later structures are produced by earlier actions.

Of course, any general acceptance of such a standpoint is still far away, and perhaps not easy to attain, but in the pluralist panorama of contemporary sociology, historical orientation is clearly in the ascendant. The scope and rapidity of this paradigmatic shift may be judged by comparing some opinions. In 1968 Erikson despaired: 'Sociology in the US continues to lack historical focus . . . Most of what passes for sociological research in this country is not informed by much in the way of a historical perspective' (1971: 61). Only twelve years later Burke declared: 'Historical sociology is now a stream' (1980: 28). A year later Tilly noted: 'Some of America's best sociological talent is going into historical studies (Tilly 1981: 43), and in 1984 Skockpol proclaimed 'a golden period of historical sociology' and concluded: 'By now . . . a stream of historical sociology has deepened into a river and spread out into eddies running through all parts of the sociological enterprise' (1984: xii, 356).

In the image of social reality as endowed with a 'historical coefficient' the old dichotomies of continuity and change, statics and dynamics, synchrony and diachrony are finally superseded. The historical process is seen as agential accomplishment, the accumulated effect of the productive and reproductive efforts of human actors, undertaken in the structural conditions shaped by earlier generations. As we have seen, the notion of human agency as the ultimate motor of the process appears quite explicitly in the works of historical sociologists. And even though for them it is of residual interest, overshadowed by the problem of stability and transformation, in fact their work also contributes to bridging the gap between action and structure.

The historical coefficient and the agential coefficient prove to be two complementary or even coextensive characterizations of social reality. The legacy of the theory of agency converges with the inheritance of historical sociology in outlining the contours of the new vision of the social world. From different points of departure, theorists of agency as well as historical sociologists are increasingly contributing to the common image of society as a dynamic process in which people, by their own actions, persistently produce and reproduce the context of their existence, the social structures, which later become the initial conditions – constraining or facilitating – for further actions. Social life as a process of structural emergence via actions, and the tension between actions and structures as the ultimate moving force of the process – these ideas form the core of recent theories of agency as well as of historical sociology.

In the following chapters I shall try to take this continuing theoretical evolution further forward, attempting not only to add up but also to integrate, unify and synthesize those two theoretical traditions. The concept of social becoming explicated and advocated later in this book is intended as the link between the two theoretical currents. As they themselves are already synthetic, the theory of social becoming to be proposed here can rightly be treated as a second-order synthesis, a synthesis of syntheses. It aims to link all four poles (or corners) of sociological theoretical space: action with structure, and continuity with change.

3

On the shoulders of Marx

Why Marx?

Authors working within both the traditions which make up 'the new theoretical movement', the theory of agency and historical sociology, differ on many points, but there is striking agreement when it comes to identifying the classical roots of their efforts. Almost without exception, the name of Karl Marx appears among their chosen masters.

Consider some examples. Anthony Giddens, the leading exponent of the theory of agency, introduces the volume summarizing his own idea of 'structuration' with the following remark:

> This book, indeed, might be accurately described as an extended reflection upon a celebrated and oft-quoted phrase to be found in Marx. Marx comments that 'Men (let us immediately say human beings) make history, but not in circumstances of their own choosing'. Well, so they do. But what a diversity of complex problems of social analysis this apparently innocuous pronouncement turns out to disclose! (Giddens 1984: 21)

The authors of another important variant of agential theorizing, Tom Burns and Helena Flam admit: 'Rule system theory draws on the rich theoretical traditions of Marx and Weber' (1987: xii). Quite similar acknowledgements come from leading representatives of historical sociology. Norbert Elias, a contemporary classic himself, points to Marx as the forerunner of the historical approach: 'Marx tried to throw into better relief what he regarded as the most urgent problem of his time, by

28

presenting his own time as a stage between the past and possible futures' (1987: 223). Christopher Lloyd, analysing the methodological bases of historical sociology admits: 'By far the most important influences on the members of this tradition are Marx and Weber' (1988: 280), and adds: 'The idea of structuration comes ultimately from Marx' (p. 283). Another historical sociologist, Philip Abrams, identifies the core of Marx's position as stressing 'the two-sidedness of history – the ways in which history is at one and the same time a product of both the chosen action of individuals and the forceful constraint of social structure' (1982: 34). Additional testimony comes from Roy Bhaskar, who looks at the debate about the 'transformational model of society' from the heights of pure philosophy and yet notices the same fact: 'The principal historical forebears of the model, as I understand it, are Aristotle and Marx' (1986: 122).

Of course that does not mean that modern agential theorists or historical sociologists are Marxists in any meaningful sense of this much abused word. Most of them are as distant as can be from ideological or political allegiance to Marx's doctrine, but they are open enough to recognize the themes and emphases characteristic for their theory as already present in Marx's work, and therefore are ready to treat it as a fertile source of heuristic intuitions.[1] They treat Marx seriously and critically – not on their knees but with their brains – as the founder of an intellectual tradition which cannot be ignored, even though in the hands of later Marxists it often produced a caricature of its initial premises, and in the hands of Marxist politicians became the betrayal of its founding values.

I have always shared this attitude.[2] But there is a special reason for turning to Marx when one attempts a synthetic task of the sort I have set myself in constructing a theory of social becoming. Marx's theory may plausibly be considered the paradigmatic case of early synthetic, multidimensional theorizing. This is what the elusive term 'dialectics' primarily means for me. Consider the obsessive and perennial debate about the 'two Marxes'. If we take a bird's-eye view of the developments in Marxism after Marx, the persistent theme is division. There are clearly divergent and even opposed lines of theoretical development originating in Marx's work. As Steven Lukes puts it: 'Marxist tradition is no monolithic unity but a contested terrain' (1985: 2).

For our concern, one variety of the split is particularly important. It divides two lineages of Marxist theory, which may be given brief names drawn from contemporary debate. One will be called 'Marxist historicism'[3] – the term alluding to the devastating critique by Karl Popper (1966 [1945], 1964 [1957]); the other will be called 'Marxist humanism', after the brilliant exposition of Erich Fromm (1968 [1956]). The former sometimes also known as 'structuralist Marxism' (and by its critics called

29

'orthodox' or 'vulgar') focuses on the themes paramount in Marx's mature work (and particularly *Capital* [1863] and *The Critique of Political Economy* [1859]). It develops an image of society and history based on the assumptions of determinism, fatalism and finalism – as a super-individual system and mechanistically evolving process. The latter, sometimes also known as 'individualist Marxism', draws inspiration from the themes typical for Marx's early opus (particularly *The Philosophical and Economic Manuscripts* [1844]). It emphasizes the creativeness of individuals, with the resulting indeterminacy, voluntarism and contingency of the social world, which is seen as wholly reducible to individual actions. Up to now, those opposite readings of Marx have appeared time and again in sociological literature. Let me mention two examples from the 1980s.

It is not by accident that in his magisterial reappraisal of classical theory, Jeffrey Alexander squeezes Marx into one volume together with Durkheim. He clearly perceives the core message and internal developmental pattern of Marx's theory to be collectivist and 'historicist' (in the Popperian sense). Even in the youthful period – Alexander claims – 'Marx is, from the very beginning, anti-individualist' (1982a: 16). Also, 'because he retains his commitment to collective order, Marx must move, ineluctably, toward an antivoluntarist position' (p. 23). This is of course, even more true of his later work. There 'individual or group action is pictured, at every point, as the result of such conditional pressure, not as its creator' (p. 59). In effect, 'instead of maintaining a respect for the individual actor, Marx has actually eliminated individual intention from his theoretical scheme' (ibid.: 210), and 'dispenses with the very notion of an autonomous self' (p. 86).[4]

Tucker argues precisely in the opposite direction. 'Marx's methodology is characteristically individualist', he claims (1980: 11). And this is because the Marxian image of society and history is focused on individuals, rather than holistic entities: 'Marx conceives of the driving forces of history as resulting from the actions of individuals, their choices and goals, and not as something metaphysical' (ibid.: 42); 'he cannot, without contradicting himself, allow for any causal agency other than acting individuals' (p. 32). Social wholes do not have a reified quality: 'Marx tells us, we must resist the temptation to treat structures as an objectively given, unchanging reality, and we must retain the sense that they are constituted by relationships between persons, which are subject to change' (p. 42). Similarly, history is not predetermined of finalistic:

What Marx emphasizes is that history has no meaning (in the sense that we cannot say that there are designs or purposes at work which are independent of human actors), but that the impact of institutional practices on individuals is something which can best be understood as resulting from the unintended consequences of those choices that the majority of individuals are likely to make in any given set of circumstances. (p. 30).

Thus we find here a reading emphasizing opposite traits of the Marxian image to those picked out by Alexander.[5] Marx appears as a humanist rather than a 'historicist'.

I have no intention of entering this debate. Here I am merely making the meta-theoretical point about continuations and interpretations of Marx. As we have seen, they are mutually opposite, inconsistent and even contradictory. Marx is invoked as an intellectual source by the proponents of strikingly different views. The explanation of this fact may follow two tracks. Most students (and particularly the critics) of Marx usually trace it to the alleged internal inconsistency of his theory. The sources of later divergences are sought in the antinomies of Marx's original work (either as the opposition of biographical periods, with 'mature Marx' negating 'young Marx', or – even less excusable – as the opposition of themes haunting him all his life, running parallel through all his theories). This may be called 'the hostile explanation'.

But there is also the alternative 'sympathetic explanation', which I would like to put forward. It gives Marx the benefit of the doubt. Is it not possible that the divergence of continuations and interpretations results from the errors of followers and interpreters, rather than from faults in Marx? Is it not possible that their one-sided emphases are due to the myopia of pre-synthetic thinking, whereas Marx was a forerunner of the synthetic, multidimensional view of society?[6] Is it not the case that later theorists pick out either 'historicist' or 'humanist' themes from Marx's work, because they treat the focus on structures and processes and the focus on individuals and actions as mutually exclusive alternatives, whereas Marx himself treated them as complementary, embracing two sides of the same complex reality? Thus, what the 'hostile explanation' would call incoherence, and treat as Marxian weakness, the 'sympathetic interpretation' calls 'dialectics' and treats as his major strength, in fact pre-dating the much later evolution of sociological theory toward a multi-dimensional, many-sided image of the social world.

The latter view finds some corroboration in a certain peculiarity of the Marxian method. He manifests a remarkable aversion to one-sided, extreme points of view, and persistently applies the strategy of dialectic overcoming (*Aufhebung*) inherited from Hegel. This is noticed by Rubinstein: 'Throughout he emphasizes the conceptual interdependence of factors that other theorists consider to be discrete' (1981: 122). In similar vein Lukács suggests that 'it is of the essence of dialectical method that concepts which are false in their abstract one-sidedness are later transcended' (1971: xlvi). Gramsci believed that 'it is legitimate for

31

Marxism to use other forms of thought but these must be digested and synthesized at a higher level of development' (Femia 1987: 72). Marx used this synthesizing approach *par excellence* long before modern sociology had moved toward synthetic attempts to link structure and action, continuity and change, consciousness and 'being', spontaneity and planning, theory and practice. Is it not likely that, using a dialectical (synthesizing) method, he arrived at a dialectic (synthetic) image of society? But the times were not yet ripe for this effort, the intellectual climate was not ready for synthesis; instead it was pervaded with positivistic, analytical methodology. The pre-synthetic, non-dialectic mentality of Marx's followers led to the petrification of two opposite streams of Marxist scholarship, uncritically and one-sidedly extracting selected themes from his multidimensional theory. This long tradition, marked by a succession of great names, still entraps contemporary readers and interpreters of Marx.

But there is one lineage in the post-Marxian tradition which has never ignored or neglected the original multidimensionality of Marxian thought. Here we clearly find the 'third way'; the interpretation of Marx contrary to both the 'historicist' and the 'individualist' reading. It is sometimes called 'activist Marxism'.[7] Its most famous proponents are Antonio Gramsci and Gyorgy Lukács. This is the tradition which from the beginning attempts to bridge the gap between social totalities and individual action at the level of 'praxis', and to mesh continuity with change in the context of historical process. For the attempted synthesis of these four problematic poles of contemporary social theory in the theory of social becoming, 'activist Marxism' suggests itself as a natural source of heuristic insights. In a sense, it was already going beyond both agential theory and historical sociology, merging them together, long before those brands of social theory appeared on the stage, and long before SB undertook the task of reuniting them.

Levels, aspects and modalities

Taking a bird's-eye view of the Marxian heritage, one is immediately faced with the extreme heterogeneity of his contributions. The duality of levels is substantive in nature, and has to do with the various objects on which Marx focuses his attention. On the one hand, there is the level of individuality, where human individuals and their conduct are conceptualized by means of abstract-theoretical categories of 'species being' and 'labour'.[8] This focus dominates in Marx's early, Hegelian period, in the *Economic and Philosophical Manuscripts* [1844], *Theses on Feuerbach* [1845], *The Holy Family* [1845], *The German Ideology* [1846]. It is here that we shall find the two significant and complementary theories of human nature (or 'species-being') and of alienation. On the other hand, there is the level of totality, where social wholes and their movements are conceptualized, by means of abstract-theoretical categories, as structures and transformations.[9] This focus dominates in Marx's mature, 'scientific' period, in *The Communist Manifesto* [1848], the *Grundrisse* [1859] and *Capital* [1863–94]. It is here that we shall find another pair of complementary theories, those of socio-economic formation and of class structure.

Cross-cutting with the duality of levels, there is the duality of aspects, points of view from which both social wholes and human individuals are approached. Sometimes Marx focuses on their functioning, their internal operation. Large parts of *Capital* or the *Grundrisse* deal with the economic mechanisms (internal functioning) of capitalist society, and in various parts of the *Philosophical and Economic Manuscripts* we shall find ample disussion of how human action (particularly labour) is conducted. But in other places Marx is primarily concerned with development rather than functioning, the directional transformation of one type of society into another, as well as the permanent evolution of individual human endowment. Look for example through the pages of *The German Ideology*, or *The Communist Manifesto*, or the *Contribution to the Critique of Political Economy*. Hence we may speak of the opposition of the static (synchronic) and dynamic (diachronic) aspects.[10]

Finally there is the third duality. It has to do with the modalities on which Marx focuses. Sometimes he is speaking about potentialities inherent in societies or individuals, tensions or contradictions, capacities or 'powers', which open up the possibility of particular modes of functioning or specific direction of development, but need not necessarily be realized. For instance social conflict is seen as a potentiality for change, but it may be suppressed instead; creativeness is seen as a potentiality for production, but it may be blocked or deflected into non-productive expression. In other places Marx addresses the actualities, concrete ways in which potentialities become realized, e.g. concrete stages of development, concrete forms of labour etc.[11]

To see how Marx ultimately overcomes the analytical division of these levels, aspects and modalities, raising bridges between them or merging them together, we have to reconstruct the building blocks for his synthesis: the image of human individuals and the model of social wholes.

The portrait of a human actor

The ultimate components, the basic ontological substratum of society, are humans. This is a platitude, which Marx certainly accepts, together with

33

most social thinkers, as the point of departure for social theory.[12] 'The premises from which we begin – he says – are the real individuals, their activity and the material conditions under which they live, both those they found already existing and those produced by their activity. These premises can thus be verified in a purely empirical way' (in McLellan 1971: 127–8). To put it simply: 'Because he is of a corporeal nature man must produce in order to live' (Rubinstein 1981: 107).

But common sense ends here, and the concept of an individual is expressed in a highly original way. First of all it is not substantive but relational (contextual). Human nature is not characterized by means of a constant set of universal properties, but rather by a specifically human relationship to the environment, a way of relating people to the social and natural context in which they exist. It is a derivative of the network of those relationships to society and to nature in which a human individual is enmeshed. Those exclusively human ways of relating oneself to the environment are universal and constant, but of course they may vary in their concrete forms and produce historical and cultural diversity. Relational aspects of human nature are universal, substantive aspects – historical, and idiosyncratic. One of the messages carried by the sixth of Marx's famous *Theses on Feuerbach* is, I presume, immediately relevant here: 'The human essence is no abstraction inherent in each single individual. In its reality it is the ensemble of the social relations' (Marx and Engels 1968: 29).[13] A contemporary commentator reads this thesis: 'Marx's point, of course, was that human nature is not a property which simply inhabits man, such as the egoism of the "economic man", but rather is a relation between men' (Swingewood 1975: 95). Thus a human individual appears as a nodal point, a knot in the wider network of social relationships. This social location – and the consequent fact of social moulding of individuals, as well as the reciprocal impact of individuals on the context of their social life – is a universal property of the human condition, whereas the typical combinations of relational networks vary historically, and idiosyncratic bundles of such relations vary individually.

There are two kinds of relation by means of which Marx defines human nature. To facilitate further discussion I shall call them *participation* and *creation*. Characterizing the first, Marx focuses on human relations with other people ('social relations' in the strict sense). But it could be extended, without violating Marxian meaning, to relations with nature, participation, harmonious belonging to the natural world. Conversely, characterizing the second kind of relation, creation, Marx focuses almost exclusively on human relations to nature. But again, it could be extended to attitudes toward other people and social objects, meaning for example the urge to change, educate, convince others, to reform social organizations, or to construct new groups etc. Thus, participation and creation

34

can manifest themselves with respect to both contexts of human life: social (other people) and natural (objects).

Because of Marx's emphasis on the relation of participation, his concept of human nature is not psychological but sociological. It is a common misunderstanding that focusing on an individual inevitably implies a psychological perspective. Agreeing with Tucker that 'no other major writer has displayed such a lack of curiosity about the psychological dimensions of social life' (1980: 22), one should not draw the mistaken conclusion that Marx neglected the study of individuals. An individual can be seen from various points of view. For a psychologist, the individual *per se* is the crucial subject matter, and the focus is on the functioning of the mind or personality in its cognitive, emotional, volitional, motivational, attitudinal or other aspects. For sociologist, the crucial subject matter is composed of specific super-individual or inter-individual objects: interactions, social relations, social collectivities, communities, groups, societies etc.

The sociological perspective applied to *any* phenomenon comes down to perceiving that phenomenon in the context of such specific super-individual or inter-individual wholes, as an element in them or at least as related to them in patterned ways. Therefore the individual is a subject matter relevant to sociology only in so far as she/he is implicated in some wider social fabric. From the sociological perspective an individual will therefore be seen not as a fully-fledged person (with specific, unique internal psychological make-up), but rather as an abstract, one-dimensional 'slice' of a person: as (a) an actor in a social action directed toward other people or oriented by their reactions; (b) a partner in social interaction; (c) a participant in the social relationship; (d) a member of a social collectivity or a group; (e) the incumbent of a social position; (f) the performer of a social role. For sociology, the issue of human nature concerns the characteristics of a person in his/her partial capacities as actor, partner, participant, member, incumbent or performer, and in those capacities only.

The direct proof that Marx was studying human individuals from a sociological perspective may be found in his numerous declarations that people (capitalists, proletarians) interest him only as representatives of social classes (members of specifically defined groups), as embodiments of economic categories (occupants of specific positions in the system of production and distribution), or as representatives of historical tendencies (carriers of wider historical processes).[14] Marx often emphasizes the equivalence of humanness and social existence. There is no person outside society; each individual is bound to others by innumerable relationships of interdependence, and thus the social bond is constitutive of the human condition and human nature.

Man is in the most literal sense of the word a *zoon politikon*, not only a social animal but an animal that can develop into an individual only in society. Production by isolated individuals outside society . . . is as great an absurdity as the idea of the development of language without individuals living together and talking to one another. (Marx 1971: 17–18)

An even more telling indirect proof of Marx's consistent sociological approach will emerge if we consider the necessary method of characterizing human nature implied by such a perspective, and so demonstrate that Marx did apply that very method. If a truly sociological perspective requires looking at people as participants in wider social wholes, then the focus has to move toward human action as people participate in wider wholes by means of activity of various sorts. Some specifically directed or oriented activity makes up the social action; mutually oriented and coordinated activities make up an interaction; persistent, repeatable and regulated activities *vis-à-vis* one another involve individuals in social relationships; activities creating a bond with some people and a distance or hostility to others make an individual a member of a social group; a unique set of activities defines a social position (e.g. an occupation); and a unique set of expected, prescribed activities delimits a social role. To perform all those activities, individuals must possess specific capabilities, abilities, skills, talents. 'An analysis of social action might start with a model and then ask what sort of actors are needed for it' (Hollis 1987). In other words the properties of an acting, participating individual (an actor) are derivable from the properties of a typically human, participative activity (action). This point was clearly grasped by Gramsci: 'one can say that man is essentially "political" since it is through the activity of transforming and constantly directing other men that man realises his "humanity", his "human nature"' (Gramsci 1971: 360).

Turning to the second kind of uniquely human relation to the environment, which we labelled 'creation', it will easily be seen that it also is constituted by specific types of activity. In creative activity individuals externalize their 'powers', abilities, talents by producing objects. In those objects they confirm themselves and find the objectified expression of their individual potential. As Marx puts it, '[Man] duplicates himself not only intellectually, in his mind, but also actively, in reality, and thus can look at his image in a world he has created' (in McLellan 1971: 142). Obviously, to do all that, human individuals have to command certain capacities, abilities and skills, or, as Marx would put it, special 'powers'. Again, the properties of an acting, creative individual (an actor) are derivable from the properties of that typically human, creative activity (action).

To sum up, in Marx's work the logic of constructing the image of man, of building the concept of human nature seems to follow the following pattern: 'If the nature of human activity is such and such, than there are some necessary qualities that human beings must have to perform that activity.' The nature of man (as an actor) is derived from the nature of human conduct (action).[15] Or, to put it otherwise, an actor is treated as a *potentiality* for action, and action as *actualization* of that human potentiality.

Marx clearly conceives the properties of human action to be the key to an understanding of human nature; he 'sees persons as preeminently actors' (Rubinstein 1981: 139). He claims explicitly: 'As individuals express their lives, so they are' (Marx and Engels 1975: 61), echoing almost literally the Hegelian belief that 'Spirit is what it does, and its nature is revealed only in the sum of its activities' (Plamenatz 1975: 64). Marx elaborates this idea: 'The whole character of a species . . . is contained in the character of its life activity, and free, conscious activity is man's species character' (Marx and Engels 1960, vol. 1: 553). And here again he seems to paraphrase Hegel, for whom 'Mind or Spirit is nothing apart from its activities, and its nature is revealed only in them, and exists only as so revealed' (Plamenatz 1975: 63). As a modern commentator aptly observes: 'For Marx man manifests himself as a species being through activity of a kind, quality, and pace that could only be done by human beings' (Ollman 1975: 84).

This emphasis on action as the primary, constitutive dimension of human beings is even more pronounced in the 'activist Marxism' after Marx. Gramsci answers the question: 'What is man?' in a most telling way: 'What we mean is: what can man become? That is, can man dominate his own destiny, can he "make himself", can he create his own life? We maintain therefore that man is a process, and, more exactly, the process of his actions' (1970: 351).

There is a counter-image that provides a strong corroboration of the foregoing picture of a healthy human nature. Thus alienation is the substantial reversal of the relationships binding people with the natural as well as the social milieu; it is the severing of the relationships of creativity and participation. Man is no longer creative: 'Species life, productive life . . . turns into a mere means of sustaining the worker's individual existence' (Marx and Engels 1960, vol. 1: 553). Again: 'The worker does not confirm himself in his work; he denies himself, feels miserable instead of happy, expends no liberal physical and intellectual energy, but mortifies his body and ruins his mind' (p. 550). He no longer participates in free cooperative associations, but instead becomes isolated, estranged from other people, and hostile to them – alienated from his fellows. Thus, alienation means forfeiting sociocentric impulses (theme of egoism, atomization), lack of creativity (theme of monotony), and, in consequence, abdication of control over actions (theme of passivism), resigning of autonomy (theme of reification, fetishism of commodities etc.), and, in short, the decay of human 'species potentialities'. Human nature becomes inhuman. In the reading of Marx's powerful criticism of the fate of an individual in a class society, the image of human nature from his early philosophical writings reappears, but in a reversed mode.[16]

Having presented an analytic reconstruction of the Marxian idea of human nature, one is tempted to find some synthetic principle of its operation, some generating mechanism making people actualize in action their inherent potentialities *qua* actors, and to develop those potentialities in the process. We find a promising suggestion in two recent appraisals of Marx's work. Erich Fromm believes that 'For Marx man is characterized by the "principle of movement" . . . The principle of movement must not be understood mechanically but as a drive, creative vitality, energy; human passion for Marx is the essential power of man striving energetically for its object' (Fromm 1966: 30). Mc Murtry seems to follow the same track:

> What is most striking about Marx's concept of human nature is the inherent generative force it imputes to man. Man is, for Marx, by the very needs of his nature impelled to ever more productive undertakings, which his special intrinsic capacities are uniquely able to prosecute . . . Hence man is by his very constitution continually excited into activity, forever pressed by intrinsic demand into vital material expressiveness whose most truly human form is work in its 'unadulterated' form, or productive activity akin to creative art. (1978: 35–6)

I will label this fundamental drive or mechanism 'the human tendency toward transcendence and self-transcendence' overcoming limitations, opposing constraints, fighting enemies, crossing frontiers, breaking barriers (both external, environmental, and internal, imposed by limited human endowment) by means of intensive activity.

The vision of social wholes

Human actors and their actions do not exist in a vacuum, but rather in the context of wider social wholes. When Marx turns to characterizing these wholes, he seems to apply the same approach as in his study of individuals, which we described as relational and not substantive. In the view of several modern commentators, this is the most characteristic trait of Marxian ontology. For example Ollman says: 'Every factor which enters into Marx's study of capitalism is a "definite social relationship".

The relation is the irreducible minimum for all units in Marx's conception of social reality. This is really the nub of our difficulty in understanding Marxism, whose subject matter is not simply society, but society conceived of "relationally"' (1975: 14–15). A similar observation is made by Swingewood: 'The stress is on society as a definite structure within which human intentions and actions occur' (1975: 37).

If we look closely at the statements of Marx himself, a full corroboration of the relational view of social reality will easily be found. He claims for example: 'The relations of production in their totality constitute what is called the social relations, society, and specifically, a society at a definite stage of historical development, a society with a peculiar, distinctive character' (Marx and Engels 1968: 81). In the *Grundrisse* we find an even more explicit statement: 'Society is not a sum of individuals, but it expresses the totality of those relations and situations, in which the individuals mutually confront each other' (Marx, 1953: 176). Perceiving the totalities as relational structures is just the other side of perceiving the individuals as structurally implicated (what was earlier called the Marxian 'sociological' approach to human individuals). Marx's consistent structuralism is manifested with reference to both levels of social reality; totalities as well as individualities (Sztompka 1979: 287–323).

There are other interesting parallels. It seems that Marx uses a directive similar to the one we identified in his study of actors and action, namely he attempts to derive the characteristics of structures from the study of their motion. Marx's focus is always dynamic, his structures are always in movement, he studies processes rather than entities, becoming rather than being, diachronic developments rather than static objects. And only from such dynamic studies, by means of the reverse logic, do the traits of structures emerge. Structures are seen as potentialities for operation, and operation as the actualization of such potentialities.

The third parallel has to do with the impact of operation on structures. Again, there is a sort of positive, amplifying feedback which produces permanent, 'quantitative' modifications (changes *in*), or even fundamental, 'qualitative' reshaping of structures (revolutions, changes *of*) in the course of their functioning. The emergence of new forms of social life is a universal phenomenon.

Finally the same question that we asked about actors may be posed about structures: What is the ultimate stimulus, drive, mechanism producing their incessant operations and transformations? It is obviously parallel to the question we posed earlier: What makes actors act? The answer is to be found in the Marxian idea of dialectic contradictions, strains and tensions permeating every structure, and producing the endogenous, immanent tendency to change. Thus at the level of structures

39

we find the same ultimate, underlying principle which was indentified earlier by the label 'tendency toward transcendence and self-transcendence'. In the Marxian account, social totalities are auto-dynamic, exhibiting a constant propensity to change.

Praxis as the context of mediation

So far I have been discussing two levels of social reality studied by Marx as if they were separate, mutually independent and manifesting only some formal parallelisms. But this simplifying assumption, whatever its heuristic use, cannot be maintained any longer. We must trace the mutual, dialectic links, interrelations, interpenetrations of the two levels. Actual human actions do not occur in a vacuum, but in the context of the ongoing transformations of wider structures. Conversely those transformations are not automatic but due to human actions. Similarly the potential capacities of human actors are not given, but determined by the wider structures in which they are implicated; and conversely the potential, self-transforming capacities of structures are determined by the traits of the actors who make them up. Marx does not rest content with positing the mutual interaction of these opposite levels. Rather he seems to strive for the resolution of their opposition in ontological terms by finding an area of social reality where they are fused. I shall follow his suggestions, sometimes only implicit and often not fully articulated, and try to grasp a third level of social reality, where dialectic interrelations of individualities and totalities could be anchored, a level where actors and structures, actions and transformations merge in one multidimensional form of being.

Marx is clearly aware of the mutual dependence of his two levels. In the most general language he claims: 'Circumstances make men in the same measure that men make circumstances' (in McLellan 1971: 129). This can be read as referring to the level of totalities ('circumstances'), both in its aspect of potentiality (structures) and in its actuality (operation) as counterposed to the level of individualities ('men'), again in both of its aspects: potentialities (actors) and actualities (actions). The same message is carried by the third of the *Theses on Feuerbach* [1845]: 'The materialist doctrine that men are products of circumstances and upbringing, and that, therefore, changed men are products of other circumstances and changed upbringing, forgets that it is men that change circumstances and that the educator himself needs educating' (in McLellan 1971: 204).

In the context of such considerations Marx introduces the most significant notion of 'praxis'. He seems to focus on the actual, dynamic operation of social reality (what we labelled the aspect of actualities) and defines 'praxis' as the area where human actions and structural transformations mutually interpenetrate, as the process whereby they mutually co-determine each other. To quote Marx: 'The coincidence of the changing of circumstances and of human activity or self-changing can be conceived and rationally understood only as revolutionary practice' (in McLellan 1971: 204); and elsewhere: 'In revolutionary activity, the changing of oneself coincides with the changing of circumstances' (p. 199).

Thus praxis is where action and transformation meet. It provides the bridge between acting individuals and changing structures. As such, it is doubly conditioned (constrained and facilitated): 'from below', by the actions undertaken by societal members, and 'from above', by the quality of operation of wider society (stage of structural transformations reached). But it is not reducible to either. It is something more than the sum of individual actions, and it is something more than the outcome of ongoing operation. With respect to both levels – individualities and totalities – it is a new emergent quality. Having its own specific ontological quality as reality *sui generis*, it emanates in two directions, engendering actors' conduct and originating systemic tendencies. It is the true core of social life.

Some commentators believe that Marx's theory of praxis 'provides the key for understanding his basic outlook from his early speculations to his mature thought' (Bernstein 1972: xi). They claim that it is the exemplar of his efforts to attain a synthetic, multidimensional model of society: 'Marx sought to overcome the extreme one-sidedness of both the idealist and materialist doctrines in a new dialectical synthesis of his own' (Zeitlin 1981: 2). The idea of praxis as bridging the gap between individuals and social totalities was taken up by the 'activist Marxists', and particularly Gramsci and Lukács. The former referred to the whole of the Marxian opus as 'the philosophy of praxis' (Gramsci 1971),[17] and devoted most of his own work to showing that 'effective human action is the consequence neither of pure will nor of inexorable forces, but of [a] particular kind of interaction between objective circumstances and the creative spirit of man' (Femia 1987: 121). The latter explicitly refers to praxis as the 'central concept' of his major book (Lukács 1971: xviii), in which the dialectical fusion of subject and object is a leading preoccupation. Drawing from Hegel, he finds the fusion effected in history, and he indentifies its embodiment in the proletariat.[18]

History as the mechanism of mediation

Up to this point we have been dealing with a three-level model of social reality believed to represent in general outline the Marxian image of society. In line with Marx's consistent dynamic orientation, the model was constructed as in constant internal movement; it includes incessant changes elicited by specific endogenous forces. In this sense, the factor of *time* is already present in the model, but it is restricted to relatively short duration, to a single cycle in its operation. The picture is not yet dynamic, in the full sense of the term. Now we have to extend the time dimension toward a long-range historical duration. The 'riddle of history' is precisely how single phases in the operation of the model link in a cumulative sequence, producing a series of regular, patterned, directional transformations. The problem of 'making history' is how human agency influences not only the actual functioning (operation) of a society but also its long-range development (transformations). It is only here that a truly dynamic perspective is introduced.

Such a historical dimension of social life is a central preoccupation of Lukács. Taking the hint from Marx, who once said that there was no other science but history, Lukács ascribes a processual, irreversible nature to all forms of being (1985: 52, 152). The recognition of processuality in most fields of science allows rejection of the dualism of objects and changes, statics and dynamics as totally outdated (p. 139). In the case of human society, the historical process provides the continuity between the past, the present and the future at the fundamental level of being (pp. 111–12). The incessant, irreversible process of history is driven by human praxis, and its primary form – labour. The historical emergence and self-transformation of the human species is measured by 'pushing away natural barriers' (p. 59) and enriching human self-consciousness. It brings about the widening and diversification of the field of opportunities (options) facing human actors (p. 281). Even though irreversible, human history is by no means necessary. Rather it takes the form of a tendency. It is also open-ended and eternal; it does not stop at any ultimate point (p. 182).

Social process is also at the core of Gramsci's account of Marxism. He refers to Marxian theory as 'absolute historism' (1971: 417). The processual extension of social reality is visible at all levels. At the individual level it is expressed in 'the idea of becoming (man "becomes", he changes continuously with the changing of social relations) . . . The nature of man is "history"' (p. 355).[19] It extends to all other areas of human life: 'just as man is an historical process of becoming, so also knowledge and reality are a becoming, and objectivity is a becoming, etc.' (1972: 197).

Does Marx consider history as produced by agency, as humanly made? The 'activist interpretation' rejects any fatalist or finalist assumptions or mechanistic models and focuses on the active role of human agents (masses, classes, social movements, leaders etc.) in making crucial choices influencing the course of history. There is some good textual evidence that the activist image of history *is* present in at least some of Marx's writings. Consider the following statements: 'The first premise of all human history is, of course, the existence of living human individuals' (in McLellan 1971: 127); or more specifically: 'The whole of what is called world history is nothing but the creation of man by human labor, and the emergence of nature for man; he therefore has the evident and irrefutable proof of his self-creation, of his own origins' (in Fromm 1966: 26); or, when Marx quotes Vico in an unmistakably approving context: 'Human history differs from natural history in this, that we have made the former but not the latter' (in Fromm 1966: 15). Thus a general hint of the creative, constructive nature of the historical process is clearly given by Marx, both in his early, youthful work and in his mature analyses.

This is taken up by both the leaders of the 'activist' interpretation. For Gramsci 'History is the will of men who act on nature in order to change their world, to effect their goals, to satisfy their needs' (in Femia 1987: 64); or 'History is a continuous struggle of individuals and groups to change that which exists in any given moment' (p. 99). He explicitly opts for a reading of Marx which 'postulates as the dominant factor in history not raw economic facts but man, men in societies, men who interact with one another . . . and develop through these contacts (civilization) a collective, social will; men who come to understand economic facts, judge them and adapt them, to their will, so that this will becomes the motive force of the economy, the moulder of objective reality' (p. 90). The modern commentator has a point: 'The central theme of the notebooks is the re-emphasis on man as the maker of his own history rather than as a reflection of structural determinants' (p. 64). In Lukács, the same emphasis is obvious:

> History is no longer an enigmatic flux to which men and things are subjected. It is no longer a thing to be explained by the intervention of transcendental powers or made meaningful by reference to transcendental values. History is . . . the product (albeit the unconscious one) of man's own activity . . . It contains nothing that does not lead back ultimately to men and to relations between men. (1971: 186)

Marx develops the idea of human historical creativeness, specifying two frontiers, parameters delimiting its field. The first limitation has to do with the endowment of human actors; what people are, and consequently what they are able to do. One may say that in this way history-making is conditioned 'from below'. Marx and Engles make a famous statement which seems to touch this limitation:

> History does nothing; it does not possess immense riches, it does not fight
> battles. It is men, real, living men, who do all this, who possess things and
> fight battles. It is not 'history' which uses men as a means of achieving – as
> if it were an individual person – its own ends. History is nothing but the
> activity of men in pursuit of their ends. (In McLellan 1971: 125)

The second limitation has to do with the circumstances, the situation of
action due to the character of the structures and the phase of transformation within which actors happen to live and act. One may say that in this
way history-making is conditioned 'from above'. As Marx puts it: 'Men
make their own history, but they do not make it just as they please; they
do not make it under circumstances chosen by themselves, but under circumstances directly encountered, given and transmitted from the past'
(Marx and Engels 1968: 97).

But what is the nature of those circumstances? Are they simply given,
encountered, provided by providence or fate? Here we reach the crux of
Marxian activism. He leaves no doubt about that: the structures limiting
present actions are themselves produced by human actors, by their past
actions, or by the actions of their predecessors. They are not superhuman, but entirely human creations. Here is Marx's most telling statement, referring to the sphere of technological development:

> Men are not free to choose their productive forces – which are the basis
> of all their history – for every productive force is an acquired force, the
> product of former activity. The productive forces are therefore the result
> of practical human energy; but this energy is itself conditioned by the cir-
> cumstances in which men find themselves, by the productive forces already
> acquired, by the social form which exists before they do, which they do not
> create, which is the product of the preceding generation. (In McLellan
> 1971: 130)

There is a cumulative sequence: actions undertaken by actors within
existing structures; then production of new structures by those actions;
and again actions within the limits provided by the new structures. In the
words of Marx himself: 'History is nothing but the succession of the
separate generations, each of which exploits the materials, the forms of
capital, the productive forces handed down to it by all preceding ones,
and thus on the one hand continues the traditional activity in completely
changed circumstances and, on the other, modifies the old circumstances
with a completely changed activity' (In Fromm 1966: 211).

In effect, the actors' endowment is gradually enriched, and the
structures undergo gradual development.

> Because of this simple fact that every succeeding generation finds itself in
> possession of the productive forces acquired by the previous generation,

which serve it as a raw material for new production, a coherence arises in human history, a history of humanity which takes shape is all the more a history of humanity as the productive forces of man and therefore his social relations have been more developed. (In McLellan 1971: 130)

To sum up: each phase of the process reshapes the initial conditions and alters the field of possibilities open for the next phase of history-making. Praxis operates under circumstances left by earlier praxis. But the ultimate causal force putting all this complex sequence in motion is the human agency with its inbuilt propensity toward transcendence and self-transcendence.

Where is the agency located? It would be a grave oversimplification to treat it in anthropomorphic terms, as synonymous with individual actors. For Marx, agency is to be found neither at the level of individuals nor of totalities, but in between, at the mediating level, where he has already placed praxis. Agency is a product of a specific configuration of actors (with their concrete endowment, capacities, drives, powers) put in specific structural circumstances (constraining or enabling). It is a social quality, the specific potentiality of a society for historically consequential praxis. Its embodiments for Marx are social classes, but for his revolutionary concerns the crucial one is the proletariat. It should not be identified with an empirical group, a concrete collectivity of workers; it is rather an embodied potentiality for the radical overthrow of existing social forms:

> a sphere that has a universal character because of its universal sufferings and lays claim to no particular right, because it is the object of no particular injustice but of injustice in general . . . It is, finally, a sphere that cannot emancipate itself without emancipating itself from all other spheres of society and thereby emancipating these other spheres themselves. (In McLellan 1971: 23)

Lukács couches his characterization of the agency in similarly abstract terms, explicitly distancing the analysis from empirical realities. He focuses on the area of consciousness, but at once makes the striking disclaimer: 'the real motor forces of history are independent of man's (psychological) consciousness of them' (1971: 47). The consciousness 'proper' for the historically consequential agency cannot be discovered but must be inferred, and 'ascribed' (Jones 1977: 17) to historical agency.

> This consciousness is, therefore, neither the sum nor the average of what is thought or felt by the single individuals who make up the class. And yet the historically significant actions of the class as a whole are determined in the last resort by this consciousness and not by the thought of the

45

individual – and these actions can be understood only by reference to this consciousness.

It consists of 'the thoughts and feelings which men would have in a particular situation if they were able to assess both it and the interests arising from it in their impact on immediate action and on the whole structure of society' (Lukács 1971: 51).

The search for the category containing the agential property of society, emergent with respect both to the individuals making it up and to the structures constituting its skeleton, also engages Gramsci. It leads him to the idea of hegemony, the establishment of the cultural, ideological and moral unity of society under the predominant impact of one class. 'An historical act can only be performed by "collective man", and this presupposes the attainment of a "cultural-social" unity through which a multiplicity of dispersed wills with heterogenous aims, are welded together with a single aim, on the basis of an equal and common conception of the world' (Merrington 1977: 162). As Merrington reads it: 'The problem was to elaborate the specific character of a "collective will", which would make possible the passage from a sectoral, corporate and hence subaltern role of purely negative opposition, to a hegemonic role of conscious action toward revolutionary goals' (p. 148). The central role in such a hegemonic, 'organic' configuration may be played by the actually ruling class, but only in the periods when it is still in the ascendant, performing a progressive role and 'causing the entire society to move forward, not merely satisfying its own existential requirements but continuously enlarging its social framework for the conquest of ever new spheres of economic and productive activity' (in Femia 1987: 46). With the gradual decay of the ruling class, the exhaustion of its progressive potential, the hegemonic role is taken up by the opposition, or a revolutionary class. It becomes the initiator, mobilizer of the agency, but is not itself an agency. Agency, in the full sense, appears only when the revolutionaries are able to acquire a hegemonic position, infuse the whole society with their ideas, interpretations, moral precepts and goals. Thus the agency is not identified with a single class, but is a quality of the whole social fabric.

Because agency is the fusion of actors and structures, it must exhibit the same tendency toward self-transcendence that Marx ascribed to human nature and social totalities. This is stressed by Gramsci: 'History is a continuous struggle of individuals and groups to change that which exists in any given moment' (in Femia 1987: 99). Lukács makes the same point: 'History is the history of the unceasing overthrow of the objective forms that shape the life of man' (1971: 186). This unceasing movement of human history is ultimately due to the self-development of human actors through their actions. The individual components of the agency – people – constantly mature: 'the greater men's power and knowledge, and the more aware they are that the change they do not control is nevertheless an effect of what they and their ancestors have done, the less resigned they are to their fate; they aspire, always more consciously, always more urgently to determine the conditions of their life' (Plamenatz 1975: 167). But a parallel mechanism operates within the structural component of agency – social relations – where structural contradictions, strains, tensions and cleavages become constantly more severe and articulated, and gradually ripen to revolutionary overthrow, only to be re-established in a higher form in the never-ending cycle of development.

Agential and historical theory?

At the close of chapter 2 I introduced the concepts of agential coefficient and historical coefficient to summarize the ontological assumptions characteristic for the modern theory of agency and historical sociology. In the foregoing reconstruction of Marxian sociology, informed by the insights of 'activist Marxism' (and particularly of Gramsci and Lukács), we can easily encounter several assumptions from my earlier list. It is even more striking that the assumptions of agential theory are integrated and fused with the assumptions of historical sociology into a consistent theoretical image.

Thus, we may summarize the Marxian view of the social world by means of six principles. First, the functioning of society and its development are linked in the incessant process, in which both the state of society and the mechanisms of its operation are undergoing change. The same is true of human individuals, who exist only in so far as they act, and through action change their character and even the mechanisms of action itself. In sum, the social world – at the systemic and elementary level – is inherently historical. Second, both society and individuals must be treated as relational structures: society is a network of changing, fluid social relationships, individuals are the drifting nodal points of wider social structures, where bunches of social relationships are 'anchored', so to say, in their integral persons. Third, both the social wholes and the individuals have an inbuilt potentiality for self-transcendence, which tends to be actualized (in the absence of blocking factors) in social and individual development, producing in effect the historical process. Fourth, this tendency is expressed by agents making history, but these agents are never isolated individuals nor automatic mechanisms of the wholes. Rather the agential capacity inheres in the specific configuration of human collectivities and systemic conditions, a fleeting balance reached in the dialectics of structural determination (when actors are moulded by structures) and structural emergence (when structures are modified by actors). Fifth, agents not only shape history but are also shaped by history, as this particular agential configuration emerges from the earlier historical process in the continuous accumulation of effects of earlier actualizations which turn into potentialities for later actualizations. Sixth, the operation of society and the course of history are not inevitable or necessary but fully contingent; they depend on what people are doing, what they have done, and even what they did long ago, creating cumulative conditions for current deeds embedded in a historical tradition.

Thus society and history are constantly being constructed, but not individually, nor automatically, nor necessarily, nor intentionally, nor from scratch. They are constructed socially, by structurally embedded actors, mostly by means of unintended effects, in a contingent and cumulative manner. The core of the Marxian contribution to sociology is 'the critical insight that humans are active, creative beings who constitute their world and thereby themselves, by means of their practical activity' (Zeitlin 1981: 1).

If our account is correct, it means that the Marxian theory sees society as endowed both with an *agential coefficient* and a *historical coefficient*; it provides at least in some measure the synthesis of both approaches, agential and historical, each of which is already synthetic in nature (linking action and structure in the first case, and continuity and change in the second). 'Activist Marxism' suggests therefore a rudimentary synthesis of the second degree, a *synthesis of syntheses*, a rough outline of the result we had declared as the goal of our intended theory of social becoming.

That was the reason for bothering with Marx at all, and our result justifies the strategy. But now we may leave Marx behind, and start the construction of SB in a systematic manner, forgetting about the heuristic 'context of discovery' and the whole rich variety of intellectual resources – classical as well as contemporary – from which this theory emerges.

Part II

The theory

4

Ontology of the constructed world

Overcoming dilemmas

There are three general lessons to be drawn for our immediate purposes from Marxian sociological theory. The first, and perhaps most important tells us that in order to attain a synthetic, multidimensional (or as Marx would put it 'dialectic') theory, one has to focus four-square on the ontology of the social world. The synthesis, for Marx, is to be found in reality and not in detached reason. This seems a good antidote to the tendency, quite pronounced in modern social thought since the time of Kant, to dwell on epistemological issues and neglect ontological concerns. It is only recently that the epistemological bias has been overcome, and not accidentally, in the theory of agency and in historical sociology. I fully share Giddens's opinion that 'those working in social theory . . . should be concerned first and foremost with reworking conceptions of human being and human doing, social reproduction and social transformation' (1984: xx). And I accept Lloyd's case for 'sociological realism' and his stipulation that 'it is the task of science alone to reveal the general, hidden, structural features of phenomena, and the underlying mechanisms of their becoming' (1988: 34). Actually, the ultimate goal of my intended theory of social becoming could be perfectly summarized in those two statements.

The second lesson is more substantive. It refers to the problematic field of sociological theory as spread between the opposite poles of action and structure, as well as those of continuity and change, and indicates that those poles can be brought together and fused in an integrated model only

51

if society is seen as humanly constructed, humans as socially shaped, and both as immersed in the flow of historical time. Social being is constructed, constructing and processual. The theory of social becoming, with its synthetic intent, must obviously start from this triple insight.

The third lesson is methodological; it prescribes the strategy for a synthesis. Granted that the ultimate goal of a theory is to unravel social reality and not the mechanisms of reason, it can be done only by means of reason. And unravelling the mutlidimensional, dialectic nature of reality can be attained only by applying 'dialectic reason'. This means looking at the categories (assumptions, premises) with which human thought has been grasping reality, and overcoming their one-sidedness, their biases and absolutizations.

I shall follow these three pointers in the search for the ontological model of social reality, to be used as the presuppositional foundation for the theory of social becoming. Thus, having provided brief expositions of typical ontological standpoints put forward in sociological theory, and having arranged them as polar opposites – sociological dilemmas,[1] I shall attempt in each case to formulate a third, alternative solution, which would save what is valuable (the 'rational kernel', as Marx would say) of both extreme positions and at the same time reach a qualitatively new, synthetic level of ontological insight. To put it in Hegelian terms, the 'thesis' embedded in one of the extreme assumptions will be combined with the 'antithesis' embedded in the opposite extreme assumption to produce a dialectic 'synthesis' in the form of the third, alternative solution. In this way, each of the traditional ontological dilemmas will be shown to be spurious and will be replaced. In the resultant solution, the directive of continuity will be safeguarded by the incorporation of elements taken from both traditional assumptions, but at the same time the dilemma itself will be rejected, and the alternative assumption appear as qualitatively distinct from both traditional ones (Sztompka 1979: 34–5). This approach is in line with what Agassi believes to be the 'intuitively felt program' of social scientists: 'Many thinkers seem to have felt the need for *via media* between the two traditional views, and even for a consistent synthesis between the reasonable elements in them' (1973: 189).

Of course, I am not the first to enter this path of sociological theorizing. The last decades have witnessed various attempts of this sort, and probably even a consistent tendency to move toward new, synthetic solutions of several ontological dilemmas. This tendency seems to culminate in 'the new theoretical movement' (Alexander 1988b), and is apparently exacted by the growing concern with agency and history, as can be discovered – though often in intuitive and implicit formulations – in the works of agential theorists and historical sociologists. Thus to certain extent I shall merely be reporting on what has already been attained, trying to systematize and explicate it a little better. Only then will I make the next, meta-synthesizing move and try to show how the singular syntheses, reached as solutions to each of the ontological dilemmas, add up to a coherent, comprehensive image of the social world, the system of assumptions providing the ontological foundation for the theory of social becoming.

In this chapter I shall single out five ontological dilemmas, which have to be resolved before the idea of social becoming can be put forward. This concept, which is central to SB, cannot be meaningfully defined within any of the one-sided, traditional assumptions; it cannot be ontologically anchored in any of the polar opposites. Instead, it demands the alternative, middle-of-the-road ontology of the constructed, constructing and historical world.

The first dilemma addresses the question decisive for the identity of sociology as a separate discipline: What is society? In other words, it inquires about the status of social wholes. For a long time sociology has been entrapped in the alternatives: either society is a specific entity of a superorganic sort, or it is merely a sum of its members. It was only with the 'structuralist revolution' and the idea of organized complexity that society was found to be neither of these, but in a sense both: individuals, but more than their sum; wholes but not super-individual. Society was de-reified, individuals de-atomized. The dilemma of collectivism (or metaphysical holism) and individualism (or ontological atomism), came to be replaced by 'the focus on social structure' (Blau 1974) or 'sociological structuralism' (Merton 1976, Sztompka 1986a, chapter 6). Recently the generalized idea of social structure has entered the text-book canon and is taken to define what sociology ultimately is about (e.g. A. G. Johnson 1986, Giddens 1989).

The second dilemma results from a related riddle, which has accompanied sociology since its birth: What is a human individual? The ambivalence of the human condition, reflected so often in common-sense experience, has led to another pair of alternatives: either we are masters or slaves. The early sociologists, fascinated by their newly gained perspective, disparaged the individual. They were apt to treat human beings as totally dependent objects, devoid of any initiative or control with respect to their own activities, striving toward goals set for them, along strictly predetermined paths, guided by values and following norms imposed upon them from above. An individual as a passive object rather than an active subject, a product rather than a producer, a pawn rather than an agent, a reacting organism rather than an actor – this was the image conveyed by the proponents of passivism. But the opposite image was already waiting in the wings. Other sociologists started to treat individuals as totally autonomous and rational subjects, initiating, regulating and controlling their activities toward goals they had selected, along whatever course they believed to be most conducive to reaching those goals, guided by values and following norms of their own choosing. The human being as an active subject rather than a passive object, a producer rather than a product, an agent rather than a pawn, an actor rather than a reacting puppet – such was the image conveyed by the defenders of autonomism. This polarity still haunts sociology, even though a synthetic resolution is slowly gaining ground. The emerging alternative to both extreme positions seems to crystallize around the image of 'homo creator', who is neither fully independent of conditions, circumstances and available resources nor totally overwhelmed or paralysed by the burden of external situations. He is seen as exercising a measure of choice, freedom and discretion, but always within the possibilities and limitations of the encountered world. The idea of creativeness promises to provide a dignified but at the same time realistic portrait of the human individual.

The third dilemma has to do with the changing, dynamic quality of social life. This has probably been obvious to every member of society from time immemorial but is particularly salient in the modern epoch[2]. When sociologists face the question: What is history? their answers go in two opposite directions. The earlier approach, firmly rooted in the nineteenth-century intellectual tradition, treats history as a specific whole, and ascribes to it some immanent, pre-established form, logic, direction or meaning. The ideas of historical necessity, irreversibility, regularity, unilinearity, and finalism are corollaries of this position, which is often referred to as developmentalism or 'historicism' (Popper 1964). The opposite approach proclaims the full contingency of history, looking at it as a mere sum of concrete historical events, without any ulterior sense or goal. The notions of random accidents, chance, spontaneity and open-ended prospects come to the fore in this standpoint, which is sometimes known as eventism.[3] The replacement of both developmentalism and eventism is made possible by the idea of a contingent process, neither necessary nor random, both open-ended and regular. According to the assumption of processualism, there is no necessity, because an essential component of history is human decisions and choices. People always 'could have acted otherwise' (Giddens 1979: 56). At the same time there are regularities, because events and choices are sequential and cumulative; later ones occur in conditions shaped by earlier ones, and themselves influence the further course of the process, by shaping the conditions for future events and choices. There is some 'logic' in history, but not imposed from above. Rather, it emerges and evolves from a complex fabric of events and choices. And of course the stuff of history is made of such events and choices, but they are not isolated. Rather, they are causally linked in processual sequences embedded in time. Thus history is shown to be something more than the sum of events, but also something more contingent than eventless schemes.

The fourth dilemma refers to the closely related problem: What is the human role in the operation of society and the movement of history? Sociologists answer this question in two ways. Those who think of society and history as super-individual totalities, with their own *sui generis* principles of functioning, tend to underrate or even disparage the role of individuals in supporting their persistence or evoking changes. Even more, they see individual conduct as the epiphenomenon of the continuing operation of society and the flow of history. This is the assumption of fatalism. But those who treat society in individualistic terms, and history in eventist fashion, usually take the opposite stand. In their view, human actors have a decisive impact on the shape of society and the course of history, while they are themselves insulated from the impact of other events, whether preceding or coexistent. To put it otherwise, their choices are eventful, and they are free. This is the assumption of voluntarism. It is only by adopting the concept of possibilities, opportunities and options that sociology escapes the equally disastrous traps of fatalism and voluntarism. According to the assumption of possibilism, at each moment in life an individual is seen as located, by ascription or earlier achievement, in a specified field of opportunities, facing a set or 'repertoire' of possible actions she/he can take. Within this set of potentially available moves, there is a subset of actions which are particularly consequential, which 'make a difference' for wider society, or even the course of history. The crucial choices are those which assume super-individual relevance. Usually, they are normatively constrained and invoke questions of responsibility, conscience, guilt etc. Acting in this field, an individual is free, and in particular he/she is free to influence society and history, by stepping into the subfield of consequential actions. But neither the full field of options nor the subfield of socio-historically relevant options is fully open. They are always limited, so that the scope of possible choices is determined by earlier events or choices, made by the individual himself or by others shaping those fields for him. Thus an individual is seen as powerful but not omnipotent, free but not unconstrained. Her/his social and historical role appears as considerable but never boundless.

The fifth and last dilemma appears when sociologists face the fundamental peculiarity of society and history, the factor of consciousness, and ask about its ontological status. Consciousness, or awareness of social and historical phenomena on the part of actors, may take a whole spectrum of forms, from common sense to theoretical discourse. Thus the dilemma appears in two guises: the more general, 'Consciousness or reality?' and the more specific, 'Theory or practice?'. The question is: How does consciousness – whether common-sense or theoretical – relate to the actual socio-historical process? Two opposite standpoints are conceivable, and in fact sometimes encountered. One is the traditional assumption of similitude: consciousness provides a passive mirror image of actual reality, always only approximate, often distorted, sometimes definitely false. The causal track is seen as one-directional, from the social world to its reflex in human consciousness. Another, and contrary, assumption ascribes autonomous existence to consciousness, and goes so far as to deny (or at least suspend or 'bracket') the existence of any real substratum of consciousness. The actual world disappears, dissolved in thought. This is a modern version of solipsism, or – as Merton calls it – 'sociological Berkeleyanism' (Merton 1976: 175). But both extreme assumptions started to crumble and eventually collapsed once the crucial insight known as 'the Thomas Theorem' was recognized in all its implications (Merton 1982: 248). It stated that if people believe something to be real, it is real in its consequences. Or, in more formal phrasing, consciousness is internally constitutive of social reality, because people act on beliefs, and actions are the stuff of which that reality is made. The awareness of society or history feeds back on their very course and functioning. With respect to theoretical discourse, it means that the theory of society becomes a part of, and an influence on, the very society it purports to explain. Thus, there is a two-way causal loop; from reality to consciousness, and from consciousness back to reality. This assumption, overcoming the dilemma of similitude or solipsism, has come to be known as the principle of 'reflexiveness'.

The set of five assumptions attained by the dialectic resolution of traditional dilemmas makes up a specific multidimensional image of social reality which may be called dialectic. It is clearly distinct from the standard one-sided views, whether mechanistic or subjectivistic. It is also comprehensive, presents an overall image of the individual, society and history, and answers all major ontological questions in a mutually consistent way. The dialectic ontology of the constructed, constructing and historical world includes the assumptions of structuralism, creativism, processualism, possibilism and reflexiveness. This syndrome of interrelated assumptions forms the ontological foundation for the theory of social becoming. Now, each of the five pillars requires more detailed examination and explication.

The focus on structures

Sociology is born as a science, when a new class of objects – specific social entities – begins to be recognized and perceived as problematic. Hence, 'the mode of existence of collectivities, groups, societies, organizations and so forth is a major concern for sociological theory' (Abel 1970: 29). The existence of such super-individual objects is problematic, mainly because they are not directly observable. The situation is in some respects the obverse of that of physics; there the objects of the macroscale are directly perceived, and the components at the microlevel are not. The latter therefore become problematic, and the issue of the ontological status of atoms, molecules or subatomic particles is vigorously pursued. In sociology, the objects at the macrolevel are not directly perceived, whereas the microscale components, human individuals and their activities, certainly are. In this instance, the former become problematic, and the question of the ontological status of groups, collectivities and wider social wholes is already present at the birth of our discipline.

Naturally enough, the question 'Do the collectivities really exist or not?' has engendered two opposite answers. The affirmative answer, ascribing a specific mode of existence to social objects and treating them as some reality *sui generis*, was immediately countered by the negative answer, refusing any distinct mode of existence to social entities and resolving them completely into the participating individuals. Those were the typical, extreme solutions organizing the field of the dispute. 'No orientations to the problems of existence are more fundamental than those which take the individual as primary (individualism) and those which take the collective as primary (collectivism)' (Martindale 1964: 453).

The debate between individualism and collectivism has been going on for decades, both at the level of meta-theory (philosophy of the social sciences), and in the more implicit, 'applied' sense at the level of theory proper. I shall omit the history of that debate here[4] and move directly to the explication of both opposite positions. Two components of the question about the ontological status of collectivities may immediately be distinguished. The first is the aspect of existence. Do the social wholes 'really' exist, or, more precisely, do they constitute an ontological category separate from that of human individuals and their actions? The second is the aspect of causation. Are the social wholes causally effective agents? The distinction between the existential and causal aspects of the problem is only the first approximation. Let us probe a little deeper. The claim of existence entails several more specific assertions: (a) that a social whole possesses a certain uniqueness with respect to other social wholes and is externally distinguishable from them by means of a specified boundary; (b) that a social whole possesses a certain unity and is a real entity internally integrated to the extent that it operates as a going concern and undergoes changes as a totality; (c) that a social whole possesses a certain autonomy with respect to its parts and has properties, functions and characteristic processes that cannot be meaningfully predicated of the parts; (d) that a social whole possesses a certain continuity and identity, despite the turnover of parts, and is perceived as the same whole even though all the elements have undergone changes. In a similar vein, the claim of causation can also be dissected as asserting (e) that a social whole is causally effective with respect to other social wholes, that there exists a causal process among social wholes; and (f) that a social whole is effective with respect to its parts and exerts some independent power, influence or determining impact on the individuals who are its members.

Now, the collectivistic standpoint may be defined as the acceptance of all those claims, and the individualistic standpoint as their rejection. Thus the generalized formulation of (ontological)[5] collectivism will read: Social wholes (groups, collectivities, societies, cultures, civilizations, etc.) do really exist and act as causal agents; that is to say, they are distinguishable from other social wholes, are internally integrated or unified, are at least partly autonomous with respect to their elements, preserve some continuity independent of the fate of those elements, and exert a causal influence on other social wholes and on their own components. The generalized formulation of (ontological) individualism will be: So-called social wholes do not have an independent existence or causal potential; that is to say, they are just chaotic aggregates of human individuals and their activities, overlapping with other similar aggregates, additive in nature, lacking any separate properties other than those statistically computed of the properties of individuals, devoid of any continuity over and above the fates of individuals, causally connected only via the activities of individuals, and possessing no independent power over those individuals.

The resolution of this sociological dilemma seemed impossible as long as sociologists were searching for the specific social substance, the substratum of social phenomena and processes, a new sort of 'being'. They could choose and defend only one or the other of the contradictory positions. The debate became a stalemate. It was only with the 'structuralist revolution' in scientific thinking[6] that prospects of a synthesis and of a resolution of the dilemma were opened. Instead of the search for a specific substance, the much more promising search for a new type of organization, a characteristic network of relationships – in brief, a specific social structure – has begun.

Of course the concept of social structure was ambiguous from the start and a great variety of definitions were proposed.[7] The earliest agreement was reached at the meta-theoretical level, which is concerned with the importance of the concept for sociology. To invoke some authorities: Goode claims that 'structural problems are central to sociology' (1973: 20); Blau echoes these words: 'The idea of social structure is at the very core of sociology' (1974: 1); Nisbet is even more emphatic: 'Of all contributions that sociology has made to contemporary thought none is greater than, if indeed as great as, its envisagement of human behavior in terms of social structure' (1974: 73); and Coser adds his voice: 'I consider the study of social structures to lie at the very center of the sociological enterprise' (1975b: 218). In addition to such declarations, there is also an area of emerging substantive consensus; most authors emphasize that structures are (a) relational networks, which (b) exhibit patterned regularities, (c) are to be found at some deep, hidden level of social reality, and (d) exert some impact on the observable level of social phenomena and processes. Therefore, for our purposes, the following generalized definition of social structure may be proposed: Social structure is the hidden network of persistent and regular relationships between components of social reality, which significantly controls their operation (Sztompka 1989).

If the dispute between collectivism and individualism is rephrased in terms of the structuralist approach, the crucial question becomes whether the social wholes (groups, collectivities, societies etc.) represent a distinctively new, emergent organization of human individuals and their activities. The traditional standpoints, seeking a specific social substance, may be marked by the subscript '1', and the reformulated standpoints, seeking a specific social structure, by the subscript '2'. Thus, four standpoints in the dispute can be distinguished:

COLLECTIVISM$_1$ = There exists a specific social substance, the reality *sui generis* over and above acting individuals, who are only its epiphenomena or emanations.

INDIVIDUALISM$_1$ = No specific social substance exists; human individuals in their manifold activities are the only real substratum, and constitute the basic components of society.

COLLECTIVISM$_2$ = Social wholes have a distinct structure; they represent a complex, emergent relational network, an organization that binds acting individuals but exhibits specific traits and regularities of its own.

INDIVIDUALISM$_2$ = No patterned, structural organization can be discerned in a society; it consists solely of an amorphous, random aggregate of human individuals and their actions.

My strategy in seeking for a synthetic, 'dialectic' standpoint able to overcome the traditional dilemma, is to cross-tabulate both dichotomies (see figure 4.1). It can be done without danger of internal contradiction

The aspect of substance

	INDIVIDUALISM$_1$	COLLECTIVISM$_1$
COLLECTIVISM$_2$	STRUCTURALISM	REIFICATION
INDIVIDUALISM$_2$	ATOMIZATION	METAPHYSICS

The aspect of organization

Figure 4.1

because the aspect of substance and the aspect of structure are logically independent.

Let us describe the resulting combinations. The conjunction of INDIVIDUALISM$_1$ and INDIVIDUALISM$_2$ renders an extreme version of fully consistent individualism, which perceives society as an unorganized, formless aggregate of individuals. 'Atomization' seems a fitting name for this image. Another consistent pair is the conjunction of COLLECTIVISM$_1$ and COLLECTIVISM$_2$, an extreme version of collectivism, which treats social wholes as real objects, super-individual entities in which human individuals are embedded as the ultimate elements of a complex internal anatomy.[8] 'Reification' is the good term for expressing the flavour of this position. The mixed combinations are also of two sorts. The conjunction of COLLECTIVISM$_1$ and INDIVIDUALISM$_2$ entails a claim that society represents a completely specific domain of reality, which has simply nothing to do with the world of individuals and has to be treated as totally separate and autonomous.[9] I suggest the term 'metaphysics' in its common-sense meaning, to grasp the core of this strange, counter-intuitive viewpoint.

Finally the combination of COLLECTIVISM₂ and INDIVIDUALISM₁ yields an ontological position which appears truly synthetic, fusing the content of both, initially opposed assumptions rather than mutually enhancing their different aspects (as in the case of 'atomization' and 'reification'), or merely putting them side by side, as mutually irrelevant (as in the case of 'metaphysics'). This solution, to be called 'structuralism', claims that the only really existing objects in a society are human individuals and their actions. But pluralities of individuals are interlinked in complex fashion by networks of social interactions and social relationships. Such a structure or organization endows the groups, collectivities and societies with new, emergent properties and regularities, as compared to the traits and patterns of individual behaviour. Structures do not have any substantive, ontological existence; they are only attributes of reality, forms in which it manifests itself. Thus there is nothing else in a society but people. At the same time society is something more than the plurality of individuals. The 'something more' is precisely the structure of their mututal relationships. To put it another way, sociology is certainly about people, but it does not follow that it must be written in terms of people, because its proper focus is the emergent traits and regularities of structured, organized collectivities.[10]

The standpoint of structuralism will be taken as the dialectic solution to the dilemma of collectivism and individualism. It preserves some significant insights of both traditional positions, but at the same time avoids their one-sidedness. From traditional collectivism it inherits the belief that social objects are 'something else' or 'something more' than a simple sum of individuals, but unlike traditional collectivism, it avoids the danger of reification, or the even graver metaphysical separation of social reality from the world of living people. From traditional individualism it takes the claim that the ultimate components of society are individuals, but unlike traditional individualism it avoids the danger of treating individuals as unconnected atoms, still less as detached from the social context.

The structuralist position allows us to conceptualize and answer all those riddles, which gave birth to the dispute between collectivism and individualism in the first place: (a) the uniqueness of social wholes, by referring to the unique structural organization of components; (b) the unity or integration of social wholes, by emphasizing the particular intensiveness of structural relationships within them, as opposed to the much looser relationships with the outside; (c) the autonomy of a social whole *vis-à-vis* its parts, by specifying properties and regularities of structured totalities which cannot be predicated of the elements; (d) the idea of a continuity of social wholes in spite of the changes in their human components, by invoking the notion of structural invariance, which preserves the form and pattern in the flow of substantive transformations; (e) the causal impact of one structure on another, by referring to the mediating activities of individuals across the boundaries of structures within which each of them is implicated, or to the even more immediate links between two structures by virtue of a single individual participating in both of them (as in the case of pluralistic memberships in groups, role-sets or status sets); (f) the independent power of the whole over its parts, by invoking the notion of structural constraints and facilitations, determining the opportunities for individual action in dependence on the position people have within the wider structural network.

The assumption of structuralism in the sense set out above will be adopted as the first ontological foundation for the theory of social becoming.

Individuals; autonomous but bridled

Another perennial problem of social thought, and later of sociology, has to do with the essence of human beings. Whatever social entities were studied, however social facts were conceptualized, the individual always reappeared as a basic component. When sociologists focused on social actions, the individual was there as an 'actor'. If they focused on social interactions, she/he was involved as a 'partner'. If they focused on more established social relationships, she/he appeared as a 'party' or a 'side'. If they focused on social groups or collectivities, she/he was seen as a 'member'. If they focused on collective behaviour or social movements, she/he was found as a 'participant'. If they focused on social structure or social system, she/he was there as an 'incumbent' of positions or 'performer' of roles. And whether they were aware of it or not, in all these cases the students of society had to make assumptions about human nature. Hollis is right: 'There is no dispensing with a model of man' (1977: 3). Skidmore confirms him: 'Models of man, far from being only minor or unimportant aspects of sociological theory, constitute sets of premises foundational to sociological accounts' (1975: 4).

Of course a human individual is an utterly complex and segmented entity. Of his/her many aspects, dimensions or 'faces', there is only one fundamentally important for the sociologist. Seen from a sociological perspective, a human being will always appear as a component of social wholes, or at least as regularly related to such wholes. Thus a sociologist will always look at an individual from an external perspective of wider, super-individual or inter-individual totalities, and treat her/him as embedded in various social contexts – networks of interaction, groups, institutions, organizations, structures, systems etc. An individual as a participant in something larger than him/herself – that is a typical sociological angle of vision.

But if we think for a moment what it really means 'to participate' in social wholes, it will become clear that it comes down to acting in particular ways. Activity is the means by which an individual participates in larger social contexts. Mutually directed or oriented activities make up an interaction; persistent, repeatable and normatively regulated activities *vis-à-vis* one another involve individuals in social relationships; activities creating a bond with some people and distancing oneself from others make an individual a member of a social group; and a specific set of activities defines the social role that an individual is expected to perform by virtue of her/his structural position. Thus for a sociologist, action is a core aspect of an individual, who is viewed only in the capacity of an actor.[11] The 'sociological model of man' (or woman) is in effect a set of premises about human action, and only by derivation does it allow the capacities of human actors to be specified as prerequisites for conducting action of that type.

As usual, the question 'What is the character of human action?' (and consequently 'What are the traits of an actor?') has engendered two opposite answers. One typical standpoint claims that action is basically reactive; adapting or responding to stimuli (pressures, requirements, expectations) coming from the outside; human conduct is released by environment. This is countered by those who believe that 'Much of human behavior does not have the character of things happening to a person. Instead it consists of things that people have made happen for various reasons' (Harre and Secord 1972: 39). Thus the opposite standpoint claims that human action is constructive, self-initiated, actively coping with the environment (defining, interpreting, selecting incoming stimuli) and, in effect, shaping the outside world.

The images of an actor differ accordingly. Hollis gives them apt names: 'Plastic Man' and 'Autonomous Man': 'Whereas Plastic Man, being formed by adaptive response to the interplay of nature and nurture, is only spuriously individual, his rival is to be self-caused. Where Plastic Man is an object in nature, his rival is the "I" of the I and Me. Where Plastic Man has his causes, Autonomous Man has his reasons' (1977: 12). Or, in a less poetic idiom, the main criterion concerns 'the extent to which the person is regarded as an agent directing his own behaviour. At one extreme he may be seen simply as an object responding to the push and pull of forces exerted by the environment. At the other, he may be seen as an agent guiding his behavior toward some explicit goal by some means of which he is thoroughly aware' (Harre and Secord 1972: 136).

As before, I shall leave out the rich story of the debate between the supporters of Plastic Man and Autonomous Man as it has been evolving in sociological theory for more than a century.[12] Instead I shall move immediately to the explication of the dilemma. Both opposite stand-points – let us call them activism and passivism from now on – accept a relational perspective. They assume that an individual is necessarily related to the outside world, the external environment (supposedly in-cluding natural as well as social components, various objects and other people). Thus each of the opposite assumptions involves two distinct aspects, says something of the individual as such (and his actions) and of the context (environment) in which she/he lives and acts. Let us define the possible partial assumptions, dealing with those aspects separately. Obviously activism and passivism will mean different things if seen from the point of view of the actors, as compared to the point of view of the external environment. We shall first handle the aspect of the immanent drives and tendencies of the individual.

PASSIVISM$_1$ (DEPENDENCE) = human action is purely reactive, released or evoked by external stimuli. An actor is a passive being, with a ten-dency to adapt to the outside world.

ACTIVISM$_1$ (AUTONOMY) = human action is self-initiated, self-directed and self-controlled, actively shaping the environment. An actor is a choosing and deciding being, with a constant drive to remake the out-side world.

Now let us take the second aspect, the assumed character of the environment as related to human beings.

PASSIVISM$_2$ (RESTRAINT) = an environment provides a closed pool of limited, scarce resources (both constraints and enablements) for human action to use, or stimuli to influence their action.

ACTIVISM$_2$ (LIBERTY) = an environment provides an open, limitless pool of resources or stimuli for action.

Both aspects are logically independent and therefore the pairs of assumptions may be cross-combined as in figure 4.2.

The combination of PASSIVISM$_1$ and PASSIVISM$_2$ defines the extreme version of Plastic Man. An individual appears as fully enslaved by nature and society, is seen as a total marionette, a puppet on a string, pushed and pulled around by external pressures. He is the direct product of the actually existing, concrete circumstances in which he happens to find himself. The opposite combination of ACTIVISM$_1$ and ACTIVISM$_2$ defines the extreme version of an Autonomous Man. Here, an individual is an unrestrained master of circumstances, shaping them at his will. He is like God, an ultimate free subject, or, to use Hollis's term, a 'sovereign artificer' (Hollis 1987: 1). But there are also mixed combinations of assumptions. The combination of ACTIVISM₂ and PASSIVISM₁ produces the image of an individual not only resigning any use of unlimited resources easily available, but insulating himself against the impact of environmental stimuli, refusing even to react and thereby withdrawing into inactivity, in the strict sense. Here we have the complete reification of a human being, turning him into a pure object. As long as we consider action of some sort as a definitional trait of being human, this logical combination does not refer to human nature any longer; at most it describes a dead individual. Therefore, it is irrelevant for our purposes. But we still have one logical option left.

It is only with the combination of ACTIVISM₁ and PASSIVISM₂ that we achieve the dialectic surmounting of the dilemma. It presents the image of an individual who is facing the environment with incessant transforming intent, but it is an environment pervaded by scarcity; there are only limited resources, and therefore only some things that can be done. Furthermore the environment raises barriers, constraints on human

The aspect of immanent drives

	ACTIVISM₁	PASSIVISM₁
PASSIVISM₂	CREATIVISM (HOMO CREATOR)	PASSIVE REACTANT
ACTIVISM₂	SOVEREIGN SUBJECT	REIFIED OBJECT

The aspect of ernal resources

Figure 4.2

65

efforts. In taking action directed at such an environment the individual is reflectively influenced by its limitations, has to adapt to them by changing his/her actions, and even – in the long run – curbing and re-shaping the very tendencies to act, her/his immament drives. In a word, the individual modifies his/her actions and also changes her/himself under the impact of the clash with 'hard' realities. He/she is seen as a subject, but also as an object at the same time. In short, she/he embodies 'agent sovereignty in a constraining world' (Hollis 1987: 14).

To be more specific, the combined assumption gives equal emphasis to human autonomy and dependence. The autonomy is revealed in the relationship to the natural environment, where men and women show creativity, ingenuity, originality – constantly transforming nature to suit their needs. They construct objects, produce goods, create civilizations. In this process they also creatively shape their own biological endowment (a significant fragment of the natural environment, even though seeming-ly located 'inside' the individual) by developing their skills, abilities, powers, by creating new needs and aspirations etc. Human autonomy is equally revealed in their relationship to the social environment. They constantly produce new associations, groups and collectivities, establish new institutions, introduce new patterns of social organization, initiate new ways of life, new social norms and values, create political and cul-tural systems, religious doctrines and artistic creeds, science and ideology.

But at the same time, human dependence is equally stressed. The encountered conditions predetermine to a large extent what can be done. The limitations are inherent in the given natural environment that pro-vides certain raw materials, resources and facilities, and is deficient in others. The special case of those natural and limited resources is of course the individual genetic endowment or biological constitution, which can facilitate certain activities and hamper others. Limitations are also in-herent in the social environment, where the established patterns, norms, values, institutions etc. may act not only as stimulants but often as power-ful constraints on action.

Thus an individual is seen as Autonomous Man and Plastic Man at the same time. He is a Janus-like creature with two faces. I suggest the term 'creativism' to describe this dialectic assumption. The word seems fitting because creation, at least when carried out by humans and not gods, is precisely an attempt to mould, produce something new, but out of existing resources, within given conditions. It is never *creatio ex nihilo*. Creation exemplifies well this fundamental existential tension that emerges in our dialectic image of human nature; a contradiction between human effort and limited resources, active drive and defiant conditions. This seems to reflect a universal and inevitable circumstances of human life.

The assumption of creativism, the image of an individual as a 'homo creator', will be taken as the second foundational premise for the theory of social becoming.

Sequential logic of the process

The third puzzle that sociologists have faced since the birth of the discipline has to do with social change. In fact, one of the main reasons for the emergence of sociology was the pervasive experience of rapid and fundamental transformations in nineteenth-century Europe. No wonder that all the founding fathers, from Comte to Weber, gave much of their attention to 'social dynamics'. In this area, their accounts still have a tremendous impact on the thought of our own times; 'In the analysis of social change, we cling loyally to the ideas built up by nineteenth-century intellectuals' (Tilly 1984: 2).

What is the core of the problem? Of course, the self-evident observation that social reality is in some sort of constant movement is trivial and has never been seriously contested. The very term 'social life' with its unmistakable origins in an organic metaphor, carries clear dynamic connotations. People are born, mature and die; they wake up, drive to work, return home and rest; they travel, migrate and settle down; friendships are made and broken; groups are formed, crystallize and disperse; social movements mobilize, struggle and (sometimes) win etc. Allen is right: 'There can be no doubt that the static society, involving no movement at all, is at the best an ideal type analytical category and at the worst a fantasy' (Allen 1975: 179). The truly problematic area is entered only when a different scale of movement is considered; no longer the 'changes in' society, the minuscule, repeatable, periodical occurrences within the bounds of a persisting whole, but 'changes of' society, the transformations of the whole 'social organism', 'social system' or 'social structure' occurring in time. As opposed to social life, these can be referred to as history.

The dispute about the nature of human history has engaged the best minds and is far from being ended. In the course of the dispute two analytically discernible positions have appeared. One considered history as endowed with specific form, shape, meaning or 'logic'. It was perceived as an extended totality, with consistency and unity, changing in specific directions, passing through regular stages toward a pre-set end, and moved by some immanent, endogenous force. The stuff of which history was made consisted of long-range trends or tendencies, engulfing – and in fact overshadowing – the concrete historical events. This image originated in the organic analogy, and found its strongest implementation in

evolutionism. As Nisbet argues: 'In the evolutionist's construction, it is
basically the metaphor of growth that is fundamental. From this come
the familiar premises of immanence, continuity, direction, and fixed succession of "normal" stages of development' (1969: 257). I shall refer to
this standpoint, rooted in the traditions of historiosophy, as developmentalism. It has shown great vitality and is still with us, both in common-sense thinking and in theoretical discourse; 'societal development
belongs to those great and important concepts around which large sec-
tions of social science theories, and often great endeavors of social praxis
have been organized' (Chodak 1973: 13). But of course, even though
dominant, developmentalism has never been the only image of history.
Almost from the beginning it met with a critique which challenged the
idea of unity, consistent design, directionality, finalism and immanent
causes. The opposite standpoint was born, emphasizing contingency,
chance, alternative scenarios, open-endedness and external (exogenous)
causation. The stuff of history was made of events, happenings and episodes. This position, having close intellectual affiliations with traditional
historiography will be referred to as eventism.

Is the dilemma of developmentalism and eventism really exclusive and
irreconcilable? If we take a closer look at both typical standpoints, we
shall see that each incorporates two distinct claims. One addresses the
aspect of substance: Is history an ontological domain *sui generis*, a specific totality, looming over and above its components – human actions,
occurrences, incidents? Another addresses the aspect of pattern: Is there
a discernible form, regularity, sequence among the multitude of historical
events? The developmentalists will tend to answer in the affirmative, and
the eventists in the negative. But these are clearly separate questions, and
therefore, analytically, four variants of the answer may be singled out,
and ordered in two pairs of opposite assumptions.

Thus, in response to the riddle of substance, we may discover two
opposite, typical solutions:

DEVELOPMENTALISM$_1$ = 'History'[13] is more than the sum of events; it is
  a separate domain of reality, running its own course, independent of
  (and even causally prior to) events, which are only its emanations or
  epiphenomena.
EVENTISM$_1$ = History is a congeries of events; there is nothing in history
  but occurrences, happenings, episodes.

And in response to the riddle of pattern, another pair of typical answers
appears:

DEVELOPMENTALISM$_2$ = History exhibits discernible regularities, trends, forms; its components are linked, interrelated in a sequential mode.

EVENTISM$_2$ = History is a fluid, shapeless chaos; its components appear in accidental permutations, unique, concrete and localized in time.

Cross-combining the two logically independent aspects – of substance and of pattern – allows us to discover four possible standpoints facing the initial general question: 'What is history?' (See figure 4.3.).

There are two consistent combinations which represent the extreme, radical endorsements of opposite positions. Thus the combination of DEVELOPMENTALISM$_1$ and DEVELOPMENTALISM$_2$ stipulates that history is a time-extended totality, evolving on its own along a predetermined path, and its immanent tendencies are reflected in the orderliness or regularities of actual historical events, which somehow follow the 'logic' of the overall historical trend. The central message of this position may be grasped by the term 'historicism' introduced in a critical context by Popper (1964 [1957] and 1966 [1945]). But because a fully-fledged

The aspect of substance

		EVENTISM$_1$	DEVELOPMENTALISM$_1$
The aspect of pattern	DEVELOPMENTALISM$_2$	PROCESSUALISM	HISTORICISM$_1$
	EVENTISM$_2$	RANDOMNESS	TRANSCENDENTALISM

Figure 4.3

69

'historicism' means, for Popper, something more – touches on another sociological dilemma, to be discussed in the next section – in the present context I shall label the reconstructed combination as historicism$_1$. The opposite, mutually enhancing fusion of EVENTISM$_1$ and EVENTISM$_2$ gives us another radical standpoint. It suggests that history is nothing other than the sum of historical episodes, which are fully contingent and accidental, and do not show any inherent, sequential regularities. The term 'randomness' seems fitting to grasp the core of this view.

Now we come to the mixed standpoints, combining contrary solutions to original queries. The first is not very promising for our synthetic purposes, as it totally severs the link between composite assumptions instead of merging them. The combination of DEVELOPMENTALISM$_1$ with EVENTISM$_2$ means that history is a region completely detached from events, the domain of fate, existing and regularly evolving in some metaphysical realm, not only in total independence of, but also in total indifference to, the chaos of earthly happenings. The word 'transcendentalism' may serve as a name for this rarely encountered but analytically conceivable image of history.

Thus we arrive at the last mixed solution. It is truly synthetic, linking together, and even fusing, the components of opposite positions. The combination of EVENTISM$_1$ and DEVELOPMENTALISM$_2$ will be treated as the dialectic surmounting of the initial dilemma. On the one hand, it does not ascribe any reified or metaphysical qualities to history; there is no specific historical substance *sui generis*. Ontological existence is located solely in the area of events; history exists only *via* events, it consists of nothing but events. On the other hand this standpoint does not treat historical events as a formless, fluid chaos. There is something more to history than events. Namely, there is a pattern, a regularity among them. First, they are causally interrelated and influence each other. Second, they are sequentially ordered, linked in multiple chains of causally related episodes spread in time – earlier and later. Third, most importantly, the sequences are cumulative. Earlier episodes leave a residuum, imprints, memory traces, which enter into the initial conditions for later episodes, and – although selectively – are preserved in them and enriched, only to be passed on as a new context for future events. In this way, the present is always in 'not merely chronological but also genetic relation to the past' (Nisbet 1969: 256). The obvious illustration of this sequential and cumulative flow is the passing on of historical tradition, memories, ideas, and images, values, norms and rules, institutions, organizations and structures, objects, products and artefacts, resources, skills, knowledge etc. (Shils 1981)

I shall refer to such an assumption as 'processualism', and use it as one of the ontological pillars of SB. It conveys a realistic and fruitful image of history, disposing of several fallacies of the traditional positions. First of all, history does not posses any metaphysical, substantive reality. Thus, in this image, the pattern of history is not superimposed or pre-established, but rather emerges out of the intermeshed plurality of events. Such a pattern is not treated as unique or singular, but rather emerges as the combined product of multiple sequences, overlapping and parallel, convergent and divergent, contradicting and complementing each other. It is not seen as a uniform and unidirectional process, but may change direction, course and speed. It is not viewed as approaching any fixed final goal, but is open-ended and contingent, allowing of alternative scenarios.

In effect, history loses its imposing stature as something far above the mundane realities of everyday life. Quite simply, it *is* everyday life, coalescing in sequential patterns of gradually growing complexity. Thus the processual perspective implies a continuity between the smallest-scale occurrences at the level of personal biographies and the grand events of historical dimensions. Causal interrelatedness and the sequential cumulation of events, the intermeshing of sequences and enhancing of tendencies – all these mechanisms demonstrate that even the smallest individual deeds count, in the long run, in producing the greatest historical transformations. Such a conclusion has not only theoretical but also moral significance.

Choosing in the field of possibilities

The three questions considered so far – 'What is society?' 'What is an individual?' and 'What is history?' – prepare the ground for approaching the most fundamental ontological problem of the theory of social becoming: the nature of human agency. Now the three basic aspects of social reality – structures, people and processes – treated separately in the earlier discussion, must be linked in a coherent picture. This can be done in various ways, taking each of the aspects as the basis for integration. But our realistic premise, that the ultimate ontological substance of society and history comes down to acting people, dictates the approach starting from the level of individual agents. Thus, the problem may be phrased as the question 'What is the human role in society and history?'

Society and history are two contexts of human action. We ask how human individuals fit into these contexts. Neither is immutable, petrified, or stable, but, as we saw earlier, they are in perpetual movement; societies function or operate (all kinds of 'changes in' are going on at any moment of time), history moves on (all kinds of 'changes of' occur in any span of time). Individuals fit into the operation of society and the course of

71

history not just by being there, but by acting in specific ways, entering or joining the ongoing processes. Their actions may have some significance, probably they make some difference. That is why we ask about the role they play in society and history.

This question, in implicit or explicit formulations, seems to assist all human reflection, and certainly makes a perennial problematic current running underneath, and occasionally emerging to the surface of all social philosophy and sociological theory. As a rough approximation, one may distinguish two typical answers. The first is optimistic and ascribes a crucial role to human beings. The other is pessimistic; it denies any significant role to humans. These standpoints may be called voluntarism and fatalism respectively. Their opposition, seemingly irreconcilable, makes up our next 'sociological dilemma'.

But if we look closer, it will become apparent that both standpoints are internally complex, hiding in themselves several partial assumptions. Let us break down this complexity by distinguishing two aspects of the problem. Asking about the human role in society and history, one may have in mind two separate questions. The first inquires about the functions of human action (Sztompka 1974a): what are its consequences for the wider context in which it is implicated, i.e. for the operation of society and the course of history? In other words, is it causally effective, or rather ineffective for the processes in which it participates? The second question is quite different; in fact it takes the reverse form and inquires about the causes and determinants of human action: What is the impress of the wider context (i.e. the operation of society and the course of history) on the action occurring within it? In other words, is human action causally determined, or is it free from determination by the processes in which it participates?

The distinction of functional and causal aspects allows us to phrase four ideal-typical assumptions. Thus, the question asked in a functional mode engenders the following opposite answers:

FATALISM$_1$ = human actions have no significant functions with respect to society and history; they are ineffective as causal factors, and the social and historical processes are insulated from any human intervention, having their own momentum, direction and goal.

VOLUNTARISM$_1$ = human actions have decisive functions with respect to society and history; they are crucially effective causal factors, and the social and historical processes are basically shaped by human intervention, which constitutes their driving and controlling force, giving them momentum, direction and goal.

72

The question asked in a causal mode engenders another pair of opposite answers:

FATALISM$_2$ = human actions are causally dependent on the social and historical context; they are determined (enabled or constrained) by the operation of society and the cumulated effects of earlier phases of the historical process (historical tradition).

VOLUNTARISM$_2$ = human actions are causally independent of the social and historical context; they are insulated against the operation of society and earlier historical tradition.

It becomes obvious now why the problem is so crucial for social philosophy or sociology (and also common sense); it concerns the issue of human freedom. VOLUNTARISM$_1$ affirms and FATALISM$_1$ negates positive freedom (or 'freedom to' influence society and history). VOLUNTARISM$_2$ asserts and FATALISM$_2$ denies the negative freedom (or 'freedom from' the social and historical influences).[14]

The functional and causal aspects are logically independent; one can obviously be 'free from', but not 'free to' and vice versa. Therefore, let us apply our standard strategy of cross-combination, as in figure 4.4.

There are two consistent, mutually enhancing combinations. That of FATALISM$_1$ and FATALISM$_2$ describes a condition of enslavement: an individual is fully determined by socio-historical circumstances, and has no way of influencing them. The mirror-image of this is a condition of God-like independence and omnipotence; an individual decisively and freely shapes society and history but escapes any social or historical determination affecting himself. He does not depend on anything, but on him everything depends; his actions are at the same time absolutely unconstrained and absolutely consequential; on his whims the fate of the world hinges. This describes an eternal – and never fulfilled – dream of absolute freedom. The term 'deism' may be used to refer to this position.

There are also two mixed combinations. VOLUNTARISM$_1$ together with FATALISM$_2$ describes the paradoxical condition of useless freedom or inconsequential permissiveness. People are seen as insulated from any constraints of society and history, but at the same time have no say in changing them. They are allowed to do whatever they want, but it does not make any difference to the operation of society or the course of history; their actions are entirely irrelevant. To put it in other words, the world of acting individuals and the world of ongoing processes, social and historical, are mutually impenetrable, separate and occupying different domains of reality. The term 'parallelism' expresses this dissociation of the individual and socio-historical levels well. Clearly it is not very promising for my search for a dialectic synthesis.

73

The aspect of function

	VOLUNTARISM$_1$	FATALISM$_1$
FATALISM$_2$	POSSIBILISM	TOTAL ENSLAVEMENT
VOLUNTARISM$_2$	ABSOLUTE FREEDOM (DEISM)	PERMISSIVENESS (PARALLELISM)

The aspect of cause

Figure 4.4

Thus it is only with the final combination of VOLUNTARISM$_1$ and FATALISM$_2$ that we find a truly synthetic path. Here a strong and mutual link of individual action and the socio-historical context is emphasized; actions significantly influence what is happening in society and history, but are themselves shaped by the operation of society and the heritage of earlier history. People appear as producers and products, shaped and shaping, subjects and objects, puppets and puppet-masters at the same time. The central concept for interpreting this ambivalence is 'possibility'. Thus, people may be seen as placed in a certain field of possibilities, given to them by society and history, endowed with a certain repertoire of actions that can be taken. The field or repertoire is not of their own making; it is encountered. But within that field they are free to take any action included in the repertoire; choices and decisions are theirs to make. And whatever they decide or choose makes a difference to the further operation of society and the future course of history. This image of the human condition, absolutely fundamental to the theory of social becoming will be called the assumption of possibilism.

But it can easily be seen that the assumption is highly imprecise and requires further analytic explication. We do not yet know how strongly the field of possibilities is determined, nor do we know how consequential human decisions are in making use of available possibilities. In other words, both constitutive assumptions, VOLUNTARISM₁ and FATALISM₂, have to be specified. Let me consider the latter first.

The field of possibilities is delimited in many ways. First of all, part of it is given not by society or history, but by nature (the physical, chemical and biological constraints and enablements, e.g. the fact that people have limited life-spans, limited energy, limited physical capabilities, a limited capacity of memory; that they can walk and swim, but cannot fly unaided, that they can read only a certain number of books, and remember only a certain number of songs, and travel only a certain number of miles per day etc.).[15] We shall abstract from this kind of limitation here.

The proper socio-historical field of possibilities is set in two ways, negatively and positively. Negative constraints rule out actions that cannot (or at least should not) be taken, by means of proscriptions, prohibitions and taboos, or by means of a more tangible withdrawal of the requisite resources (people may abstain from killing because of the first commandment or because they do not have a gun). Positive facilitations encourage actions that can (or should) be taken, in the same way, by means of prescriptions or availability of resources. Both methods of delimitation, negative and positive, may operate from without, externally, by circumscribing the situation in which action is taken, or from within, internally, by circumscribing the constitution, endowment of the actor (his/her knowledge, motivations, attitudes, talents, skills, imagination, perseverance etc.).

To what extent do those various barriers and opportunities determine what people actually do? Let us break this question into its components. In my view, it has at least two distinct aspects. The first refers to the object of determination and concerns the scope of the qualities being determined. It may be expressed as the question of what properties of action are determined. The second aspect refers to the mechanism of determination and concerns the nature of the causal link between determining conditions and the object of determination. It may be expressed as the question of how human action is determined.

To the question specified in the first way (concerning the properties of action determined), two opposite answers can be given. (a) The action is determined in its whole concreteness and specificity; all the properties of an action are the object of determination. To put it briefly, what is determined is that a given person performs a certain concrete action. (b) The action is determined only in its generic, typical features, which are decisive for its membership of a particular class of actions. To put it briefly, what is determined is that a person of a certain type performs an action of a certain type. To the question specified in the second way (concerning the strength of the causal influence) another pair of opposite answers can be given. (a) The action is determined in the strict, necessitarian fashion. There is an unfailing one-to-one causal correspondence between the determining factors and the resulting action. To put it briefly, in such-and-such circumstances a person will invariably perform such-and-such an action. (b) The action is determined in a loose, probabilistic fashion. In the given determining conditions, a certain specifiable proportion of people belonging to a particular class, will be likely to take a given action. There is a certain, specifiable probability that, in the given circumstances, an action of a specified sort is apt to appear. To put it briefly: in such-and-such circumstances some members of a certain category of people will perform such-and-such an action.[16]

Both specifications of FATALISM$_2$ – describing the scope of determination and the strength of determination – are clearly independent. Therefore without the risk of contradiction we may recombine the two pairs of options, and derive four concrete interpretations of what fatalism could mean, as in figure 4.5.

The scope of determination

		PARTIAL	COMPLETE
The strength of determination	PROBABILISTIC	AUTONOMY	SELECTIVE BONDAGE
	NECESSITARIAN	ALLOWED VARIATIONS	TOTALISTIC TYRANNY

Figure 4.5

These interpretations may be placed along a continuum, from strong to weak determinism. The strongest version combines complete and necessitarian determination. The field of possibilities is strictly delimited, and actual actions taken within the field are strictly and precisely defined. People find themselves in a condition of totalitarian bondage or tyranny. A slightly weaker version treats the determination as complete in scope but probabilistic. Those who fall under the determination are bound totally, but not all do. For some there is a chance to escape determination. This is still bondage, but selective. The weaker version combines partial and necessitarian determination. People are seen as strictly determined to take actions of certain type, but all idiosyncrasies of style, application and execution are allowed. There are permitted variations, but only on the prescribed theme.

Finally the weakest version combines partial and probabilistic determination. People have considerable leeway to perform actions in variable, individually flavoured fashion, and a good chance of evading determination altogether. In other words, people are left with considerable autonomy; only some people among those belonging to a certain category are apt to choose some action out of those belonging to a certain type. Nothing can be definitely said about the determination of concrete specific action, taken by a concrete, named person. Determination of human action by the socio-historical context is general and not specific, and it is collective, not distributive. This interpretation will be called autonomism, and taken to represent the human condition more adequately than the alternatives. It is only in this sense that FATALISM$_2$ will be adopted in SB.

Let us turn now to the second composite assumption of possibilism, namely VOLUNTARISM$_1$. How do the choices and decisions taken within the limits of autonomy that actors possess in the field of possibilities influence the wider social and historical processes in which they participate? To say that human action has significant consequences (functions) for the operation of society and the course of history is still to leave the door wide open for the various interpretations of the scope that human intervention may have. To put it otherwise, the extent of effective human influence on society and history may still be questioned.

This question has two distinct aspects. The first refers to the aspirations and capacities of actors, and can be put as the question of what they want and what they can do. This defines what may be called their subjective potentialities. For example it may refer to human ambitions, skills, talents, competences. The second aspect refers to the receptiveness of the socio-historical reality to human intervention, and may be expressed as the question of what can be done. This defines what may be called the objective possibilities inherent in the situation. For example, it may refer to the inertia, resistance to change and rigidity of social and historical processes.

The question asked in the active voice (concerning the potentialities of an actor) engenders two opposite answers (a) Human actors are omnipotent; their repertoire of actions is unlimited; the actions they actually perform depend exclusively on their decisions (once the decisions are taken). They are also over-ambitious, never satiated, restless in their attempts to influence the outer world. In short, individuals want and can do everything. (b) Human actors are always limited, both in aspirations and capacities; there is only a certain restricted repertoire of actions available to them, and their ambitions are bridled by realism. In short, individuals want and can do some things, but by no means everything.

The question asked in the passive voice (concerning the inertia or resistance of socio-historical processes) engenders another pair of opposite answers. (a) The social and historical context is completely flexible, totally amenable to change; the operation of society and the course of history depend exclusively on the kind of actions that people take. To put it briefly, everything is attainable. (b) Social and historical processes are to some extent inert, rigid and resistant to change; there is only some area within which human intervention makes any difference and is effective; beyond that area it becomes ineffective and futile. To put it briefly, something is always attainable, but by no means everything.

Both specifications of VOLUNTARISM$_1$ – describing the subjective and objective potentialities – are clearly logically independent. Therefore without the risk of contradiction we may recombine two pairs of options, and derive four concrete interpretations of what voluntarism can mean (see figure 4.6).

As before, we have a continuum here, from the strongest to the weakest assertion of human power over social and historical processes. The strongest version claims the full and unlimited sovereignty of actors, who are seen as omnipotent against a totally flexible socio-historical world. Whatever they want can be reached. The more restricted version points to limited aspirations and capacities against a potentially malleable world. People do not want and cannot attain what is potentially attainable. This is a condition of negligence. The weaker version describes actors as omnipotent but blocked in their efforts by the inertia of rigid socio-historical processes. They want and can attain what unfortunately is not attainable. This is a condition of helplessness.

The weakest version ascribes to actors limited aspirations and capacities against an only partly malleable context. They are subjectively and objectively constrained, but within the borderlines of those constraints, there is always some field of opportunities for consequential action. The extent of those opportunities, always restricted but never vacant gives individuals variable efficacy in shaping the society and history in which they participate. This seems to present the most realistic depiction of the human condition. And it is only in this interpretation that the assumption of VOLUNTARISM₁ will be adopted in SB.

Thus, by a long analytical detour, we have returned to the assumption of possibilism, constructed as the dialectic solution to the dilemma of fatalism and voluntarism. Answering the question about the human role in society and history, we have defined possibilism as the condition in which human actors possess autonomy and efficacy. It means that they are acting in a field of possibilities which is always partly open, and by taking partly indetermined decisions and choices, they influence in a limited but not inconsiderable measure the operation of their societies and the course of history. The assumption of possibilism makes up the fourth, and pivotal, ontological foundation of the theory of social becoming.

Actors' aspirations and capacities

		LIMITATION	OMNIPOTENCE
Resistance of processes	RIGIDITY	EFFICACY	HELPLESSNESS
	FLEXIBILITY	NEGLIGENCE	SOVEREIGNTY

Figure 4.6

79

The theory

Reflexive consciousness

The last ontological problem arises with the recognition of the unique aspect of social reality, setting it apart from nature, namely the consciousness or awareness of social and historical phenomena on the part of their actual participants. Trees and stones do not reflect about forests or mountains; people do reflect about their society. Social consciousness takes on a great variety of forms, from common sense, rules of thumb or 'practical discourse' at one pole to sophisticated philosophical and sociological accounts or 'theoretical discourse' at the other. In one form or another, it always accompanies social life. Apart from the intricate epistemological puzzles that the presence of consciousness produces for the philosophy of the social sciences,[17] sooner or later the question of its ontological status has to be faced.

The answers that sociologists typically gave to this query went in two opposite directions. Those who were naturalistically (or positivistically) inclined tended to ignore or at least to minimize the awkward fact of consciousness. For them society possessed hard, objective 'facticity'; social phenomena were seen as existing independently of thoughts about them, and social consciousness was treated as a residual category. The ontological status of social consciousness was defined as derivative from objective facts. Those who embarked on the anti-naturalist (or anti-positivist) revolution took the opposite stand. They tended to focus on the domain of consciousness and to neglect the 'hard' social reality. Values, meanings, beliefs, creeds, reasons, goals of acting people – these were their main preoccupation. The objective roots of consciousness were often neglected or 'bracketed', and the world of objective social facts disappeared into the shadows. In this orientation the ontological status of social consciousness was treated as autonomous. As a result, another sociological dilemma was born, and it has haunted sociological theorizing ever since. Its crux was aptly grasped by Merton: 'It is one thing to maintain, with Weber, Thomas and the other giants of sociology, that to understand human action requires us to attend systematically to its subjective component: what people perceive, feel, believe and want. But it is quite another to exaggerate the sound idea by maintaining that action is nothing but subjective' (1976: 175). A similar warning against the dangers of one-sidedness is given by Giddens: 'action – reflexivity – has to be regarded as central to any comprehensive attempt to provide a theoretical explanation of human social life. At the same time it is of first importance to avoid the relapse into subjectivism that would attend an abandonement of the concept of structure' (1977: 117).

If we examine the dilemma of objectivism and subjectivism[18] more closely, it will be noticed that the dispute concerns two distinct aspects. One has to do with the ultimate substratum, the building blocks of the social world. Does it consist of people, their actions, groups and organizations treated as corporeal, material, real entities, located in space and time? Or rather does it resolve in consciousness, images, visions, projections and illusions, which constitute its ultimate fabric? Another aspect has to do with the causality operative in the social world. Is social consciousness purely receptive, fully derivative from the objective world, shaping and forming itself under its one-way impress? Or rather is social consciousness causally effective with respect to the objective world, intervening in the course of social events and processes?

Taking into consideration the distinction of substantive and causal aspects we may define four typical fragmentary assumptions. Thus concerning the substantive constitution of the social world the following opposition appears:

OBJECTIVISM$_1$ = social reality is made of real (material, corporeal, embodied) social objects, located in space and time (individuals, populations, groups, communities etc.), as well as their characteristic modes of functioning (individual and collective actions).

SUBJECTIVISM$_1$ = social reality exists solely in the consciousness of actors as the images, visions, constructs, especially those which are shared by pluralities of people and encoded in creeds, ideologies, doctrines, *Weltanschauung* – etc.

Now, concerning the direction of causality, another opposition may be defined:

OBJECTIVISM$_2$ = social consciousness is only a passive, more or less adequate mirror-image of the existing social world.

SUBJECTIVISM$_2$ = social consciousness exerts a causal influence on social reality; it significantly affects all that is going on in society (individual and collective actions, social events and processes etc.).

The substantive and causal aspects are clearly independent. Therefore the cross-combination of the two pairs of assumptions is a valid procedure. It will generate the four possible standpoints about the ontological status of social consciousness shown in figure 4.7.

What is the meaning of those combined solutions? Two of them are homogeneous, representing extreme forms of objectivism and subjectivism. Thus the combination of OBJECTIVISM$_1$ and OBJECTIVISM$_2$ makes up a standpoint asserting the objective, real existence of the social world, which imprints itself on the shared consciousness of societal members, resulting in images of some degree of similitude with their objects. The

The aspect of substance

	Objectivism$_1$	Subjectivism$_1$
Subjectivism$_2$	Reflexiveness	Solipsism
Objectivism$_2$	Similitude	Meta-awareness

The aspect of causation

Figure 4.7

opposite combination of SUBJECTIVISM$_1$ and SUBJECTIVISM$_2$ locates social reality exclusively in the domain of consciousness, where autonomously existing images, ideas, concepts, doctrines etc. are interconnected and influence each other in quasi-causal fashion. The term 'solipsism' may be borrowed from philosophy to refer to this extreme variety of subjectivism. The third standpoint is mixed; it merges SUBJECTIVISM$_1$ with OBJECTIVISM$_2$. It seems to imply that in the autonomously existing world of ideas there are components of different orders; in particular one may distinguish a narrower class of meta-ideas, reflections about reflections, images of images. In other words, it asserts the existence of meta-awareness. This solution is clearly not synthetic, as it simply specifies or even extends the 'solipsist' view.

It is only with the fourth mixed standpoint that we reach a truly synthetic solution, which presents a dialectic replacement of the dilemma. The combination of OBJECTIVISM$_1$ and SUBJECTIVISM$_2$ will be called the assumption of reflexiveness and incorporated into SB as the last of its ontological premises. It claims that society has a real, spatial and temporal existence, but that social consciousness is neither its epiphenomenon nor its passive mirror image. It is causally active, influencing the course of social events and processes, and in this sense it is not external to society, but rather internally constitutive of society. In other words, it is as real as other more tangible social objects – people, groups and actions – and it enters the causal net, leaving an impress on the operation of society and the movement of history. It is not only about society, but in society.

How does this come about? The answer is that human beings, and human beings only, act on beliefs; they take into account various ideas about themselves, their place in a society, the mechanism of social functioning and social change, the prospects for the future – and incorporate them into their motivations and reasons for acting. On this basis they make decisions and choices. In other words, they act on the basis of their subjective perceptions of the situation, whether those perceptions are true or false, adequate or inadequate. As Lichtman observes: 'Only men can reconstitute themselves in accordance with the newly acquired knowledge of their own situation' (1967: 143).[19] Human actions are ultimately what society is made of, the elementary stuff of social events and processes. Via this link, images of society causally influence society. 'What people believe about the way the world works can contribute to making it work that way' (Bell and Mau 1970: 220).

This peculiarity of the social world is beautifully grasped in what came to be known as 'The Thomas Theorem': 'If men [or women] define situations as real they are real in their consequences' (Merton 1982: 248). This statement by W. I. Thomas, with its emphasis on the objective outcomes of human subjectivity, is rightly singled out by Merton as 'probably the single most consequential sentence ever put in print by an American sociologist' (1973: 262). Of course not all human actions are informed by self-awareness of social and historical processes. Much happens in a blind fashion, via unintended consequences, latent effects or the 'cunning of reason' (Hollis 1987). Merton emphatically notes that the reverse of the Thomas Theorem does not hold. It is not true that 'If men do not define situations as real, they are not real in their consequences' (1976: 174). To avoid the fallacy of total subjectivism he proposes a counterpart: 'And if men do not define real situations as real, they are nevertheless real in their consequences' (p. 177). The Thomas Theorem indicates the peculiar human potential of extending reality by means of the independent causal power of interpretation, definition, imagination and projection. It does not presuppose the insulation of individuals from the impact of reality.

So far we have been discussing the common-sense consciousness or everyday self-awareness of societal members. But the same mechanism of reflexivity applies to theoretical consciousness, the sociological knowledge formulated by specialists. In recent decades this perplexing and unique property of social knowledge has come to the fore of sociological debate, as both a difficulty and a challenge. Hollis jokes: 'That molecules have no thought about molecules must be of great relief to the physicist' (1987: 4). On the other hand Popper looks at it as a cognitive opportunity: 'Nowhere is the fact that the scientist and his object belong to the same world of greater moment than in the social sciences. . . . We are faced, in the social sciences, with a full and complicated interaction between observer and observed, between subject and object' (1964 [1957]: 14).

Whether they like it or not, students of society do not stand in a detached external position *vis-à-vis* their subject matter; rather they are studying something which is in part their own creation and which undergoes changes dependent in part on their own activities. Each student of society is thereby in a sense a student of himself. This is even more true if we think of the collectively acquired, shared knowledge of society, produced by the scientific community and more or less widely available to societal members. It is the internal experience of a society by itself, the form of collective self-knowledge, the true union of the subject and object of cognition. As McRae puts it: 'Sociology is a major form of human self-consciousness, a kind of imperfect looking glass in which we may see reflected back the visage of society' (1974: 7).

As a result, social theory has intimate, immediate relevance for social events and historical processes. The theories of Kepler, Newton or Einstein, do not, by themselves, influence the orbits of the planets: a theory of human action, social order or social development may directly influence the human beings who are at once its ultimate referents and its ultimate addressees, and in effect transform the very processes about which it makes its assertions.

> Of critical import to the social and behavioral sciences alone is the fact that the very discovery of an order in the realm of the social must inevitably, by the very grammar that adheres to social or behavioral research, act to some degree as a new and unique element in the stream of empirical events that make up human interaction . . . Such social knowledge stands as a new and unique factor entering into the social matrix that includes both the researcher and his subjects, transforming it in some measure from the matrix that might have been if the order had not been revealed. (Friedrichs 1972: 266)

Other authors make similar observations: 'Theories in action become a material force . . . Once they enter into collective knowledge and consciousness, they affect beliefs, orientations and actions and, therefore, become real, that is social facts' (Burns 1976: 6). 'Among the ideas which move people are ideas about what moves them. Social theory, being itself in circulation among its subjects, is tied to its own tail' (Hollis 1987: 4).

The important implication of this peculiar trait of social theory is its direct, immediate applicability. In the natural sciences the relationship of theory and practice is normally mediated by the formulation of the directives of action (know-how) derived from basic knowledge (know-that), and the translation of basic knowledge into directives is a quite complex task, requiring special subdisciplines of the so-called practical, technical or applied sciences. In the social sciences this is not necessarily the case. Very often, descriptive, explanatory or predictive knowledge, by virtue of being in a significant respect the self-knowledge of society, may become immediately relevant for social practice, for the shaping of human conduct from the simplest everyday acts to the most complex political decisions.

This immediate influence of social knowledge on social practice is discussed by Merton as the mechanism of self-fulfilling and self-destroying prophecies, where the sheer fact of a prediction becoming known among those whose behaviour it concerns can validate an initially invalid claim and invalidate an initially valid one. The former case occurs when 'an initially false but widely shared prediction, expectation, or belief is fulfilled in practice not because it was at the outset true, but because enough people took it to be true and, by acting accordingly, produced the outcome that would otherwise not have occurred' (Merton 1982: 103). The latter case refers to the pattern in which 'public prediction of future social developments [is] frequently not sustained precisely because the prediction has become a new element in the concrete situation, thus tending to change the initial course of developments' (1976: 154).

Thus theories in the social sciences may have an immediate practical impact. Theorizing, therefore, may be equivalent to a practical influence. This truth should not escape social scientists, as it burdens them with particular responsibility: 'The writing of history merges imperceptibly into the responsible act of creating history . . . The formulation, as well as the act of describing the image of the future, may influence the future itself' (Polak 1961, vol. 1: 57). In the field of our immediate concern, 'In recent years, sociological "truths" have come . . . to influence the way people see themselves and their societies and, thus, have been consequential for the behavior that emerges from such conceptions' (Bell and Mau 1970: 208). Therefore 'sociologists can help to change the world through their reinterpretation of it' (p. 239).

I have devoted considerable attention to the assumption of reflexiveness, because it seems to be another of those ontological insights without which contemporary sociological theory simply cannot do. The richness of its implications, many of them still unexamined, has been recognized only recently. Reflexiveness will act as one of the core premises of SB.

This closes our discussion of the five ontological foundations on which the theory of social becoming will be built. They were constructed by finding synthetic, dialectical solutions to five pervasive ontological dilemmas present in social thought and sociological theory from their very beginning. In effect, a coherent image of the constructed, constructing and historical social world has slowly emerged. It is a world in which reflexive individuals are seen as creatures and creators at the same time, social wholes as fluid relational networks humanly made, but also affecting people, and historical processes as the stream of incessant interplay of emergence and determination, in the course of which both individuals and society undergo cumulative transformations. Such a world clearly embodies what we identified earlier as two crucial dimensions of 'social becoming', namely the agential and historical coefficients. Now we have to unravel how society, so depicted, actually operates, and this will require constructing the model of social becoming. This will be our task in the next chapter.

5

The model of social becoming

Setting the layout

In my understanding of a theory, its central part is made of a general, comprehensive image of the subject matter: the conceptual model embracing the main principle of its constitution, operation and transformation. In this chapter I shall try to present a conceptual model of society; a set of logically interlinked categories representing how society is built, how it functions and how it evolves. The model will be rooted in the five ontological assumptions explicated earlier: structuralism, creativism, processualism, possibilism and reflexiveness. It will attempt to show how the social mode of being, conceived in these terms, can actually manifest itself in its complex dynamics.

Obviously the task is quite involved. I shall approach it step by step, gradually and carefully, by a series of successive approximations. The full picture will appear slowly, become more and more complicated, and incorporate more and more dimensions, levels and aspects. In this way it will become more realistic, coming closer to actual human experience. But the point of departure must be most abstract, a mere frame to be filled later.

Let us start by distinguishing two levels of social reality: the level of individualities and the level of totalities.[1] The former is made of people, as individuals or as members of concrete collectivities (groups, associations, communities, movements etc.). The latter is made of abstract social wholes of a super-individual sort, representing social reality *sui generis* (societies, cultures, civilizations, socio-economic formations, social systems etc.). In terms of our ontological assumptions of structuralism and creativism, the social wholes are interpreted neither as mere congeries nor as metaphysical entities, but as STRUCTURES; and social individuals are seen neither as passive objects nor as fully autonomous subjects,but as bounded AGENTS.

Now a second distinction may be added. It has to do with two modes of existence of social reality; the mode of potentialities and the mode of actualities. We refer to the former when speaking of inherent tendencies, germs or seeds of the future, capacities, abilities, 'powers' etc. We refer to the latter when speaking of processes, transformations, development, conduct, activities etc.

Both modes can be taken by each of the major components of the social world. Structures may be treated as potentialities actualizing themselves (unfolding) in OPERATION; and agents as potentialities actualizing themselves (mobilizing) in ACTION. Thus, by cross-cutting the two dichotomies – of levels and of modes – we arrive at four concepts making the cornerstones of our model: structures and agents, operations and actions (figure 5.1).

	POTENTIALITY	ACTUALITY
TOTALITY	STRUCTURE	OPERATION
INDIVIDUALITY	AGENT	ACTION

Figure 5.1

Let us consider the relations between the cells of this fourfold table. In the vertical dimension we postulate the complementary relations of *emergence* and *autonomy*. Structures are seen as emergent with respect to agents; even though they embrace agents, they possess their own, specific properties and regularities. They are inter-agential networks, not reducible to the sum of agents.[2] But agents also are not reducible to their structural location; they possess some measure of autonomy, integrity, relative freedom to choose and decide. They are self-contained entities, with specific properties and regularities, and not only nodal points of structures.[3]

Similarly, the operation of structures (functioning of society) must be treated as emergent with respect to actions taken by agents. Even though actions make the ultimate stuff of societal operation, the latter is not reducible to the former; combining numerous interrelated actions it acquires its own specific momentum, pattern or sequential logic. It is more than a sum of actions. We defined structures as static emergents with respect to agents, even though without agents there would be no structures. In a parallel fashion operation is a dynamic emergent with respect to actions, even though without actions there would be no operation. As Peter Blau puts it: 'Although complex social systems have their foundation in simpler ones, they have their own dynamics with emergent properties' (1979: 20). Those properties may be analytically considered at their own level, in abstraction from the fact that the ultimate substratum of societal operation is made of social actions.

I would suggest three forms of such independent dynamics of structures. Thus one may observe a 'principle of inertia': it is usually more likely that the functioning will continue in the same fashion rather than taking a radical turn[4] (e.g. in the countries of 'real socialism', raising prices and taxes had for a long time been a more typical response to economic shortages than switching from a planned to a market-oriented economy; changing leaders was much more common than replacing totalitarianism with democracy; building another coal mine was a standard investment decision, rather than turning to nuclear energy etc.). One may also observe a 'principle of momentum' (or continuation): when a certain phase or stage of operation is reached, it is likely to proceed to the next stage, rather than stopping or turning back[5] (e.g. if some policy is started it tends to continue at least for some time; if investments are made in some area of economy, they engender further related investments; if disorganization appears in some domain of social life, it tends to widen and engulf other domains; if people's consumption needs are already satisfied to some extent it is hard to lower the level of need-satisfaction).[6] Finally there is also a 'principle of sequence'; phases of the operation are patterned, and often cannot be omitted.[7] There are routines of all sorts in social life, which have to be followed in regular sequence to be effective (e.g. the economy cannot be modernized without educating the labour force first; consumption-patterns cannot be changed without producing or importing new, original products). Those are only hypothetical illustrations, intended to show that emergent structures may be seen as unfolding in emergent fashion, according to their own principles.

Conversely actions are not mere embodiments of societal functioning fully embedded in the momentum of operation. They have some measure of autonomy, a relative independence of the dynamic social context in which they participate. At least a part of what agents actually do may not fit the actual mode of social functioning; they may 'go against the current', act in anachronistic ways or anticipate the future by exhibiting imagination, originality or innovativeness.

If we turn to the horizontal dimension of our fourfold table, the relation between agents and actions is quite intuitive. It is covered by the concept of 'mobilization'. Agents mobilize their potential capacities, abilities, needs, attitudes and dispositions in taking actions of various sorts. They eat when hungry, quarrel when angry, compose symphonies when talented, make revolutions when 'relatively deprived', wage wars when armed etc. Of course there are multiple factors which decide whether they actually do all these things or abstain from action, keeping their potentialities latent. Some of the intermediate variables entering the causal nexus between agential potentialities and their manifestation in action will be discussed in the next chapter, when the model will be operationalized.

Much less obvious is the horizontal relation at the upper level: between structures and their functioning (operation). It will be grasped by the concept of 'unfolding'. Structures unfold in operation, discharge their inherent potentialities, tendencies, dispositions in functioning. For example, they are apt to break down and change when pervaded with contradictions, tensions or strains; conversely, they are likely to operate smoothly when internally homogeneous and harmonious; or they are likely to produce stagnation when undifferentiated and centralized whereas they are likely to develop when pluralistic and decentralized. Of course there are several intervening variables which decide whether the potentialities of structures will actually unfold or not.[8] Their tentative consideration has to be put off till later chapters. For the moment the simple examples given are intended only to prove the general point, that actualization of structures may be analytically conceived as separate from the actualization of agents, even though in reality both are intimately linked.

The model of social becoming

In the middle: agency and praxis

All analysis must be a step toward synthesis. Having defined the level of structures (in their operation), and the level of agents (in their action) as distinct and separate, we must attempt now to bring them together, to conceptualize their linkage. This is a crucial move in the construction of our model. It is here, at the 'interface' (Archer 1988: xviii) between structures and agents, operations and actions, that the riddle of social becoming must be traced.

Several authors have taken the search in this direction by emphasizing the 'duality of structures' (and its logical corollary, the duality of agents) or more generally, the 'analytical dualism' of social reality. For Giddens: 'duality of structure . . . expresses the mutual dependence of structure and agency' (1979: 69). Thus 'the constitution of agents and structures are not two independently given sets of phenomena, a dualism, but represent a duality. According to the notion of the duality of structure, the structural properties of social systems are both medium and outcome of the practices they recursively organize' (1984: 25). The 'duality of agents' could be proposed as a complementary principle, meaning that the properties of agents are both the products of structures and the resources for structure-building. A similar suggestion is made by Bhaskar: 'If society is the condition of our agency, human agency is equally a condition for society, which, in its continuity, it continually reproduces and transforms. On this model, then, society is at once the ever-present condition and the continually reproduced outcome of human agency: this is the duality of structure' (1986: 123).

Archer challenges the 'duality of structure' and opts for 'analytical dualism': 'the attempt to conceptualize how certain properties of the "parts" and certain properties of the "people" actually combine at the interface' (1988: xviii). She proposes to examine their interaction, their mutual interplay, rather than conflating them as 'tightly constitutive of one another' (p. xiii), because 'the whole point of analytical dualism is to be able to investigate the relations between them' (p. 141). I shall not enter this debate, because, utilizing the insights of both parties, I shall propose a slightly different conceptualization, a third solution.

In the model of social becoming, the levels of structure in operation and of agents in actions will be treated neither as analytically separable nor as mutually reducible. Instead a third, intermediate level will be postulated, and it will be claimed that it represents the only true substance of social reality, the specific social fabric. If we think of any empirical event or phenomenon in a society, anything that is actually happening, is it not always, without exception, a fusion of structures and agents, of

91

operation and action? Show me an agent who is not enmeshed in some structure. Show me a structure which exists apart from individuals. Show me an action which does not participate in societal operation. Show me societal operation not resolving into action. There are neither structure-less agents nor agentless structures. At the same time structures do not melt away into agents, nor agents into structures.[9]

I have always been struck by the wisdom of a sentence written by Charles H. Cooley: 'Self and society are twin-born' (quoted in Fletcher 1971, vol. 2: 486) and by Marx's earlier claim: 'Circumstances make men in the same measure that men make circumstances' (in McLellan 1971: 129). Why should we not take seriously the full implication of these insights that there is neither agential nor structural reality *per se*? Nor is there any conceivable mode of real interaction between those two realities, between agents and structures treated separately. In fact, they are fused together in one human–social world, the agential *cum* structural fabric of society. It is not the case that separate agents and structures interact to produce effects. Rather, the agential–structural reality in its internal, immanent unity appears in various permutations, various combinations of agential and structural ingredients, making up social events.[10] The ultimate stuff, the real components of which society is made is events, neither individual acts nor 'social facts', but their intimate, concrete fusions.[11]

This standpoint finally departs from some illusions clearly inherited in sociology from common sense. The first is the 'illusion of egocentrism'. We think of ourselves (and by implication, of other people) as self-contained, integral, separate entities, possessing independent existence. But it is only an illusion of our egocentric self-consciousness. If we are separate at all, it is only as things: those skin-bound bags full of flesh (if I may use the expression). All that is human in us is neither separate nor independent. C. H. Cooley made this point at the very beginning of our century: 'The individual is not separable from the human whole, but a living member of it, deriving his life from the whole through social and hereditary transmission as truly as if men were literally one body. He cannot cut himself off; the strands of heredity and education are woven into all his being' (1964 [1902]: 35). At another point he says: 'Self and society are twin-born, we know one as immediately as we know the other, and the notion of a separate and independent ego is an illusion, (Cooley 1962 [1909]: 5). Our truly human nature is derived from society, expressed through society, existing only through its links with society. We can live only with other people, for others, alongside others, together with others, against others. Even when physically alone or isolated, we still preserve those links in our minds – in our language, education, morality, attitudes, motivations, loyalties, self-identifications, dreams, plans etc. As Fletcher comments on Cooley:

We cannot define the boundary of an individual self by throwing a kind of sheath about his skin. A human mind is not like that. It is not limited to the boundaries of the body. A person cannot be so defined. The dimensions of his mind are spread along all avenues of his perception and social awareness. (Fletcher 1971, vol. 2: 485)

There is no escape from society, except by death, which takes us back into a non-human, material state. Why not draw ultimate conclusions from this fact? Why maintain that the individual and society are separate and opposed entities? Why not see ourselves as merely parts, components and elements of a wider social fabric? Why not admit that we have only a virtual individual existence?

The second is the 'illusion of reification'. We think of states, bureaucracies, economies, political regimes, social systems etc. as super-individual, towering, often oppressive edifices, standing above us, distant from us, independent of our will and yet controlling our lives. But it is only an illusion of our distorted imagination, the product of our tendency to create hypostases. If social objects are super-individual at all, it is only in their material, physical substratum in the form of barracks and tanks, offices and courtrooms, prisons and hospitals, aeroplanes and cars. Their truly social, institutional nature consists entirely of people and their actions. They exist only so long and only in so far as individuals fill the material shell with actions. Without them, there are no social wholes; at the most, there are dead physical skeletons of societies – as in the sad museum of Pompeii or in that terrifying scene from *The Last Shore* when, after nuclear war, the buildings of a city remain intact but there are no people. Homans makes the point with typical clarity: 'The characteristics of social groups and societies are the resultants, no doubt the complicated resultants but still the resultants, of the interaction between individuals over time – and they are no more than that' (1974: 12). Societies are made of individuals and exist only through individuals. Why not recognize that fact? Why maintain that social wholes are somewhere above us living their own, separate lives? Why not admit that they have only a virtual social existence?

The transmutation of those illusions at the level of theoretical discourse produces the fallacy of epiphenomenalism, in its two pervasive versions. One is the 'fallacy of individualistic epiphenomenalism', which treats social wholes as emanations of individual minds, imagined concepts rather than tangible objects. Here only individuals are endowed with true existence and societies exist only in human heads. The other is the 'fallacy of collectivistic epiphenomenalism', which treats individuals as emanations of society, as puppets, marionettes, fully absorbed and not separately distinguishable in society. Here, only societies are endowed with true existence, and people exist only as the raw material of society. Both views are wrong. Why not admit that both societies and individuals are real, only integrated so closely that there is no way to disentangle the fabric, to separate the threads? Let us quote Cooley again:

> A separate individual is an abstraction unknown to experience, and so likewise is society when regarded as something apart from individuals . . . 'Society' and 'individuals' do not denote separable phenomena . . . Through both the hereditary and the social factors in his life a man is bound into the whole of which he is a member, and to consider him apart from it is quite as artificial as to consider society apart from individuals. (Cooley 1964 [1902]: 36–8)

Elsewhere he says: 'Self and society go together as phases of a common whole' (1962 [1909]: 5). Why not recognize that neither individuals nor wholes are even conceivable apart from each other? There is no way to think of human individuals outside some social context, because the very definition of what it means to be an individual must contain reference to some social whole, be it family, tribe, local community, nation, professional group etc. Similarly, there is no way to think of social wholes apart from the individuals who make them up, because the very definition of any social whole must include some reference to its components, members of groups, incumbents of positions, performers of roles etc.

This leads us back to our central claim: what truly exists in society, in the full ontological sense, is the *unified socio-individual field*, the 'third level of reality' between traditionally conceived levels of totalities and individualities. Social wholes and human individuals in isolation have only a virtual existence, their separation and mutual opposition are the product of false, distorted imagination, common-sense illusions and theoretical as well as meta-theoretical fallacies.

The concept of a socio-individual field provides the solution to the first dichotomy that we distinguished at the outset: it overcomes the opposition of the individual versus society (or individualities versus totalities). But what about the two remaining dichotomies: statics versus dynamics, and potentiality versus actuality? It will be shown that the oppositions they convey are equally illusory and fallacious, and that the concept of a socio-individual field brings a bonus, allowing us to surmount them as well.

Thus the separation of the static and dynamic aspects of social reality, of persistence and transformation, stability and movement, order and change, must also be seen as fully artificial. No social entities (whether wholes or individuals) exist in a timeless void; they are always located in the temporal context, as moments, episodes or phases in the continuous, sequential chain of a process. But conversely, no social process exists *per se*, devoid of some substratum, without something that is changed, transformed, modified. All social objects undergo constant movement, they are in the process of incessant change – to use somewhat metaphorical language, they are living. But they also retain identity; they are different, and yet remain the same objects for varied spans of time – in metaphorical terms they have their particular lives. 'Life' in this wide, liberal meaning is simply constant self-transformation. If we think of social reality as a unified socio-individual field, we may now extend this notion as a 'living socio-individual field'.

The last dichotomy, the opposition and separation of potential and actual modes of social being, is equally misleading. In fact they are intimately linked by mutual feedback loops. Potentialities (capacities, abilities, skills, facilities, resources etc.) are manifested in conduct, but they are not given. Rather they are shaped by earlier conduct (experience, training, learning etc.), themselves produced by actualizations. In turn, their actualizations reshape the potentialities for future conduct (enrich tradition, resources, possibilities). There is an incessant back-and-forth oscillation between what is possible and what actually occurs, and it extends in time. This I propose to identify by the concept of *becoming*. Thus we arrive at the ultimate characterization of social reality, as a *living socio-individual field in the process of becoming*.

To avoid this long and awkward phrase I propose the simple category of *social becoming* as the comprehensive term covering the peculiar socio-individual constitution and the peculiar processual mode of existence of social reality. In this idea all the six poles of ambivalence so pervasive in the perception of society (whether in common sense or in theoretical discourse) are merged and fused: persons and groups, order and change, possibilities and realities. Society in the image proposed here, exists only as social becoming. In its very essence it is multidimensional, ambivalent, dualistic, 'dialectical'. This is the peculiar, unique mode of social being which provides the specific subject matter for sociological science.

Let us examine the anatomy of social becoming a little more closely. What is this peculiar reality made of? We have to identify its ultimate components, and then the forms in which they are combined and aggregated. There are numerous candidates for the status of elementary 'social particles' that have been proposed in sociological theory: persons, actors, actions, behaviours – in various brands of individualism; interactions, joint actions, social relations, roles, status-roles – in various versions of structuralism; groups, collectivities, communities – in theories informed by holism or collectivism; symbols, values, norms, beliefs, interests – in subjectivist theories. Perhaps this list is incomplete. But none of the 'received' ideas fits the ontology of social becoming. For this perspective, the ultimate atoms of social reality are *events*.[12] Society is made of social events. Why events? Because they are the only elementary ontological objects bridging all the three dualisms or dichotomies which we have found illusory and fallacious. In their own constitution social events fuse individualities and totalities, persistence and change, potentiality and actuality. Events always have this synthetic quality, comprising three dimensions of being; they are located at the crossing of three axes organizing human experiences in society. Whatever event we take, on the microscale (e.g. eating breakfast) or on the macroscale (e.g. waging war), it relates to some person (persons) acting in the context of some social whole which is supported or reshaped by the action; it involves some sequential changes but preserves the relative continuity of their subject; and it displays capacities transformed in their realization, and turning into new capacities.

Events do not occur in isolation from others. They make up clusters and sequences, routines and procedures, chains and processes, spatiotemporally connected, and involving pluralities of people in diversified social contexts. Taking the suggestion from Marx, Gramsci and Lukács, we shall call the actual manifestations of the social fabric – the ongoing social events – by the term 'praxis'. Praxis is where operation and action meet, a dialectic synthesis of what is going on in a society and what people are doing. It represents the confluence of operating structures and acting agents, the combined product of the momentum of operation (at the level of totalities) and the course of actions undertaken by societal members (at the level of individualities). To put it in other words, it is doubly conditioned (constrained and facilitated): from above, by the phase of functioning reached by wider society, and from below, by the conduct of individuals and their groups. But it is not reducible to either: with respect to both levels – of individualities and totalities – it is a new, emergent quality. In this way the concept of praxis is anchored vertically to the two core concepts of our model referring to actualities: operation and action.

Now, remaining at this intermediate level, let us employ a sort of backward reasoning. If 'praxis' is the actuality, the manifestation of social fabric, then there must be something which is actualized, or manifested, the inherent potentiality for praxis, or more precisely, a set of capacities, dispositions, tendencies immanent in the social fabric and allowing praxis to emerge. The concept of agency is proposed as correlative to praxis, located at the same level but referring to a different mode of existence, namely bearing upon the potentiality for praxis. Let me represent this phase of our reasoning on a simple diagram (figure 5.2).

Agency so conceived is an attributive notion; it summarizes certain properties of the social fabric, this 'really real reality' of the social world. It is where structures (capacities for operation) and agents (capacities for

96

action) meet, a synthetic product, a fusion of structural circumstances and agential endowment. As such, it is doubly conditioned: from above by the balance of constraints and limitations, resources and facilities provided by existing structures; and from below by the abilities, talents, skills, knowledge, attitudes of societal members and the organizational forms in which they are pooled together in collectivities, groups, social movements etc. But it is not reducible to either; with respect to both levels – of totalities and individualities – it makes up a new, emergent quality.[13]

So far we have anchored the concept of agency vertically, in two other core concepts of our model referring to potentialities: structures and agents. But it must also link itself horizontally, with the concept of praxis. As a potentiality, agency is actualized in praxis, manifested in social events. This horizontal link between agency and praxis will be covered by the term 'eventuation'. It is again, a confluence of actualizations going on at other levels; a fusion of the unfolding of structures, and the mobilization of agents. Thus, it is conditioned from above and from below, but

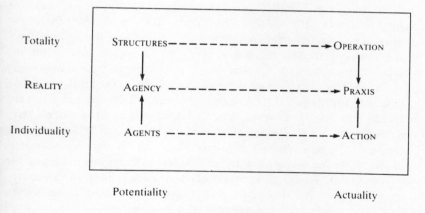

Figure 5.2

is not reducible to either of the processes, and represents a new, emergent quality. Like those constitutive processes, it is also contingent; eventuation is only possible or probable, but never necessary. Agency may be actualized in various measures, it may also remain latent or dormant. We shall suggest some variables relevant here in the next chapter, when the task of operationalization will be faced.

Three sequences linking potentialities and actualities, namely structures-unfolding-in-operation, agents-mobilizing-in-action and the synthetic process, agency-eventuating-in-praxis, have been treated as linear, working in one direction only. We must correct this by recalling the ideas of 'duality of structure' and 'duality of agents'. Piaget focuses on the level of totalities, writing of 'the constant duality, or bipolarity, of always being simultaneously structuring and structured' (1971: 10), and Plamenatz focuses on the level of individualities, saying of an agent: 'he is the product of his own activities . . . what he has done and its effects upon him' (1975: 76). As I read them, those formulations convey an important insight concerning the feedbacks that must be included in the model. The first refers to the self-modifying propensity of structures: they are reshaped by their own operation, so that we may speak of the process of structure-building. The second refers to the self-modifying propensity of agents; they are reshaped by their own action, and we may speak of the moulding of agents.[14] Applying the same idea *mutatis mutandis* to the mediating, third level of agential–structural reality, we may say that agency is significantly reshaped by praxis. We may speak of agency-construction. To bring this point home, I shall allow those three feedbacks into our model, indicating them by reversed arrows. But the questions: 'How does this come about?' 'How may the potentialities may be influenced by their own actualizations?' 'How does the self-generative mechanism really operate?' must be postponed.[15] They have to await the moment when the dimension of time is introduced into the model. Then the misleading image of causation working backwards will disappear.

New categories of agency and praxis, as well as the addition of linking processes and feedbacks at all levels, have considerably enriched the model of social becoming. Agency and praxis have been shown to constitute two sides of the incessant social functioning; agency actualizes in praxis, and praxis reshapes agency, which actualizes itself in changed praxis. We may summarize the present stage of conceptual elaboration by means of the extended diagram in figure 5.3.

Because my use of the terms does not always coincide with earlier conventions, which themselves are ambiguous and sometimes contradictory, it is time to reiterate the definitions of three crucial concepts, the triad of 'A's – actors, agents and agency – as they appear in the context of the model. All three are taken to refer to the mode of potentiality; they are attributive concepts. The term 'actor' signifies this core aspect, the dimension of a person – a fully-fledged, living, integral human being – which manifests itself in acting, the core form of human existence. 'Actor' is the potentiality of an individual for action, a set of specific drives, skills, abilities, 'powers' which may be mobilized and manifested in action. The term 'agent' is more comprehensive; it includes not only individuals but also concrete, bounded collectivities, groups, social movements etc. It refers to those aspects of individuals and collectivities which enable or dispose them to act, to perform individual or collective action respectively. They include all the individual capacities for action mentioned earlier, and also the means by which those capacities are pooled together in collective conduct: cooperation, coordination, division of labour etc. Finally, the term 'agency' refers to the capacity of society as such – that specific agential-structural fabric – to conduct praxis and produce social events. It covers all those and only those traits of society – abstracted from its full, limitless complexity – which are relevant for praxis, the core form of social existence.

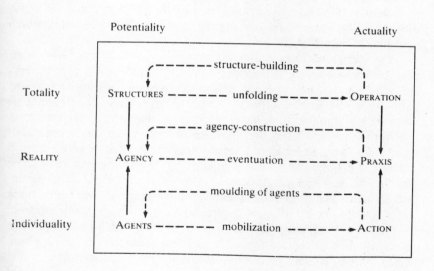

Figure 5.3

Environments: nature and consciousness

The model of social becoming, as constructed so far, is suspended in a vacuum. Our next step must consist in supplying it with a wider context. Social becoming must be placed in the environment. I postulate two kinds of environments. The first is quite intuitive; it is nature. The second is less so; it is consciousness. Contrary to appearances, there is a striking similarity between the two, as concerns their general status *vis-à-vis* human actions and societal operation. Because humans are natural corporeal beings, living in space and time, utilizing natural resources, affecting natural conditions etc., nature is an inescapable 'container' in which social life flows. People cannot exist outside it. Hence, it is the first necessary environment of the social world. But humans are also thinking beings, utilizing symbols, communicating with others, formulating beliefs etc. They are always immersed in the milieu of ideas, their own, as well as those of their contemporaries and predecessors. Again, people are not even conceivable outside that. Hence, consciousness can be treated as the second necessary environment of human society. In sum, the given, inevitable duality of the human constitution – as natural object, and conscious subject at the same time – entails the duality of environments which surround human praxis.

Let us start from the more obvious side, from the natural environment. It appears in two guises: as the external natural conditions in which agents and structures act and operate, and as the internal constitutive traits of individuals, who are the ultimate substratum of society. The first may be illustrated by climate, topography, ecology, geology etc. These are clearly relevant to human actions. But they are also relevant to the operation of structures. Some networks of interrelations are enabled or even enforced and others precluded by natural conditions. Think of migration routes, trade paths, communication networks or settlement patterns in mountainous areas, as opposed to the plains, those emerging in valleys or along rivers, and those established at the seashore or on islands. Or think about hierarchies of inequality of wealth or power, typical for areas poor in resources, as opposed to those emerging in conditions of natural abundance. Those are only random illustrations that come to mind.

Nature, however, affects society not only from without but also from within, via the biological constitution and genetic endowment of populations. Much of what goes on in a society depends on the mental skills, inborn talents, physical strength, endurance, health, fitness etc. of each member, as well as on the recurrence and distribution of those biological traits across various segments of the population. Even though, literally speaking, these influences operate from inside individuals, they may also be treated as part of the environment in a more abstract sense – an environment with respect to what is irreducibly, specifically human in people and their societies.[16]

In both forms, as external and internal influences, the natural environment may appear as negative constraints (barriers, blockades), or positive enablements (facilitations, resources). To complicate matters even more, the relationship of nature to society must be seen as two-sided and reciprocal. Nature provides parametric conditions, but at the same time interactive conditions for human agency and praxis. It sets the field for the possible actualizations of the agency, but via praxis it can be shaped itself, and therefore the field can be modified. On the one hand, it may be extended. That is what technology, civilization, and in general 'humanized nature' are all about. Note that the 'internal environment' – the inherited, biological or psychological endowment – can also be extended via action. That is what training, mental exercise, self-improvement, cultivation of fitness etc. refer to. On the other hand, the feedback of praxis on the natural environment need not be positive or beneficial. It may also narrow the field of possibilities for the actualization of the agency. It is only recently that we have widely recognized the detrimental, even disastrous, impact of human praxis on nature. Pullution, depletion of resources, shortages of energy, ecological destruction etc. are illustrations of this phenomenon as it affects the external, non-human environment, while the so-called diseases of civilization, the deterioration of health, stamina or psychological well-being of populations, show how the internal, hereditary constitution of individuals may also be adversely affected by their own actions.

Let us turn to the second type of environment, the social conciousness or 'ideological milieu' in which social becoming operates. Immersion in consciousness must be treated as one of the distinguishing attributes of social systems. As Jarvie puts it: 'The social world is peculiar in that its entities, processes and relations emerge from, and are constituted by, the actions of its members, and these in turn are predicated on the theories and pictures of it which they entertain from time to time' (1972: 10). Another formulation is given by Boulding: 'Social systems are what I call "image-directed", that its, they are systems in which the knowledge of the systems themselves is a significant part of the system's own dynamics and in which, therefore, the knowledge about the system changes the system' (1964: 7).

Consciousness manifests itself at various levels of our model. Primarily, it is of course the attribute of individual actors. I follow Giddens in attaching great importance to what he calls 'human knowledgeability': 'Human agents or actors . . . have, as an inherent aspect of what they do, the capacity to understand what they do while they do it' (Giddens

1984: xxii). Therefore, 'To be a human being is to be a purposive agent, who both has reasons for his or her activities and is able, if asked to elaborate discursively upon these reasons (including lying about them)' (p. 3). Elaborating some insights of Alfred Schutz, Giddens distinguishes two forms of consciousness, practical and discursive: 'Human actors are not only able to monitor their activities and those of others in the regularity of day-to-day conduct; they are also able to "monitor that monitoring" in discursive consciousness' (p. 29). This is undoubtedly a fundamental ontological fact, which must be taken into account in any picture of social reality.[17] Consciousness, or awareness in this sense may be ascribed not only to actors, but to other kinds of agents: collective ones. We speak of 'group culture', 'idioculture', 'group ideology' (Ridgeway 1983: 252), having in mind the characteristic distribution of ideas in the group, the typical, dominant, widespread, average beliefs of group members. All this is fairly intuitive, and we have to turn toward a more abstract conceptualization.

Moving from the bottom level to the top level of our model, we may consider consciousness in less individualistic terms, no longer as the content of human minds, but as super-individual relational networks binding ideas, beliefs, concepts into the comprehensive blocks of ideologies, doctrines, creeds, theories and traditions. These obviously endure longer than their individual carriers (people or groups who accept parts of them in their individual or collective consciousness), they are encoded, materialized and petrified in texts, and they serve as constraints or resources for individual thinking. They also have their own dynamics, and the principles of inertia, momentum and sequence proposed earlier seem to apply here as well. In this sense, consciousness is treated as Durkheimian 'collective representations', as 'social facts *sui generis*' or as a Popperian 'Third World' (Popper 1982: 180).

From both sides consciousness impinges on the core ontological level of agency and praxis. The agential potentiality is significantly shaped both by what people in a given society actually think and believe (in their individual or collective consciousness), and by what ideological structures (ideologies, creeds and the traditions embedded in social consciousness) make them think and believe. The former may be treated as the internal environment of the agency, as it resides inside human heads. The latter may be treated as the external environment of the agency, as it has a sort of super-individual existence, outside individual minds. Both, in their subtle and shifting mutual balance, delimit the field for the actualization of the agency, provide constraints and facilitations by defining what sort of praxis is possible and what is impossible, which means are available and which precluded, which goals are feasible and which utopian.[18] Praxis in turn, via a sort of feedback, crucially affects consciousness. It is in and through praxis that people acquire beliefs as well as test them, verify and falsify claims, confirm and reject their cherished ideas.[19] It is in and through praxis, by proving their vacuity, ineffectiveness or anti-human effects, that ideological and doctrinal structures disintegrate and disappear, utopias are discredited and dogmas broken, even though the process may take generations or ages, as the principle of inertia operates here with particular viciousness.

The fact that the operation of agency and praxis is immersed in the 'sea of consciousness' – the external and internal environment of thoughts, beliefs, ideas – has one more important implication. Consciousness not only exerts its own, proper impact on the agency and praxis, but mediates in the impact exerted by other environments as well as in the actual dialectics of agents and structures. People are not passive 'reactants', but they face reality with an active, anticipating attitude. They define, interpret, select the factors of their situations, and act on the basis of their perceptions and evaluations. As Merton puts it, 'we respond not only to the objective features of a situation, but also, and at times primarily, to the meaning that situation has for us' (Merton 1982: 249). Consciousness – individual, collective and social – is a pool of resources in the form of concepts, symbols, codes, frames etc. for such interpretations. It may keep people blind to some constraints or opportunities, or open their eyes to them. It may cheat them, supplying inadequate intellectual tools for grasping reality, or serve the exposure of illusions by offering sharp critical notions. Thus the natural conditions, in their constraining or enabling influence on the agency, are to a large extent mediated by the 'ideological millieu'. The agency has to be 'awakened' to natural threats or promises in order to eventuate in relevant praxis. Or it may remain dormant, ignore limitations and neglect opportunities as long as they are not perceived. By way of example, think of 'ecological awareness' as born only recently and moving large masses to counter-action against pollution, even though, objectively speaking, the world had been polluted much earlier, at least since the dawn of industrial era. Or think of aerobics or the 'fitness craze' appearing only when people recognized that physical exercise is beneficial, even though inaction and sedentary habits had been shortening their lives at least since the beginning or urban civilization.

But it is not only the impact of the natural environment which is mediated by consciousness. The same mechanism is present also when any kind of social structural conditions merges with agential endowment at the level of agency and praxis. Social structures do not constrain or enable people in any straightforward, immediate, mechanistic fashion, but only to the extent that people recognize them and define them as impediments or resources. For instance, as Alexis de Tocqueville observed long ago, people may be exploited or deprived for ages, and rebel only when an

103

egalitarian ideology is born, with its concept of human rights, freedom, injustice etc. (Tocqueville 1955 [1856]). In a word, their revolutionary praxis emerges only if 'revolutionary awareness' is awakened. In a similar fashion, for many millennia women had been dominated by men, but only recently have they mobilized against their subjugation. The indispensable condition was the articulation of the 'feminist consciousness'. Structural blocks, barriers and obstacles evoke reactions and galvanize the agency only if they are defined as such. The same is true of structural opportunities resources, facilities. The economic structures of the market and the political structures of democracy have proved their value in many parts of the world for a considerable time, but their full adoption in Eastern Europe became possible only when a large degree of 'democratic consensus' emerged, a widespread agreement on the necessity of initiative, competition, pluralism, representation etc. Before the democratic opportunities could truly be utilized, they had to be acknowledged as opportunities.

Recognizing the crucial role of consciousness in the functioning of society, we must guard against a one-sided absolutization. It would be an illusion to think that all that occurs in a society is intended and recognized by its members. Many authors have emphasized the important latent dimension of social life. There are structures, environmental conditions and even their own endowment of which actors are unaware. And they are quite often unable to envisage the outcomes, especially the long-range or indirect ones, of their own actions. This is stressed in Popper's account of 'situational logic' (1982 [1974]: 117). For Merton it is the unintended and unrecognized consequences of purposive actions that are treated as the central concern of sociology: 'It is suggested that the distinctive intellectual contributions of the sociologist are found primarily in the study of unintended consequences (among which are latent functions) of social practices, as well as in the study of anticipated consequences (among which are manifest functions)' (1957: 120). In similar vein Giddens observes: 'Human knowledgeability is always bounded. The flow of action continually produces consequences which are unintended by actors, and these unintended consequences also may form unacknowledged conditions of action in a feedback fashion' (1984: 27). These limitations of agents and actions are reflected at the intermediate level of our model, in the possible characteristics of agency and praxis, which sometimes must be seen as insulated from their external and internal environments of consciousness. Thus one may postulate a spectrum of situations from 'blind agency' and 'spontanoues praxis' at one pole, to 'self-aware agency' and 'rationally-controlled praxis' at the other. Along this scale all the grades of influence that consciousness exerts on the functioning of society may be ordered.

The model of social becoming

Enter time

In the model of social becoming, the factor of time is inevitably present from the very beginning. If we speak of the unfolding of structures in operation, or the mobilization of agents for action, or eventuating agency through praxis, the time dimension is clearly assumed; all these processes can occur only in time. So far the recognition given to time in our model is deficient on two counts. First it is only implicit; the temporal extension of processes is treated as self-evident and taken for granted. No systematic implications of temporality have yet been drawn. Second, it is limited to what may be called the 'internal time', as opposed to 'external time', the time of functioning as opposed to the time of transformation. The action of the agents, the operation of structures and their synthetic fusion in the praxis of the agency are not yet seen as producing any novelty, but rather as reproducing the same conditions. Thus the functioning of society is still static[20] and not truly dynamic; covering only 'changes in', and ignoring 'changes of'. The model, therefore, is still synchronic, and not truly diachronic. We have to overcome both deficiencies now, incorporating time into our model in a more explicit and less limited way.

In this we find good precedents. A strong emphasis on the factor of time is clearly visible in both the lines of earlier theorizing that I am trying to synthesize in SB, the theory of agency and historical sociology. They share the crucial insight that the linkage of the level of individualities and totalities is possible only if history is brought into the picture. Giddens calls for the 'incorporation of temporality into the understanding of human agency' (1979: 54), and in this connection introduces his core concepts of 'recursiveness' ('In and through their activities agents reproduce the conditions that make these activities possible') (1984: 2), and 'structuration' ('the ways in which the social system, via the application of generative rules and resources, and in the context of unintended outcomes, is produces and reproduces in interaction') (1979: 66). This emphasis inevitably pushes the theory of agency toward historical sociology: 'with the recovery of temporality as integral to social theory history and sociology become methodologically indistinguishable' (p. 8).

No wonder that in the first manifesto of historical sociology we find full support for 'the need to reconstitute the action and structure antinomy as a matter of process in time, to re-organise their investigations in terms of dialectics of structuring' (Abrams 1982: xvi). Abrams claims that 'the social world is essentially historical' (p. 3) and defines historical sociology as 'the attempt to understand the relationship of personal activity and experience on the one hand and social organisation on the other as something that is continuously constructed in time' (p. 16). Lloyd claims that 'human agency and social action relate dialectically to social structures over time' (1988: 11). He proposes to 'retain a temporal dimension as intrinsic to any study of society since structure, action, and behaviour are interrelated in a dynamic, transforming, manner' (p. 314), and specifies a sequence in which those three aspects appear: '(1) Given circumstances, which are enabling and disabling of action, (2) Conscious action that is historically significant, (3) The intended and unintended consequences of action, which turn into objective and seemingly unalterable conditions of action and thought' (p. 283).

Roughly similar phases in this sequence are carefully analysed by Archer under the labels of 'structural conditioning', 'structural interaction' and 'structural elaboration', making up the incessant cycles of morphogenesis (1988: xxii). Already in 1986 she was 'taking time to link structure and agency', because 'without the proper incorporation of time the problem of structure and agency can never be satisfactorily resolved' (p. 2). She made a crucial point, which seems self-evident now, but only after it has been stated: 'structure and action operate over different time periods . . . structure logically predates the actions that transform it and structural elaboration logically post-dates those actions' (p. 22); or in more poetic idiom: 'the future is forged in the present, hammered out of past inheritance by current innovation' (1988: xxiv).

We can see that all the conceptual components necessary to incorporate time explicitly and fully into our analysis are already there. We have only to express them in terms of our model. If we recognize that the model as elaborated so far depicts only one, single cycle of social becoming, we can approximate historical reality better by placing several replicas of the model side by side, along an axis of time. Each is seen as internally functioning (reproducing itself in 'internal time'), and also as extending its impact to the next one (producing it in 'external time'). The functioning of the earlier one is seen as causally related to the functioning of the later one, transforming it in significant respects.

How does this causal nexus work? To put it simply, praxis at a certain time, moulds the agency at a later time, which is actualized in changed praxis at a still later time, and this process continues interminably. More concretely, the sequence can be dissected into a number of phases. Thus, ongoing social events, merging structural operation and agential action (or simply praxis) at any given time, influence both structures (modifying or shaping new relational networks) and agents (modifying or shaping their immanent capacities) at the later time. As a result, a modified or new agency emerges and societal potentiality for praxis is changed. If and when the agency is actualized through eventuation, it is manifested in new praxis, itself expressing the fusion of the operation of new structures and the actions of new agents. In turn, new praxis at a later time begins an

The model of social becoming

analogical cycle, which, via changed structures and agents, modified agency and its actualization, results in the emergence of further modified praxis. This sequence goes on endlessly, producing incessant cumulative transformations of society. It represents what we mean by human history, as opposed to the internal functioning of society.

To drive this important point home, let us repeat it in a slightly different phrasing, linking it with our earlier discussion of the 'third level' of truly social reality. Events (praxis) leave effects, material residues, memory traces, structural arrangements, institutional forms etc. which make up historical tradition. They are intended and unintended, recognized and unrecognized, but together they make up real circumstances, conditions, situations for further events (praxis). The network of events extends beyond direct co-presence in praxis, and acquires continuity thanks to the indirect mediation of conditions produced by earlier praxis as the foundation for later praxis. In terms of our conception, this is precisely what is meant by *history*. History is the continuous chain of praxis mediated by tradition, the latter representing the results of praxis and conditions for praxis at the same time. The crucial property of history is the cumulativeness of tradition, the permanently growing scope of received heritage from earlier praxis, constraining but also facilitating (providing enriched resources) for later praxis.

Any existing state of society is therefore only a phase of a historical sequence: a product of past operation (accumulated historical tradition) and a precondition for future operation. Similarly any social event (as a component of praxis) is in a sense a reflection of all previous history, and a germ of future history. It is localized in the flow of historical time. Social becoming treated in the dimension of 'external time' or '*longue durée*' could be called *making history*. We shall represent this most complex historical dimension of social life in a schematic form in figure 5.4.

This image requires some comments. In this version of our model, to simplify the picture, we have included only the main lines of causation, indicated by arrows, and omitted internal causation relevant only for the functioning of society rather than its transformation. But one omission is not only for didactic reasons. From now on, we may erase the feedbacks, introduced tentatively earlier to express the important point that structures are reshaped in their operation, agents remoulded in their actions, and, in effect, agency reconstructed in its praxis. The backward arrows indicating feedbacks in the earlier scheme, can be straightened out now, when we recognize that the structures, agents and agency on which they feed back are different structures, agents and agency – namely, they exist later in time. It is true that operation feeds back on operating structures, actions feed back on acting agents, praxis feeds back on agency which it manifests, but no teleology is implied by our speaking of later

107

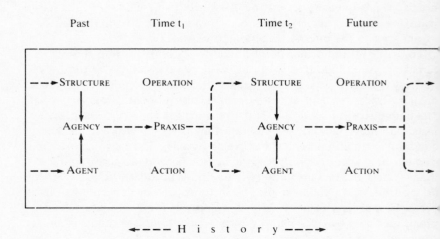

Figure 5.4

structures, later agents and later agency causally influenced by earlier operations, earlier actions and earlier praxis.

We must also not be misled by the didactic necessity of drawing side by side the models representing societal functioning at various moments of time. It does not mean that we are speaking of various societies, interacting between them, or one influencing the other. In fact, they are not different societies, but different states or phases of functioning of the same society. The sequence represents therefore the self-transformation of society between various moments in time, in and through its functioning at any moment in time.

The sequence of such self-transformation is continuous and interminable. Therefore, it is only for practical reasons, that the scheme depicts only two consecutive phases; it could be extended in both directions, toward the future and toward the past. Changing the scale, and neglecting all internal details of social anatomy and physiology, the picture of social self-transformation through time would look like figure 5.5. As can be seen the model now allows us to define precisely three concepts crucial to the inclusion of social dynamics. 'Functioning' covers all that is happening in society at some moment in time. 'Social change' describes the single transformation of society from one, earlier state to the next, later state. And 'historical process' refers to the sequence of self-transformations that society undergoes in a long span of time. Accordingly we may enrich the earlier distinction between internal and external time by indicating two important varieties of the latter: the short-range time of social change, and the truly historical time of the *longue durée*.

This whole discussion proceeds as if the previous section had not yet been written. We still ignore, or 'bracket', the fact that society does not exist in a vacuum, but rather in the double environment of nature and consciousness. Releasing this simplifying assumption will allow us to discover an additional important mechanism through which the historical process works. We have noted that both nature and consciousness enter into a mutual relationship with society, as shaping and shaped at the same time. Richer by the recognition of time, we may now disentangle this dialectic as well. Let us start with nature. Praxis leaves an obvious imprint on nature, changing natural conditions (depleting forests, regulating

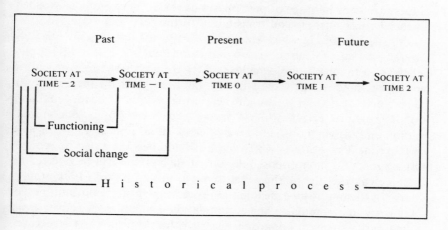

Figure 5.5

109

rivers, ploughing land, polluting air etc.), but also adding a whole new domain of transformed nature ('humanized nature', 'artificial nature') made of products and artefacts, technology and civilization (houses and roads, bridges and factories, gadgets and furniture etc.). This is a remnant from earlier praxis, which provides the conditions for later praxis. More precisely, it co-determines both the capacities of agents (what actions can be taken) and the potentialities of structures (what modes of structural operation are feasible), and in effect influences the synthetic quality of agency. The agency eventuates in changed praxis, which in turn reshapes the natural environment, and so the cycle continues. One may say that the remnants of the earlier functioning of society are encoded in the natural environment and passed on to the next phases of functioning.

A similar mechanism of continuity will appear when we turn to another environment of society, social consciousness. Ongoing praxis at any given time is reflected both in the ideas, beliefs and convictions held by agents (individuals or groups), and in the ideologies, creeds, doctrines acquiring more objectified, super-individual existence. Changed consciousness feeds back on the capacities of agents (redefining what actions are possible), and on the potentialities of structures (specifying what structural arrangements are feasible). In effect, the agency is significantly reshaped. In its actualization, it results in changed praxis at a later time, and this in turn brings about changes in consciousness. Again, the cycle repeats itself, and the process of incremental modifications of consciousness continues. Thus the heritage of past phases of social functioning is encoded in social consciousness and transmitted to the future.

This mechanism, in which the historical process involves the continuous remodelling of environments – nature and consciousness – is supplementary to the main one, which operates through reshaping structures and agents (and in effect their fusion, the agency). Thus there are four causal loops that can be distinguished in the process of history-making: (a) via structural effects, (b) via agents' capacities, (c) via 'humanized' nature, and (d) via modified consciousness. In all four cases praxis at a certain time leaves effects which outlast it and become an active, conditioning force for later praxis. The sum of such effects can be referred to as historical tradition, in the widest sense of this term (Shils 1981). In the course of the multi-stage, sequential process, the historical tradition has a tendency to accumulate. The accumulation is of course selective; some remnants of earlier periods are carried on, others vanish. Thus, structures may disintegrate, agents may lose their previously acquired capacities, artefacts may perish or become obsolete, and ideas may be forgotten. This depends on a number of variables, some of which will be suggested in the next chapter. But there is always a core of tradition, which is transmitted from generation to generation for long stretches of time. As a

result, the process is endowed with considerable continuity and cumulativeness, and we witness the emergence of sequential patterns in history.

Most often, though not unexceptionally, the engendering of lasting
effects by ongoing praxis, and the cumulation of these effects in transmitted tradition, is unwitting; it operates without intention, purpose or
even awareness. The effects are unintended and unrecognized by the
members of a society, even though praxis itself is purposeful, intentional
and often rational. As Giddens puts it, 'Human history is created by
intentional activities but is not an intended project; it persistently eludes
efforts to bring it under conscious direction' (1984: 27), or in the more
metaphorical language of Hollis, 'Actions have many consequences,
which are systematic but initially unnoticed by everyone. They can be
deemed the work of the Cunning of Reason if, when they surface, they
are found to be the collective effects of individually rational decisions
taken by role-players in the course of games' (1987: 205). In this case, if
any pattern emerges in history it must be credited to the rule of the 'invisible hand'. But it cannot be denied that sometimes visible, and even all
too visible, hands operate in history – dictators, tyrants, reformers, legislators, revolutionaries, prophets etc., who try to push the historical
process along a preconceived path, in an intended direction, by means
of planned transformations. Whether those attempts are successful or
not, they present an alternative variety of history-making.

In both cases the historical process is contingent and not predetermined
or necessary. The residues of earlier praxis make up a field of possibilities
(agential, structural, environmental) for later praxis. The field is always
bounded but never optionless. There are always possible alternative paths
of further process starting at each of its phases. Some are actualized in
praxis, some are rejected; hence some historically present possibilities are
used, and others abandoned. Ultimately it depends on the decisions taken
and choices made by the agents, who always 'could have acted otherwise'.
If there is any necessity in history, it is a conditional necessity: if people
decide to act in this or that way. The semblance of necessity appears only
ex post facto, once decisions and choices have been taken and actions
made. Before that, the process is always open-ended.[21] As Tilly puts it:
'a process constitutes a series of choice points. Outcomes at a given point
in time constrain possible outcomes at later points in time' (1984: 14). In
the long run, this contingent mechanism, produces all kinds of twisting,
variable trajectories along which history moves. The mechanism
described shows 'how people do indeed make their own history but also
how particular circumstances, which are the result of people having made
history in the past, condition that history-making' (Lloyd 1988: 301).

Let me summarize the significant elaboration of the model attained by
now. Social becoming has been shown to occur in time. Praxis at any

given time produces consequences (intended and unintended, recognized and unrecognized) at the level of totality, modifying structures, as well as at the level of individuality, changing people. It also influences the environments – nature and consciousness. As a result, the changed agency emerges and is implemented (via changed actions and modified operations) in the new praxis at any later time. Such cycles repeat themselves, the effects accumulate, and the pattern of societal self-transformation emerges. The resulting process is continuous, cumulative and contingent, opening successive fields of possibilities before human agents, whose choices and decisions ultimately set its course. The process so described represents in terms of our model what is normally referred to as history. Thus already at this stage of our construction, the model incorporates the two fundamental traits of society which we set out to synthesize: the agential coefficient and the historical coefficient. At least a part of our promise seems to be fulfilled, but the construction does not stop here, and further successive approximations must be made.

The becoming of social becoming

In our discussion so far we have built a multi-level model of social reality and endowed it with the double dynamics of internal functioning and self-transformations. Society is seen not only as built in particular way, but as having a particular mechanism of self-movement. Through the operation of that mechanism society is constantly changing, but is the mechanism itself immutable? Is it permanent and historically universal, or does historical relativization perhaps touch not only the parameters and variables of the model but the very principles of its dynamics?

In a different language, this is a variant of the old question, whether historical change means only the change of facts (states of society) or also the change of regularities obtaining in a society (social laws)? (Gewirth 1969 [1954]). I opt for the latter solution (which may be called 'radical historism') and reject the notion of ahistorical, universal social laws (Sztompka 1984a). Translated into the terms of our model, it will mean that historical transformations embrace not only the agents, structures and agency, not only the actions, operations and praxis, not only the environments of nature and consciousness, but also the links among all those, the ways in which they combine in producing social dynamics. In short, I shall claim that with the passage of time, the very principles of operation, the mode of functioning and change of human society, undergo significant transformations.[22] The ultimate, most complex feedback loop is added to the model; it is not only the case that agency changes itself in the course of its own praxis, but that social becoming changes its mode in the course of history. We enter here the domain of meta-dynamics. Poetically one could speak of the becoming of the very mechanism of becoming.

There are several hints in the literature showing that scholars have vaguely perceived this peculiarity of the social world. Marx and Engels had already spelled out the opposition of the 'kingdom of necessity' and the 'kingdom of freedom', or the 'prehistory' and 'true history' of human society, meaning by that a fundamental change of the principles of operation at the borderline dividing the class societies of the past from the expected classless society of the future. Contemporary Marxists speak of 'naturalistic history' as opposed to 'humanistic history', alluding to the growing role of human, rational intervention in modern epochs (Topolski 1978). Think of Ward's opposition of genesis and telesis, as two distinct principles of evolution, the latter involving purposefulness, awareness, and knowledge (Fletcher 1971, vol. 1: 479). A similar message is carried by other, commonly counterpoised pairs of concepts: market and plan, spontaneity and deliberation, the invisible hand and rational control, the cunning of reason and the realization of projects. They indicate not only a change of society, but the meta-change, the change of its most fundamental modes of changing.

Following hints in the earlier literature, I shall postulate that the mode of social becoming evolves in a way that depends on the kind of relationships linking society with its environments (nature and consciousness). The common denominator of the historical tendency embracing the mechanism of social becoming will be found in humans' growing control over environments, in the sense of command over them and insulation from them. With respect to nature, this tendency is fairly obvious. The history of human civilization and technology is nothing if not the gradual subjugation of natural resources to human needs and the growing protection of human society against natural threats. With respect to consciousness, the growth of human knowledge means among other things, the evolving consciousness of social phenomena, regularities and mechanisms of social functioning and change, and the exposure of myths, illusions and 'false consciousness'. This allows for more anticipation, planning and purposeful shaping of social life. As the mechanism of social becoming grows less opaque to its own participants, it inevitably incorporates more human intervention.

But as we know all too well, both tendencies produce not only beneficial effects, the improvement of social becoming, but also considerable side-effects or even counter-effects, distorting, endangering, or even blocking societal functioning and change. The excessive conquest of nature has led to ecological disaster, pollution, depletion of natural resources etc. Excessive belief in reason, knowledge and planning of social life has led to human enslavement, poverty and even extermination under a variety of 'scientific' totalitarian projects. Thus the historical tendency seems to evolve toward a higher form of control/the recognition of the limitations of control, or in other words, the self-control of the very aspirations to control.

The costs, dysfunctions, side-effects, long-range dangers of control over both kinds of environments – nature and consciousness – are perceived ever more clearly in modern society. Think of the rapid growth of ecological awareness, with its idea of harmony with nature and the imperative of bridling excessive ambitions to conquer it. Or think of the wave of anti-totalitarian, liberal-democratic awareness, with its idea of pluralism, tolerance, participation, spontaneity, and the renunciation of all attempts to impose preconceived, dogmatic blueprints on human history.[23]

In terms of our model, those may be taken as indicators that the new mode of social becoming is slowly emerging, providing human society with more autonomy as well as more self-conscious, critical and realistic control over its own fate. It is like the next mutation on the eternal path from the fully objectified, blind existence of primitive people, through the naïve megalomania of human power and reason, to the fully creative, wide-awake existence of the expected future society, living in harmony with nature, and reconciled with the limits of thought. This is the path of the historical emancipation of human agency.

The ultimate premise: human nature

Our model of social becoming is almost completed. We have analysed its complex internal constitution, provided it with the mode of internal functioning, placed it in historical time and endowed it with the mechanism of self-transformation; we have even supplied it with the meta-mechanism through which its very principles of functioning and transformation undergo historical change. Thus the most radical dynamic perspective has been applied; society appears as an incessant, perpetual movement. We may start from any part of the model and see how it evolves in time. Whatever component we choose, it is seen as operating; any fact turns out to be an event; any agent resolves into actions; any state is only a phase of the ongoing process. But one crucial question remains: what moves it all? What is the motor, the dynamic force, the propelling power, the ultimate mover that activates human society and pushes it along its historical path of social becoming?

Of course we may try to play with backward regress. Why is there a certain praxis? Because it actualizes a certain agency. And why has that agency such potentialities? Because they were shaped by earlier praxis. But what about that earlier praxis? It is the manifestation of an earlier agency. And so on, *ad infinitum*. It does not lead us far. Sooner or later we have to reach some limit of backward reasoning, to postulate some constant, ultimate, activating factor. We must find some force that prompts the agency to actualize itself in praxis, causes the praxis to continue long enough to reshape the agency, induces the new agency to exhibit its potentialities in praxis, and replicates those cycles in the continuous and cumulative process of history, eventually emancipating the agency itself.

God, or Providence, Fate, Immanence or History, even though appealing, do not provide satisfactory solutions for our purposes, because of their basically unempirical, untestable character. The ambition of SB is to be a scientific, sociological theory; to postulate an image of society which has a definite, even if distant and mediated, relation to the world of social phenomena and processes. Thus we must search for some emprical component of the social world that is the seat of that driving force of social becoming. Our model is certainly 'anthropocentric'; it is founded on the assumption that the irreducible component of society, its only ultimate ontological substratum, is people.[24] Therefore we cannot but seek the ultimate, primary mover of society in their traits and properties – in brief, in human nature. As Dawe claims: 'All sociological work . . . is founded upon and derives its meaning from views of human nature, whether they are stated explicitly or remain implicit (and often unrecognized even by those whose work rests upon them)' (1978: 369).

Admittedly, we are entering very uncertain territory. Many scholars would reject the very idea of any universal, immutable qualities of human beings. Those who accept some constant human traits, paint surprisingly varied pictures. Suffice it to cite some of those high-sounding Latin denominations: 'homo sapiens', 'homo cogitans', 'homo faber', 'homo politicus', 'homo socius', 'homo ludens', 'homo reciprocus', 'homo creator', 'homo historicus' – and of course also 'homo sociologicus'. It would require volumes merely to report on that debate, let alone to make any contribution; the whole history of philosophy, social thought and the social sciences could be written around this theme. After all what can be more interesting to human beings than who they really are? Therefore I shall have to bracket all that rich and diversified heritage of conceptions about human nature and to restrict myself to postulating the minimum, most parsimonious account, proposing the image which will logically fit the model of social becoming, and supplying it with its missing ultimate component.[25]

Thus we shall be involved here in a sort of backward logical reconstruction. Assuming that the model of society we have elaborated so far is adequate, what must be assumed about its smallest 'elementary particles', human actors? In other words, granted that some traits of human beings are a prerequisite for the dynamics of social becoming, which are they? What traits must be possessed by individuals for the processes of history to continue? Only later shall we try to support this reconstructed image by independent evidence, to see if such properties of human beings fit the basic ontological conditions of the human species as we actually encounter them in the world. In other words, we shall try to see if human nature, as reconstructed in the preceding step of analysis, could have been evoked (in some evolutionary way) by that species-specific existential situation, or, briefly, by the human condition. To repeat, human nature will be reconstructed as the product of the human condition and as a prerequisite for social becoming, or, more precisely, as the set of dispositions indispensable for surviving in the world as it is given to human beings, and for producing society and history.

Let us focus on the notion of agency, as it appears in our model. It is suspended, so to speak, between earlier and later praxis. It must possess some traits in order to produce later praxis, and it must possess some other traits in order to embody earlier praxis. To put it otherwise, among its potentialities there must be some allowing it to shape and influence the future historical process, and others allowing it to be shaped and influenced by the preceding historical process. I propose to refer to the former as the capacity for self-transcendence, and to the latter as the capacity for social learning. Both are treated as potentialities of the social fabric, attributes of social reality *sui generis*, conceived at its own specific level. But, as we remember, this societal level is seen as the fusion of agents and structures, and therefore can be analytically decomposed into them. Leaving the structural component aside, we focus on agents. And these, even in their collective, group variety are made of individual actors. Thus the potentialities of agency must be some product of the aggregated traits of actors. Self-transcendence and social learning must find some ultimate roots in the potentialities of human individuals.

The first of these is normally referred to as creativeness or innovativeness, the ability to conceive and produce new objects, forms, shapes, images etc by combining existing components in original, novel ways. The second is normally referred to as educability, the ability to learn from experience, to acquire and accumulate knowledge. Both can be treated as axioms; no school of sociology or psychology seriously doubts them.[26] Their complex aggregation produces the synthetic capacity of the agency for self-transcendence and social learning (cultural transmission).

In order to move society on its course of social becoming, to activate social functioning and historical process, both capacities must be actualized. The agency must be eventuated in praxis, and the single cycles of societal functioning must be interconnected in a cumulative historical sequence. Thus we must assume that the agency embodies not only the capacity, but a need, a drive toward self-transcendence[27] and social learning. Returning to the level of actors, we shall find the ultimate roots of this societal synthetic need or drive in a human trait acknowledged by a number of sociological and psychological schools (though not all of them in this instance) as the need for self-realization or self-fulfilment, the tendency of human individuals to put their capacities, abilities and talents to some use, to externalize or actualize them. This refers equally to creativeness and learning; people not only have a capacity to create and learn, but exhibit a drive actually to do these things, to create something and to learn something. Such individual drives, aggregated vertically in a complex way, produce the actual tendency of the agency toward self-transcendence, and the actual tendency to acquire the lessons of earlier praxis by social learning. These in turn, aggregated in time, allow human society to stretch horizontally into a continuous historical process.

To summarize this complex argument, let us put it in the form of a quasi – 'calculus': (a) individual creativeness + the need for self-realization = actor's self-transcendence; (b) individual educability + the need for self-realization = actor's learning; (c) aggregation of actors' self-transcendence (in given structural conditions, treated as *constans*) = agential self-transcendence; (d) aggregation of actors' learning (in constant structural conditions) = social learning; (e) self-transcendence of the agency + social learning entail social becoming (the functioning of society + historical process).

The minimum, most parsimonious image of human nature which must be assumed as a necessary prerequisite of social becoming was found to consist of three traits: creativeness, educability and the need for self-realization. For our purposes, it is all we have to know about this most complex of God's creatures.

Let us see now, if this image can be corroborated by the human existential situation in the world, if it can treated as the equally necessary outcome of the givens of the human condition. People live in two overlapping contexts: natural and social. They are parts of nature and members of society. Both contexts place constraints, limitations and barriers on their actions. Nature provides resources, but they are always scarce, never sufficient; it also presents threats, blocks to human efforts, and it is characterized by inclemency.[28] In similar fashion, society (other people and the structures in which they interrelate) provides facilities, enablements and resources indispensable for human actors, who can live only with others, against others, alongside others, for others. But at the same time society constrains their efforts; they cannot do all they would like, nor can they do it entirely as they would like; some of their autonomy or freedom is taken away by the co-presence and co-actions of others. Thus, in the minimum, parsimonious way sufficient for our purposes, the human condition may be characterized by three universal features: scarcity, the inclemency of nature and the constraints of society.

If we abandon the objective, external perspective for a moment, and look into human heads, we shall discover subjective psychological counterparts of this existential condition. Thus, first, people are permanently dissatisfied, never fulfilled; the inclemency of nature, the pervasive scarcity of resources, the limitations of interactions with others – all these preclude satiation. And this is even more painful because people are basically insatiable; their aspirations, strivings, desires and needs have a tendency to expand proportionately to the level of satisfaction attained.[29] This is due to their capacity for learning, their inherent educability. They simply learn new needs. The second psychological corollary is the permanent experience of dependence, of unfreedom in the clash with other people and social structures; people constantly hit their heads against the hard 'facticity' of the social world. This feeling of being constrained fights againts their need for self-realization. This is the experience we referred to earlier as the 'vexatious fact of society' (Dahrendorf 1968).

Thus, the core feature of the human world, both in its objective and in its subjective dimension, may be identified as tension, strain and contradiction. There is a permanent gap between realizations and strivings, achievements and ambitions, ideals and realities. Wilbert Moore has elevated this truth to 'a universal feature of human societies which in most general form may be stated as the lack of correspondence between the "ideal" and the "actual" in many and pervasive contexts of social behavior' (1963: 18). The human condition comes down to its strainful and ambivalent location in the world, natural and social, and its subjective reflex, the dissatisfied, unfulfilled and permanently frustrated frame of mind.

This would be a sad picture were it not the key to human greatness. The trouble turns into a blessing. Finding themselves in such an existential situation, human beings have to adapt, develop traits and dispositions enabling them to cope with limitations, constraints and predicaments. Tensions and strains produce a necessity to resolve them by struggle. Human nature evolves as a response to the human condition; specific human capabilities, abilities and skills develop as instruments to deal with the oppressive surrounding world. As Cohen observes: 'Men would be among the unlucky ones, except that they, uniquely, can continually refashion their environment to suit themselves' (1978: 152). People find themselves in the existential situation where creativeness and innovativeness, are a necessity, an imperative, functional prerequisite for survival. To paraphrase Sartre's famous idea that 'Man is condemned to freedom', one may say that 'Man (or woman) is condemned to create'. In the course of this active adaptation humans constantly shape and reshape nature, engaging in material production; they produce objects and utensils, buildings and roads, vehicles and food crops. They constantly shape and reshape society, engaging in societal morphogenesis; they construct groups and associations, organizations and institutions, norms and values, symbols and codes.

There is another imperative for survival, namely that those products of people's efforts will not perish with their death, and that each generation will not have to start from scratch. The inheritance of tradition, cultural transmission from generation to generation must be made possible. The process of creation acquires continuity and cumulativeness and turns imperceptibly into history, precisely because of another human trait: educability (capacity to acquire knowledge) and the drive to learn (to realize that capacity).

Thus by two roads, following two different arguments, we have arrived at the same image of human nature, as creative, educable and self-realizing. This is the last component, the ultimate assumption of the model of social becoming, providing it with inherent dynamics. It is because people are such, and their human condition is such, that social becoming can operate, producing in effect society and history.

6

Active and passive society

The puzzle of social becoming

Even a cursory look at the panorama of human history reveals a striking fact: the rhythm of social change is extremely uneven. There are long periods of stagnation, when for decades, centuries, or in ancient times even for millennia, society remains basically unchanged.[1] The processes run slowly and are mostly limited to 'changes in', to the reproduction of existing institutions, rules, norms, values, patterns of social organization and forms of social order. People are born and die in the same social world. The passenger in H. G. Wells's Time Machine could disembark after a long period and recognize his society without any trouble: he would fit perfectly well into its framework. We may speak here of a passive society.

On the other hand, there are occasional interludes – lasting a month, a year, a decade, sometimes a whole century – when history seems to speed up. The social processes accelerate, they take the form of 'changes of', fundamental transformations of the whole social fabric. Sometimes literally overnight, regimes collapse, constitutions change, social consciousness is awakened, everyday life acquires new meaning, the network of rules, norms, values and institutions is radically reshaped. Wells's passenger would not believe his eyes, he would never have thought it possible. These are revolutionary periods, which later, with the benefit of hindsight, appear in history books under the names of 'heroic era', 'golden age', 'civilizational explosion', 'flourishing of culture', 'economic miracle', 'social reconstruction', 'renaissance', and the like.

120

Active and passive society

Take a random list of examples: Athens in the fifth century BC, the Rome of the Caesars, the Maya empire between the seventh and tenth centuries, *quattrocento* in Italy, the French Renaissance of the sixteenth century, the great French Revolution and Napoleonic wars, the 'Spring of Nations' in 1848, Russia in 1917, and what probably will come to be called the 'Autumn of Nations' in Eastern Europe in 1989. All of them make up the great puzzles of history; they always come unexpectedly, catch everybody by surprise, and only later seem to have been inevitable. For their participants, they signify unusual, exciting times, of raised activism, a feeling of potency, strengthened social bonds, optimism and hope. In such periods people seem to take their fate in their hands, their actions make more difference than normally, they feel less bound, more autonomous and free. As somebody put it, they 'take history by the lapels' and shake it. The heritage of such periods lasts longer; it is incorporated into heroic myths, symbols, oral and written traditions and fond remembrance, and survives in more tangible institutional and normative arrangements which outlive their creators and acquire their own momentum. These are the most spectacular cases of the active society.

Comparing the revolutionary epochs with eras of stagnation, the active society with the passive society, we may see strikingly different ways in which the mechanism of social becoming operates. These are of course only the extreme, polar cases, between which there are probably all shades of intermediate situations. In this chapter we must try to account for this amazing historical variety. And that requires moving from the level of a conceptual model to more concrete empirical implementations. The main categories of the model of social becoming will have to be redefined as variables, as taking differentiated forms, shapes or 'values'. The resulting differences in the modes of social becoming will have to be accounted for by the specific clusters, combinations, permutations or syndromes of such variables. In other words, we are moving in the direction of concretization and operationalization of our model, trying to endow it with an empirical interpretation.

Where should we seek for the master-variable responsible for the eruption or acceleration of social becoming, or for the contrary, its slowing down or suppression? What factors are crucial in the emergence of the active society, as opposed to the passive society? Common sense suggests that it must have something to do with the quality of the people involved in historical events. At first glance the sansculottes storming the Bastille seem to be a different brand of human beings from the peasants obediently bowing their heads to the feudal yoke. The crowds in the streets of Prague in November 1989 seemed to be made of different clay from those who in nearby Romania frenetically applauded the local tyrant as the 'Genius of the Carpathians'. But even at the level of common

121

sense, this impression is shown to be misleading if we notice that quite often the passive conformists and committed rebels are literally the same people, only at different moments of their biographies. For a long time they remain passive, then suddenly mobilize for protest, opposition or rebellion. Only a month later, in December 1989, the same seemingly resigned Romanians awoke to the most determined and bloody struggle for freedom, destroying one of the last fortresses of communist totalitarianism. The difference in their actions cannot be explained by inherent personal traits, but rather by the situations or wider context in which they happen to be placed. Again, not all people become revolutionaries, even in the most conducive situations. So we must also take account of their concrete, individual predispositions.

Even more clearly, the fully reductionist track of our search must be entirely abandoned if we move to the level of theoretical discourse. In terms of the theory of social becoming human nature was posited as universal and constant. Hence, logically, it cannot account for variation. And yet we must not remove people from our theory, because another fundamental premise of SB claims that society and history are not God-given but humanly constructed. We must recognize that human nature manifests itself historically in various forms and operates in various contexts. Thus the explanation of the various ways in which this human construction proceeds must be sought in the variable context and variable historical forms in which the *constans* of human nature manifests itself, in other words, in the social structures in which people find themselves, and in the particular, historically specific endowment of agents (actors and collectivities).

This argument leads us to the intermediate level of the model, which is precisely the area of a synthesis, the fusion of individual agential endowment and structural variation. At this level the idea of agency – the synthetic quality of the social fabric, actualizing itself in praxis – appears as the core locus of variance. The various modalities of the agency, from viable, robust, manifest, wide awake, to suppressed, weak, latent and dormant, seem to be responsible for the various modes of social becoming, from revolution to stagnation. Agency, the initial potentiality for praxis, and therefore history, the capacity of society to activate itself for self-transcendence, appears as the master-variable of SB. The quality of the agency distinguishes the active society from the passive society.

To repeat, we suspect that the various modes of human becoming depend primarily on the character of the agency present in a given society at a given time. Agency so conceived is a general, synthetic attribute of society, a historically unique mix of structural conditions and agents' characteristics. Its character decides whether society is active or passive.

Agency is of course an abstract, theoretical notion, but we claim that it has ontological reference, represents some really existing, underlying phenomenon. Is there any way to grasp it directly, to differentiate its revolutionary from its merely reproductive potential?

One tempting avenue leads to the tautological fallacy. We may say that the character of the agency is to be discovered in the outcomes it effects. 'By their fruits ye shall know them', as the Scriptures advise. Thus agency is revolutionary when it produces significant transformations, and it is reproductive when it merely preserves the status quo. Society is active when it transforms itself and passive when it does not. But at most we have definitions here, not explanations. Our aim was to find out why sometimes the agency operates in the reproductive and sometimes in the transformative mode; or why some societies are passive and others active; or why in some epochs a society remains passive only to awake for active self-transformations in the next. If we answer by invoking reproductive potential in the former case and transformative capacity in the latter, we are only playing with words, our reasoning is circular, and no knowledge is gained.

Another approach would be to search for global indicators of a state of society, reflecting its agential potentiality independently of the actual processes generated by that tendency. In other words we should look for symptoms showing which kinds of society are (potentially) active, and which (potentially) passive. One type of such indicators would comprise the level of social arousal, readiness for activism, change-oriented attitudes, revolutionary *élan*, social effervescence, etc. Another type would refer to organizational forms present in a society, e.g. a robust 'civil society', institutional pluralism, a developed 'social movement sector' (Garner and Zald 1981). The third type of indicator would comprise the intangible qualities of social consciousness, expressed by such metaphorical ideas as 'social climate', 'social atmosphere', optimism or pessimism, achievement orientation and social frustration, enthusiasm or 'disaster culture' etc. Those notions are by no means empty; they represent real phenomena, feelings, experiences, but they are vague and imprecise, and resist efforts to measure them. There is no logical reason why they should not become precisely observable and measurable some day, when proper research instruments are devised to grasp such global properties directly. But for the time being we cannot depend on this sort of indicator in our effort to identify various kinds of agency.

We have to resort to indirect, inferential indicators, to break down the potentiality of the agency into its components, aspects, dimensions and 'faces', to specify each of them precisely, and then recombine their different values into 'syndromes' or synthetic measures representing the various states of the agency as a whole. Because the agency is treated as the fusion or merger of structures and agents, we have to examine these ingredients separately, discover their various forms and then merge them again in better specified combinations typical for the active and the passive society. In the discussion that follows we must take up the systematic consideration of multiple structural and agent-related factors that constitute the agency, and show how in their particular combinations they produce stronger or weaker potentials for activating the mechanism of social becoming. If we succeed in this anatomical vivisection of the agency, we shall discover what kind of agency is the 'soul' of an active society, and what kind is embodied in a passive society. Then the puzzle of social becoming will at least be clarified, if not solved.

Four levels of social structure

We shall start from the top of our model, specifying the crucial category of social structure, which constitutes the agency 'from above'. It was defined earlier as the hidden network of patterned (persistent and regular) relationships among the various components of social reality, controlling empirical variance in the social domain. Social structure must be seen as complex and integrated, consisting of several levels (or dimensions), but bound together by specific inter-level linkages.

The variety of components linked by structural relationships allows us to distinguish four levels of social structure. Various theoretical traditions have picked out one or another for primary consideration. The first level was central for Emile Durkheim, and afterwards for the structural-functional school. It is the normative level, the network of rules, norms, values and institutions prescribing the proper, expected conduct, and proscribing the wrong, forbidden modes of human action. Such normative components cluster in various ways; in the systems of laws, mores, customs (or 'folkways', to use W. G. Sumner's classic phrase). They make up a reality of 'social facts' external to any single individual (even though ultimately produced by all of them) and exert a significant constraining and enabling impress on what people actually do.

The second level became crucial for the social phenomenologists from Max Scheler to Alfred Schutz. It may be called the ideal level, the network of ideas, beliefs, images, convictions about reality (including social reality and ideas about people and their societies). Such ideal components cluster in various ways, in creeds, doctrines, ideologies, *Weltanschaungen*. Spreading out in a society they attain a certain objectivity and externality for each single individual (even though ultimately thought out by all of them). As such they significantly constrain and facilitate human actions.

The third level of social structure was the area of pre-eminent concern for Georg Simmel, and afterwards the interactionists of all brands, from social behaviourists, exchange theorists and symbolic interactionists to modern proponents of network analysis. They treated actions as the main components of a social structure and studied the networks of interactions, the reciprocal, mutually oriented actions of multiple individuals. The form, shape or 'geometry' of such interactional networks (e.g. communication channels, lines of possible interpersonal access etc.) acquires some objective, external quality with respect to any single individual (even though they emerge from the actions of all). Therefore they significantly constrain and enable whether, toward whom, or with whom a person will act.

The fourth level fell into the focus of Karl Marx, Max Weber and later the extremely wide group of theorists studying the phenomena of classes, stratification and mobility. Here, the ultimate components of social structure are taken to be vested interests (or 'life-chances' or opportunities), i.e. variable access to valued resources or facilities (mainly wealth, power, esteem, knowledge) unequally distributed among human populations. The hierarchies of inequality acquire objective, external quality for each individual (even though, after all, they are the emergent product of the combined activities of all the members of a society). Individually people are significantly constrained or enabled by their location within such hierarchies.

The synthetic image of the social structure, combining those four one-sided foci and treating them only as four levels of a comprehensive whole – Ideal level, Normative level, Interactional level and Opportunity level – will be referred to as the INIO scheme.[2]

No level of the social structure is of course separate; each is linked to the others in complex ways. For example, the opportunity structure and the interactive structure influence the ideal structure (this is the focus of the 'sociology of knowledge); the normative structure and the ideal structure influence the opportunity structure (this is the problem of legitimation); the ideal structure influences the interactive structure (this is the problem of prejudices, stereotypes and discrimination). All other permutations of inter-structural links can easily be supplied. In general, the patterned and regular relationships among the levels of social structure produce a sort of meta-structure, the form of their integration typical for a given society.

We have to remember, that, according to one of the foundational premises of SB, structures are not static entities but rather processes of permanent transformations; they undergo incessant changes; they are constantly shaped and reshaped, produced and reproduced. Applying this perspective to our fourfold typology of social structures we may single out four sub-processes, making up the overall operation (functioning) of structures: (a) the institutionalization of normative structures (emergence and change of rules, norms, values, institutions and their clusters); (b) the articulation of ideal structures (emergence and change of ideas, beliefs, images and their systems); (c) the crystallization of interactional structure (emergence and change of interpersonal links, communication channels, lines of access and their networks); (d) the allocation of opportunity structure (distribution and redistribution of chances, opportunities, vested interests, and their hierarchies).

Acting people are anchored to this fluid and multi-level social structure by means of the social positions (or statuses) which they occupy. It is *via* social positions that structures exert their constraining or enabling influence on actors (or more generally, agents). The particular location in the social structure implies that only some selected fragments of the social structure become activated with respect to an agent, or in other words become relevant for the actions. Thus social roles, in the usual sense, describe the relevant fragments of the normative structure (norms and values typically bound up with a given position); the term 'positional mentality' would be proposed to refer to the relevant fragment of the ideal structure (ideas and beliefs typical for incumbents of certain positions); 'interactional options' would cover the relevant fragment of the interactional structure (communication and interpersonal channels open typically for incumbents of certain positions); and social rank, in the sense often assumed in the literature, would represent the relevant fragment of the opportunity structure (the range of access to resources typical for incumbents of certain positions). Of course all those aspects of a social position (status) are mutually interrelated. The complex, idiosyncratic fusion of social role, positional mentality, interactive options and social rank provides an immediate structural context, a constraining and enabling framework in which an agent is placed. Needless to add, this context is fluid and permanently changing, so that the structurally established field for action is also constantly expanding or shrinking.

Variety of agents and actions

This leads us to the bottom of our model, to the consideration of the agents who constitute the agency 'from below'. We have already distinguished individual actors (acting people) and collective agents (acting collectivities, task groups, social movements, associations, political parties etc.). Now, further specifications are needed.

Among individual actors, we notice three different types. One consists of common people in their normal, everyday activities. Most of what is happening in a society consists of people working and resting, eating and sleeping, travelling and walking, talking and writing, laughing and quarreling etc. The masses of the common people make up the ultimate stuff of which human society is made. But there are also some exceptional actors. The second type consists of such individuals who, by virtue of exceptional personal qualities (knowledge, competence, talents, skills, or even 'charisma') act as the representatives of others, in their name or on their behalf (Dahrendorf 1979). This includes leaders, prophets, ideologues, patriarchs, statesmen etc. The third type consists of those who occupy exceptional positions, endowing them with particular prerogatives (irrespective of exceptional personal qualities, which sometimes they may also possess, but quite often they do not). Their roles allow and even demand actions consequential for other people, deciding their fate (in other words making binding decisions, even exercising meta-power, and shaping rules by which others should abide). We have in mind rulers, legislators, managers, administrators, policemen etc.

Among collective agents (corporate bodies, which from the point of view of their actions and the consequences they produce may be treated as entities) there are also three types. In the first category, the collective actions are directed solely at the members, taken in order to affect the members in various ways, to help, support, mould or change them. Think of families, fraternities, self-improvement groups (therapy groups), fitness clubs, chiliastic sects, closed monasteries and redemptive social movements as fitting examples. In the second category, people get together, mobilize and act collectively to affect the wider society, not only themselves, to influence other people or more permanent social arrangements, so to speak from below, by exerting pressure. Here we can include reform-oriented social movements, revolutionary conspiracies, pressure groups, lobbies, political parties etc. The third type would comprise all kinds of bodies endowed with prerogatives to enact rules, laws, binding decisions on others, so to speak from above. Governments, legislatures, courts, boards, committees etc. fall into this category.

This typology of agents (individual and collective) can be cross-combined with another one, dealing with the characteristic modes of action (whether individual or collective). If we consider the form that actions can take, there seems to be a continuum. At one pole we shall find everyday activities, with purely egoistic motivations and intent. Unwittingly, in unintended and often unrecognized ways, each of them may have important side-effect – affect other people or even more lasting social institutions; and all of them aggregated together certainly have such far-reaching social consequences. As examples I suggest: using language, evading norms, inventing something. Then, moving along the continuum we shall find collective behaviour, a sort of additive, poorly coordinated sum of individual actions, still devoid of common intent, but because of their massiveness and combination able to produce immediate and important social consequences. Crowds, panics, hostile outbursts and riots illustrate this phenomenon. Next in line come collective actions, intended, purposeful, coordinated attempts to reach some common goal, for the participants themselves or for the wider society. Think of petitions, public manifestations, campaigns etc. A separate category is taken by enterpreneurial activities, organizing, coordinating, mobilizing, educating, indoctrinating others in order to evoke action of an intended sort on their part. Finally there are political actions, the exercise of power (or the struggle for power in order to exercise it later), ordering, manipulating, legislating, codifying (but also conspiring, campaigning, contesting elections) etc.

So much for the forms that action can take. Now if we move to the content, or target of actions – taken either by individual actors or collective agents – our model dictates another simple typology. Some actions are targeted directly on structures; they produce, change or support them. These make up the first category of our typology, the structure-building proper. It has several varieties. When new norms are imposed, original ideas devised, new interactions begun, new hierarchies of inequalities formed, we witness true morphogenesis. When norms are changed, ideas reformulated, interactional channels switched and opportunities redistributed, there is structural change. When norms are merely enforced, ideas supported, lines of interaction sustained and inequalities solidified, the actions produce structural continuation. Structure-building in those various modes does not exhaust all the types of action. Another comprises those directed at other agents rather than at structures. Here we shall find socializing, educating, indoctrinating, mobilizing, organizing, coordinating etc. By moulding, reshaping or enhancing agents' dispositions or capacities, such actions may also indirectly influence structures and contribute to the structure-building proper. Finally, we encounter actions directed at the environment, targeted on objects, either nature or already 'humanized nature' i.e. civilization. Labour is the paradigmatic example of this last category.

Forms of power: domination and hegemony

The lesson to be drawn from the foregoing typologies of structures and agents is that both levels of social becoming are extremely pluralistic and heterogeneous. Once we descend one step from the most abstract outline of the model and attempt to fill its categories with flesh, the illusion of simplicity has to be discarded. If we look at the social structure of any concrete, historically existing society, we shall see not only that it is internally split into multiple levels or types (INIO scheme), but also that each level or type is embodied in multiple concrete forms. In every society (a) there is a multiplicity and diversity of ideologies, doctrines and creeds; (b) there are many different kinds of ethos, customs and laws; (c) there are innumerable interactional networks; (d) there are numerous hierarchies of inequality. All of those coexist in some precarious balance; the end-product of convergent and divergent forces, opposition and complementarity, contradiction and coherence.

A similar picture appears if we look at the array of agents to be encountered in any concrete society. They are not only of different types – individual or collective, common or exceptional, self-contained or externally directed, spontaneously mobilized or organized from above – but each type has multiple and diverse concrete embodiments. There are masses of individual actors, and great numbers of various corporate bodies acting together or separately, cooperating or fighting, competing or struggling, agreeing or dissenting. Out of this, some precarious balance emerges, as a fluid, shifting and unstable end-product.

Now imagine how doubly complex the image has to become when we bring those one-sided analytical abstractions – structures and agents – together, and move to the central, mediating level of agency and praxis where empirical social processes actually operate. The agency, this seemingly simple quality of a social fabric deciding whether society is active or passive, turns out to be an utterly entangled synthetic fusion of multiple and diversified agents immersed in pluralistic and heterogeneous structures.

To grapple with this complexity, I suggest introducing the notion of power and its two forms, domination and hegemony. The usefulness of this concept for our purposes is suggested by Lukes: 'Power would seem to be an "agency" notion. Thus it is held and exercised by agents (individual or collective) within systems and structural determinants' (1978: 635). I propose to use the concept of power with respect to the agency in its simplest, quasi-Weberian sense as the probability that it will activate consequential praxis, and therefore the historical process. In other words, it means the 'power to' initiate and influence social becoming. Of course it allows of degrees; the strongest power of the agency is manifested in the active society, and the atrophy of its power results in a passive society.

But power so conceived, like all other phenomena located at the central, intermediate level of our model, must be treated as a synthetic product, a merger, of analytical aspects originating at two other levels, those of structures and of agents. The aspect of power manifesting itself at the level of structures, the structural power, will be referred to as domination; and the aspect of power manifesting itself at the level of agents, the agential power, will be called hegemony. The power of the agency is therefore the combined product of domination exerted over it by the structures, and hegemony exerted over it by the agents. The input from both sides need not be equal; there are all sorts of empirical possibilities, from the extreme domination of rigid structures, when agents have very little say, to the extreme hegemony of powerful agents, able to suppress the influence of weak or flexible structures. The power of the agency may derive mainly from the strength of structures (domination), or from the strength of agents (hegemony), but normally emerges as the mixed balance of both.

The concepts of domination and hegemony may be used not only in the 'vertical' direction, as 'domination over' the agency, or 'hegemony over' the agency. They may also be applied at each level – of structures, and of agents – for grasping internal tensions among its multiple and heterogeneous components. We shall speak of the domination of some structures among others, resulting in a precarious balance at the level of structures; and the hegemony of some agents among others, resulting in a precarious balance at the level of agents.

What does it mean, when in this 'horizontal' sense we say that some structures 'dominate among' others? We must be wary of the danger of hypostatization. Structures – networks of relationships – cannot by any stretch of the imagination be made to struggle, fight, compete among themselves. But they may certainly differ in comparison with others, in the constraining or enabling influence they exert on the agents and their actions. There are some core, primary or strategic structures, which have the strongest influence, and some marginal, secondary or residual structures whose impact is minuscule. Having the strongest influence over agents, those core, strategic structures may also be said to dominate among others, suppressing or overshadowing their impress.

Most sociological theories seem to assume some variation among structures in this respect. Sometimes the priority of certain structures is assumed as universal. For example, what we mean by 'economic determinism' – as exemplified by the orthodox interpretation of Marxism – is precisely the claim that the opportunity structure (and even more, its single, economic dimension) is always the strongest factor moulding the agents and their actions, as compared to ideal or normative structures, treated as derivative or secondary. Or, when Lukács or Gramsci speaks of the importance of 'political moment', and Dahrendorf borrows the Weberian concept of 'imperatively coordinated associations' (1959: 167), they emphasize that it is another dimension of the opportunity structure that acquires domination, not the hierarchies of property but rather of authority. What is referred to as the 'idealistic historiosophy' of Comte is nothing but the opposite claim, that the core level is the ideal structure, the forms and modes of justification of the dominant beliefs which determine all kinds of actions undertaken by the agents, and in effect produce the overall direction of progress. Finally what is meant by the 'normative bias' imputed to Durkheim and the structural-functionalists is their apparent obsession with normative structure – normative, or axiological consensus – as the crucial factor determining the actions of human agents, and consequently safeguarding the harmonious, equilibrated social order.

It would not be true to my synthetic, conciliatory, middle-of-the-road theoretical strategy to accept any of those universal claims. Rather, I am inclined to side with those sociologists who take them as contingent and historically variable. Which structures, or 'moments' assume predominance is not set once and for all in some essential, ontological constitution of a society. It is an empirical fact, which changes historically. There are 'economic societies', with property, wealth, ownership as organizing principles, and there are 'political societies', where authority, power and coercion assume this role. There are also 'ethical societies' where normative (religious and moral) considerations prevail. We may find examples of 'participative societies' (or at least longer or shorter episodes of this sort in the history of various societies), where the extension of interactive networks, the spreading and strengthening of social bonds, the affirmation of solidarity, widespread mobilization and mass activism set the tone of all social life.[3] Human history is too rich to be squeezed into any one-directional 'determinism' asserting the eternal domination of any single structure.

If we turn to the level of agents, the idea of hegemony that some of them may acquire among others is much more intuitive and does not entail the risk of hypostatization. Agents (individual as well as collective) fight, compete and struggle with each other, in the literal, empirically conceivable sense, and in effect some of them emerge as more powerful or hegemonic. We may ask what kinds of agents are the most important protagonists in such contests. Again, some authors are tempted to make universal claims. When Marx and Engels say: 'The history of all hitherto existing society is the history of class struggles' (1985 [1848]) they pick out a very special and utterly complex type of collective agents, and ascribe to them universal significance. A radically opposite choice is made by Carlyle who proclaims: 'Universal History, the history of what man has accomplished in this world, is at bottom the History of the Great Men who have worked here' (in Hook 1955: 14). There are other candidates for this elevated role of hegemonic agent. For some sociologists, social movements appear as crucial, especially in our century, which is commonly labelled as 'the era of social movements'. Others indicate political elites, governments, bureaucracies, parties or military leadership as the main protagonists. Those who are more idealistically inclined believe in the role of intellectual and cultural elites. There are also arguments for a central role for marginal groups, 'the outsiders', precisely because they are autonomous, not involved, or at least not yet implicated, in the operation of society and able to shape it 'from without'. The apotheoses of deviants and underdogs, of youth, or students, fit this last option. More recently the common people, the social masses in their everyday, routine actions, have come to be perceived as core agents, whose conduct pre-empts all other influences on societal functioning.

Even this cursory review of possible hegemonic agents suggests that the issue of hegemony is contingent, empirically and historically variable, and cannot be decided a priori. All sorts of agents participate in the constant struggle for control of agency 'from below', and therefore for influence on the whole operation of society, and indirectly on the course of further history. The arena of this contest for agency is normally the state, and state power is the ultimate prize. No wonder that at all those critical historical junctures when the radical transformations of society are at stake, the struggle always revolves around the possession of state power. This is the highest mark of hegemony among the whole array of agents participating in the social game.

To summarize, the dominant structures, in balance with other structures (supportive, suppressed, pre-empted, marginal etc.), exert domination over agency, constituting one side of its power. The hegemonic agents, in balance with other agents (coopted, cooperating, defeated, submissive etc.), exert hegemony over agency, constituting another side of its power. Together, structural domination and agents' hegemony make up the agential power, determine the potentiality of the agency to set society in motion and push it on the course of historical transformations.

Determinants of agency

We are only half-way in our search for the factors determining the master-variable of social becoming, the potentiality for self-transcendence embedded in the agency. We have seen how the two constitutive forces, merging in the overall power of agency – structural domination and agents' hegemony – constitute themselves in their own right, at their own levels. But we do not know yet what quality of the agency their merger will produce. Some agency is always there, but our main concern is under which conditions it is viable, robust, animating an active society; and under which conditions it is weak, fragile, sustaining a passive society. Only when we approach this question, can the puzzle of social becoming be untangled.

The answer must be sought in the variable characteristics of the whole balance reached at the structural level, the concrete network of dominant and dependent structures in their complex interplay, and in the variable traits of the whole balance reached at the level of agents, the concrete array of hegemonic and subordinated agents in their mutual relationships. The overall configuration of structures exerts domination over the agency, and the overall configuration of agents exerts hegemony over it. The power of agency emerges as the fusion of structural domination 'from above', and agents' hegemony 'from below'. We have to handle both analytical components in turn.

The crucial variable feature of the dominant structures is the degree of their determining influence with respect to actions. It may be conceptualized as a gradation from constraining (rigid, controlling) structures at one pole to enabling (loose, liberal, permissive) structures at the other. More specifically, the constraining structures may be seen as either negatively constraining (repressive, prohibitive, limiting) or positively constraining (facilitating, encouraging, enforcing). In turn, the crucial variable trait of the hegemonic agents is the strength of their disposition to change structures. It may be conceptualized as a gradation from reformist (change-oriented, active, contesting) agents at one pole to conservative agents (oriented toward preservation of the status quo, passive, acquiescent) at the other.

Agency, as the fusion of structural domination and agents' hegemony may be characterized by all possible combinations of these variables. Let us single out the six typical cases set out in figure 6.1.

The strongest agential potentiality for self-transcendence is marked as ACTIVISM₁. It is the case when change-oriented, reformist agents act within structures facilitating or enforcing change. They encounter normative structures emphasizing change, progress, achievement, and articulating values critical of existing realities, or meet ideal structures including images of the possible future society together with viable means of attaining it, or are bombarded by other agents willing to establish contacts or interactions with them, or are encouraged to advance on the ladders of stratification. In this case structures and agents mutually amplify their change-oriented potential. Agents want to change, and the change is expected, even demanded. Agency is at its peak, pushing for self-transcendence. Some of the highest-developed, democratic, market-oriented societies of our time seem to come close to this type, with the US as the paradigmatic case. In fact their economic success is the result of such an activist syndrome. Of course there are always possible dangers. One of them is the exhaustion of the reformist thrust, spreading the experience of the boredom, futility and meaninglessness of incessant effort. If the effort continues at all, it is only because of pressure from

133

above, no longer through conviction. It is a much weaker, coerced form of activism, which may easily deteriorate into passivism if the moral pressure or economic incentives are weakened. This situation is not wholly hypothetical, as may be observed at least in some segments of the most affluent societies. An alternative danger is the replacement of structures facilitating and encouraging change by those which merely allow or even prevent it. The loosening of structural inducements for change, or the introduction of counter-inducements or blocks, may lead to weaker forms of activism, and ultimately to outright passivism, even if agents still retain their change-oriented potential. This situation may be illustrated by the cases of conquest, foreign occupation and loss of national sovereignty. The tendency asserts itself even more if both processes coincide, and the demoralization of the agents is matched by a tightening of the repressive structures. Total passivism will ensue, bringing the degradation of agency to its lowest.

The weaker potentiality is marked as ACTIVISM$_2$. It is the case when change-oriented, reformist agents encounter structures which only enable

Features of structures

		ENABLING	CONSTRAINING	
			LIMITING	ENFORCING
Traits of agents	REFORMIST	RELEASED ACTIVISM (ACTIVISM$_2$)	BLOCKED ACTIVISM (PASSIVISM$_3$)	ENCOURAGED ACTIVISM (ACTIVISM$_1$)
	CONSERVATIVE	ABANDONED OPPORTUNITIES (PASSIVISM$_2$)	TOTAL STAGNATION (PASSIVISM$_1$)	COERCED ACTIVISM (ACTIVISM$_3$)

Figure 6.1

or allow change, but do not require it. The normative structure is permissive, leaving a large margin of tolerance for deviance or non-conformity; the ideal structure emphasizes free will rather than destiny, effort rather than fate; the interactional structures are opened, clearing the lines of access or communication among people; the hierarchies of inequality are loose and levelled, with considerable mobility. In this case dominant structures do not stand in the way of agents' change-oriented potential. Agents want to change, and the change is allowed. The agency is still quite robust. It may be easily 'upgraded' to ACTIVISM₁ if structures evolve toward more emphasis on change, incorporating prescriptions rather than permissions, inducements rather than enablements, and turning activism into a value rather than merely an option. But less optimistic scenarios are also possible. This situation is open to dangers similar to those facing the previous one; agents may lose their reformist motivations, structures may close down upon them, limiting their chances for activism, or both processes may occur together. Then, some form of passivism would be a likely result.

A still weaker potentiality of the agency is labelled ACTIVISM₃. This is the case when passive, acquiescent, conservative agents are coerced into change-oriented actions by structural constraints. They encounter a normative system whose laws reward initiative, originality, activism, and punish for conformity, idleness and passiveness, or ideologies which show people as the only masters of their fate, fully responsible for their failures. They meet interactional networks which engulf them in demands for reaction or response, or ladders of inequality on which one cannot stay long on one step, but may only fall down or advance. Agency is still there, but its potential is somewhat artificial. The change is enforced, imposed 'from above' somewhat against the agents' will. Think of some of the relatively underdeveloped or traditional societies of Africa, subjected to imposed, rapid modernization, or of some Eastern European societies in the period of forced industrialization. The precariousness of this situation resembles the more general dilemma of all coercion; there must be a proverbial policeman at every corner to ensure compliance, and perhaps behind the back of each policeman there must be another one coercing him, etc. – an Orwellian picture indeed. But if this form of activism can be upheld for some time and shown to produce benefits, it is likely that agents may evolve some lasting commitment to change, and turn into voluntary reformers. This may strengthen the agency, even to the highest level of ACTIVISM₁. This seems to have occurred in Japan, South Korea, Taiwan and Singapore. On the other hand, it may also easily deteriorate into passivism, and the atrophy of the agency if the coercive pressure for change is weakened for whatever reason.

With the next typical case we enter the world of suppressed, inactive agency. PASSIVISM₃ signifies a situation when reformist, change-oriented agents encounter a complete structural block to their actions in the form of rigid, strongly sanctioned norms and values guarding the *status quo*, or strong polemical indoctrination emphasizing fate rather than effort, ascription rather than achievement, stability rather than change. They face strictly delimited channels of communication and interaction, closing the circle of potential partners,[4] or immovable, caste-like, ossified hierarchies of inequality, with limited social mobility.[5] Repressive structures do not allow for change. That has been the experience of Stalinist regimes, both in the Soviet Union and in several satellite countries. They have long outlived Stalin himself, and in various post-Stalinist forms have survived till our times, fading away only in the period of *perestroika*. However, the dream of change has always remained in human heads. In this case the pressure is there, 'from below', because the agents want to change their society, though they cannot effect actual reforms, finding themselves helpless in the face of constraints and limitations. Agency is in fact dormant, but at least there are some seeds of future change, and reformers may mobilize their potential as soon as the grip of structures is released. Thus the likely escape from passivism is the move toward ACTIVISM₂. This indeed occurred in Poland, Hungary, East Germany and Czechoslovakia in 1989. Through successful reforms, the liberated agents may produce structures not only enabling but even encouraging or requiring change. The resolute attempts to institute pluralistic, democratic constitutions as well as market-oriented, competitive economic organization in Eastern Europe seem to thrust in this direction. Then the full-blown agency may reappear in the conditions of ACTIVISM₁.

Such perspectives are lacking in the case of PASSIVISM₂ when the structures are permissive, enabling change (e.g. there is large normative tolerance for innovation, ideological freedom, open communication and opportunity for advance) but nobody cares to use them; there is no willingness for change on the part of the agents. The opportunities are there, but no change ensues, as the agents ignore or neglect them and remain in a condition of resigned inertia, indifference or apathy. This situation may be illustrated by several unsuccessful attempts at economic reform and the mobilization of economic initiative undertaken by the communist authorities in Poland. There were periods where the chances for enterpreneurial activities were opened quite widely, but very few wanted to use them (partly because of the insufficient credibility of the authorities and doubts as to the permanence of the new legal regulations, partly because of the low levels of aspirations, and the expectation that they would be satisfied by the state irrespective of the amount of personal effort). In this case the agents simply do not want any changes, even though they can easily attain them. The true atrophy of the agency begins. There is no longer any inherent potentiality for change. The only prospect is the mobilization of agents, changing their inherent dispositions by moral reform, ideological appeals, re-education, illumination. This could turn the situation into ACTIVISM$_2$. Or, there is another, more practical and likely avenue; enforcing change 'from above' by introducing highly constraining structures demanding change. It is only with the success of Solidarity in 1989 that this course was taken in Poland. In this case passivism will evolve, at least temporarily, into ACTIVISM$_3$. If it lasts long enough, the chance for reforming the dispositions of agents *via* enforced activism appears, and with that some likelihood of ACTIVISM$_1$. But there is an alternative scenario, when liberal, enabling structures, not supported by activism, neglected and unused, degenerate into repressive, constraining structures, closing any opportunities for change and bringing about total and hopeless passivism. In Poland it always took the form of the proverbial 'tightening of the screw' after any cyclical 'thaw', with the imposition of martial law in 1981 as the most conspicuous example.

The full suppression of agency occurs in the case of PASSIVISM$_1$. Here passive agents live in the world of repressive structures, blocking any attempt toward change. The agents cannot and do not want to change their society. Diagnoses of the human condition under totalitarian regimes, from C. Milosz's 'captive mind' (1953), through Koestler's 'thought control' (1941), to Fromm's 'escape from freedom' (1941), emphasize various aspects of this reification. It signifies the death of the agency, which may be revived only through a long and protracted process, leading through other, less vicious forms of passivism. The first road is through PASSIVISM$_2$, when the lid of repression is released, opening some opportunities for activism. The slow revival of the agency starts from the top. This is the case with Soviet *perestroika*. The second road is through PASSIVISM$_3$, when the accumulation of grievances and frustrations passes a threshold beyond which passive agents mobilize for action. The revival of agency starts from the bottom. This was the case of the Solidarity movement born in Poland in 1980. Of course both processes may coincide, and that presents the greatest opportunity for the agency to reappear, as it leads directly to ACTIVISM$_2$. The structural changes introduced in its wake may then transform merely enabling conditions into ones demanding and sanctioning change. This ends the odyssey of the agency, back to its most vital, robust form in ACTIVISM$_1$.

All six situations described above, signifying the variable potential of agency, have been seen as the combined product of the overall character of structures (liberal, repressive or enforcing) and the overall character of agents (reformist or conservative). But we should not forget about the internal plurality and heterogeneity of structures and agents, and the constant struggles for domination and hegemony within them. It is here, in the 'politics' of structures and agents, that the secret of the permanent changes that agency undergoes is to be found. The dynamics described above, the shifts of the agency among six typical situations – either ascending toward the activist pole or descending toward the passivist – may be interpreted as the result of a power struggle among the structures and among the agents. When at the structural level the domination of liberal, permissive, or even radical tendencies is asserted, and at the agents' level, hegemony is won by innovators, reformers and revolutionaries, the agency is in full bloom. But the domination and hegemony may be contested; repressive tendencies may take hold, conservatives may get the upper hand – and the degradation of agency will start, moving along the various paths specified earlier. The contingency of agency is inbuilt in this complexity of fluid configurations and coalitions, the manifold outcomes of power contests at the level of structures and at the level of agents. Here the core determinants of agency must be sought.

They are not the only ones. If we recall the model of social becoming, the agency is 'suspended' not only between structures and agents, but between earlier and later praxis, the past and the future. And, together with the whole mechanism of social becoming, agency is also 'floating' in the environments of nature and consciousness. All are the seats of causal influences, co-determining the actual shape of agency. To represent the whole complexity of determinants impinging upon the agency, the fragment of our model may be taken out and enlarged (figure 6.2).

Some hypothetical observations may be made about the impact of the remaining co-determinants: tradition, the future, nature and consciousness.

Historical tradition reaches the agency *via* the actual structures and the actual endowment of the agents (shaped by earlier praxis), so that its substantive influence has already been taken into account in the earlier discussion. But there are some general traits of tradition which seem significant as additional variables. It is important whether the tradition of a given society is rich and complex or poor and simple. Is the intellectual horizon wide? Is the ethos well articulated? Are interactive channels comprehensive?[6] Are social divisions defined? All this is relevant for the shape of agency. It is also important whether the tradition is continuous, unbroken, stretching far into the past, or discontinuous, interrupted and short-lived. I would expect the former conditions to be conducive to the viable and strong agency, and the latter to the decaying, weak agency. But probably such regularity is not unexceptional, and must be carefully tested in each concrete case.

Turning to the other side of the time-axis, it is hard to imagine how

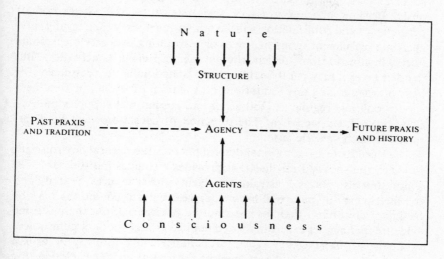

Figure 6.2

the future can influence the present, how an actual agency may be shaped by the praxis that it generates. We have happily already got rid of teleology or finalism in chapter 4. But we may recognize, with Merton, that the future may be embedded in present structures as the structurally defined expectation of continuity or discontinuity, of the duration or termination of structures. He defines this phenomenon:

> Socially expected durations . . . are socially prescribed or collectively patterned expectations about temporal durations embedded in social structures of various kinds: for example, the length of time that individuals are institutionally permitted to occupy particular statuses (such as an office in an organization or membership in a group); the assumed probable durations of diverse kinds of social relationships (such as friendship or a professional–client relation); and the patterned and therefore anticipated longevity of individual occupants of statuses, of groups, and of organizations. (1984: 266)

Applying the concept of socially expected duration to our purposes, we may suppose that the agency will be influenced by the assumption of permanence, or conversely of the transience of its constitutive structural

139

arrangements. The direction of influence is hard to specify unambiguously. Perhaps in some areas of social structures the expectation of permanence and continuation will favour strong agency (e.g. legally safeguarding permanent terms of trade, or warranting property or personal liberty in constitutions, which stimulates enterpreneurial activities). But in other areas it may paralyse the agency. Sanctioning the presidency 'for life', or abandoning any limitations on the term of office, or treating a certain political regime as God-given and eternal will suppress motivations for political activism. The direction of causation must be determined in each specific case.

The third locus of additional determinants is the natural environment in which the society finds itself. It provides resources indispensable for action, but also places constraints on agents and structures. Scarcity and the inclemency of nature allow of degrees; natural conditions may be benign or confining. Perhaps it cannot be generalized, but there is some evidence that neither exceedingly rich nor exceedingly poor circumstances evoke the strongest agency. The most conducive conditions seem instead to be found at some medium level of natural abundance. Notice, for example, how the intermediate climatic zones have engendered the strongest civilizations, or how unlimited natural resources – say in oil-rich Arabia – have not produced great advances in civilization. These observations can find some theoretical foundation if we recall our notion of the human condition and human nature. Human creativeness, innovativeness – so central for the emergence of viable agency – have been seen as instigated by strain, tension and contradiction between aspirations and achievements. In the conditions of intermediate natural abundance or benevolence this tension acquires optimum strength, stimulating and not paralysing. There is also independent psychological evidence from the area of task-solution which points in the same direction. Of course applying it *mutatis mutandis* to the abstract level of agency requires much caution. Accordingly, all that has been said must be treated only as initial suppositions requiring further study.

Finally, we come to the second environment of social becoming, the 'sea' of consciousness in which society is immersed. There are some general, formal traits of social consciousness which seem to be relevant for shaping agency. One is the scope and level of awareness of social phenomena and processes on the part of societal members. The agency may be blind or self-conscious; there are also all shades of awareness, from common-sense, practical discourse to theoretical or philosophical discourse. Another general trait has to do with the degree of realism with which people perceive the convictions of other people. On the one hand, there are the cases of utterly unrealistic appraisal, 'pluralistic ignorance',[7] where an individual feels completely isolated in his beliefs, and the 'fallacy of unanimity', when he naïvely believes that all others share his own point of view.[8] On the other hand, there are the cases of balanced, realistic judgement of dominant preferences, thought trends, ideological predilections. The third general feature of social consciousness is the self-appraisal of agential power shared by the members of the society. Again it may stretch from biased 'false consciousness' (the illusion of omnipotence), or conversely the 'Lilliput complex' (Ossowski 1962) (the feeling of utter powerlessness) all the way to the balanced, realistic judgement of dynamic potential as always present in some measure, but also inevitably limited.

More specifically, the ideas, beliefs, judgements included in social consciousness may refer to all kinds of determinants impinging upon agency. The subjective, shared and widespread perceptions of various factors influencing agency acquire the status of partly independent causal force. The 'Thomas Theorem' holds here in all its implications. Whether in fact adequate or not, the beliefs influence human motivations, and therefore human conduct and indirectly the strength of agency. Thus social consciousness becomes an important mediating determinant, catalysing the impact of all other causal factors. The ways in which those various factors are seen co-determine the agential power in their own right.

The image of social structures, and particularly the dominant structures, as repressive or liberal may coincide with the actual situation or not, but at least for some time, even the illusion of openness and freedom raises activism, whereas the fear of sanctions and restraints, even if unfounded, produces passiveness. Some outbursts of the agency in futile, brutally suppressed revolutions, so common in history, are due precisely to the misperception of opportunities. Similarly, any signal that the repressive grip of tyranny has actually been weakened (that taxes are no longer meticulously collected, that some recruits avoid conscription, that some dissidents do not land in jail, that independent expression is allowed etc.) is often the precipitant of successful revolts. Turning to the example of the turbulent autumn of 1989, is it not the case that the enormous outburst of popular resistance to the communist system in the countries of Eastern Europe started in earnest only when it was first declared (by Gorbachev) and tested in practice (by Poland and Hungary) that the 'Brezhnev Doctrine' did not hold any more, and that the Soviets would not intervene militarily?

The image of agents, and particularly hegemonic agents, held in social consciousness is equally important. If such agents are perceived as powerful, capable of challenging repressive structures and reforming the whole operation of society, or even of redirecting the course of history, they are able to mobilize massive support; whereas if they are seen as weak, their

141

calls often go unheeded. Recall the experience of the Solidarity movement in Poland in 1980–1, with almost ten million members and an escalating illusion of unmatched strength. Then, the brutal test of martial laws wrecked this perception and led to rapid demobilization. Only a decade later, under different geopolitical and internal conditions, the movement was able to regroup its forces and win a stunning electoral victory.

The third area of determinants is tradition. The subjective attitude toward tradition typical for social consciousness seems at least as important as its objective, actual constitution. The feeling of rootedness, continuity and pride in indigenous tradition, whether justified or not, seems an important factor strengthening agency. On the contrary, the presentist bias of the 'now generation', severing the link with the past, evincing indifference, hostility or a priori negativism to the historical heritage, considerably weakens the agential power. Finding the strength and pride in tradition to go forward, to transcend it, is of course a different story from slavish, uncritical conformity to received traditions, the full immersion in the 'cake of custom' – to use Sumner's apt phrase. The latter is a mark of the passive society and weak agency. The ability to distance oneself from the past and adopt a critical, relativistic view, to conduct a realistic appraisal of its merits and failures, coupled with an acceptance of selective continuity – these seem an optimum attitude for the powerful agency.

A crucial segment of social consciousness is filled with images of the future. The authors of all social utopias recognized long ago that these may be a powerful mobilizing force, even if patently unrealistic (Szacki 1980). Weber is said to have remarked that if people had not tried to reach for the impossible, they would never have won what was possible. Boulding refers to humans as 'image-directed' animals (1964: 7). Bell and Mau speak of the 'pull of the future' as typical of human society because 'expectations about the future, whether short- or long-range, may enter as a determining factor into most human behavior' (1970: 209). Via agents and their actions, so to speak 'from below', such images exert a causal influence on agency. There are two dimensions of the images which are most relevant. 'Critical differences in human behavior are hypothesized to result from images which are basically pessimistic compared to those which are optimistic, and from images which put man in the image as a causal factor compared to those which do not' (p. 222). In the human world, optimism – whether justified or not – is perhaps the strongest mobilizing factor. This is clearly true of human individuals, for whom, as we know, 'nothing succeeds better than the belief in success'; and the same seems to apply *mutatis mutandis* to the level of the agency. There is much historical evidence that societies permeated with optimism and hope (Desroche 1979) manifest high levels of mobilization, activism and participation – in a word, a viable and robust agency. On the contrary, societies which plunge into a decadent 'disaster culture', a climate of pessimism, catastrophism, hopelessness and resignation, are doomed to stagnation, and their agency quickly decays.

Another variable dimension is equally important. Nothing paralyses agency more than widespread belief in the fatalism of events and processes, which are taken to occur independently of any human effort, according to their own inevitable, irreversible and uncontrollable patterns. The fetish of providence, fate, or the iron laws of history, predetermining the future 'above human heads', is able to keep human masses in a state of passive, resigned reconciliation to existing realities. On the other hand, a vision which emphasizes that what people do matters, and matters crucially, shaping, constructing and modifying the future, has a tremendous mobilizing potential. The recognition of human 'freedom to', the voluntaristic bent of social consciousness is probably one of the strongest co-determinants of agential power. An optimistic and voluntaristic orientation toward the future is one of the components of the wider phenomenon which Giddens calls 'historicity' and which he takes to be typical for Western civilization: 'consciousness of "progressive movement" as a feature of the social life of certain societies, above all those of the postfeudal West, in which that consciousness is organised actively to promote social change' (1979: 199–200).

Finally, we come to the last area of determinants of agency: natural environment. Quite apart from its actual, objective constitution, the subjective attitude toward nature dominant in social consciousness is an important determinant *per se*. On the one hand, nature may be looked upon as an alien, threatening, external world, which must be subjected to human manipulation, control and conquest in order to be 'humanized', satisfying human needs. Or, on the contrary, nature may be seen as a valuable good in its own right, an indispensable milieu of human life, which should be preserved and cultivated, existing in full harmony with human beings. Klaus Eder traces the roots of those instrumental and autotelic attitudes to nature in two opposite 'cultural codes' underlying Western civilization: the Greek and the Jewish.

The Greek tradition utilized nature without restrictions. Nature (like a sacrificial animal) was not only an object of politics. It was treated as a means to other, namely human ends . . . The Jewish tradition on the other hand restricted the use of bloody rituals by binding the sacrificial acts to the model of a paradisiac state of nature . . . This coding implied a relationship with nature whose logic is defined by a harmonious or peaceful coexistence. (Eder 1990 [1988]: 12)

143

Obviously, most of human history has been pervaded by the utilitarian approach to nature and the theme of conquest. Only recently have the moral approach and the theme of harmony been affirmed in 'ecological consciousness', arising in response to the excesses of conquest and the dramatic dangers to human survival itself produced as its side-effects. How do those two approaches affect the agency? The answer must be put in historically relative terms. There is no doubt that for long ages the conquest of nature provided a tremendous stimulus for activism, and therefore endowed agency with vitality and power. But the historical situation changes when nature becomes 'oversaturated' with the effects of human intervention. The idea of conquest loses its appeal, and the opposite theme of conservation seems to be much more potent in mobilizing human effort and shaping agency. People recognize the need of a 'new frontier'; they shift their aspirations toward space, or, in an even more hopeful direction, toward greater self-control of their own societies or of themselves.

Closing the list of factors considered as crucial in shaping the agency, we have to make one additional reservation. So far, we have been speaking of a society – whether active or passive – as if it were a single, self-contained, isolated entity. This simplification was necessary for analytic purposes. But we should not forget that the earth has always been populated by multiple and heterogeneous societies, living side by side, cooperating, competing or fighting with each other. This global context has to be taken into account as the final area of causal influences impinging upon agency in each, single society. The importance of such supra-social, 'international' influences is raised in modern society, where globalization becomes a significant tendency. What happens in each society depends in growing measure on what is going on in other, even very distant societies. And this relates to agential capacities as well; they are no longer autonomous products of indigenous developments, but are also affected from the outside. The shape of agency in any given society is at least in part influenced by the constraints or facilitations presented by other societies, each with its own specific agency, which has been shaped in a similar process. This additional consideration allows us to understand the historical case where a society seemingly rich in agential potentialities is in fact passive for a long time because of conquest or domination by another, stronger society. Notice what happened in East Germany when the grip of Soviet influence was released. It is also relevant for the opposite case, when an internally poor or weak society is pushed into activism and exhibits surprising agential power through the backing of some strong ally. What would become of Cuba or Nicaragua, were Soviet support to be withdrawn? Taking this complication into account makes the computation of actual variables determining concrete historical situations much more intricate, but does not change their basic catalogue.

The multiple variables which we have attempted to single out in this chapter combine in multiple ways to produce the variable capacity of a society for self-transformation, its potentiality for engendering consequential praxis. The character of agency seems to explain the various courses that human societies follow in their history; to solve the puzzle of social becoming. Some combination of variables may be found responsible for the passive reproduction of society within its traditional institutional order; some other combination will be discovered in societies not able even to reproduce themselves, and therefore condemned to decay, disintegration and ultimate extinction. Both are pathological syndromes of varying gravity; they signify a blocked, suppressed or diseased agency.

But there are also some societies, and some periods in the history of every society, when agency affirms itself in its strongest, most dynamic form. A combination of variables appears which produces a powerful drive to overcome limitations, break through barriers, tear down walls, cross frontiers, literally and figuratively. Human creativeness and the push toward self-realization are at their best, and society moves by leaps and bounds, radically changing its face. Those are the golden hours of human history, when societies show their limitless potential for incessant social becoming.

Part III

The applications

7

Social movements: double morphogenesis

Two selected interpretations

The value of a sociological theory may be measured by its potentials of elaboration and application; the extent to which its general categories can be interpreted in empirical terms and applied to a wide and diversified range of social phenomena and processes. The theory of social becoming must now be put to this ultimate test. Having constructed SB in the preceding part of the book, we have to see how it relates to social life in its manifold, actual manifestations. Can it shed some new light on the concrete occurrences and developments experienced by people and their societies?

Any exhaustive treatment of this task is impossible, not only for practical reasons like the limited scope of this book or competence of the author. It is also impossible for a reason of principle. SB is a very general and abstract theory; it purports to unravel the basic mechanism of societal functioning and historical transformations. Therefore its range of elaboration and application is theoretically unlimited. If it is a good theory, it must always remain open. No conceivable evidence can ever completely fill out its framework.

Therefore we must be highly selective and focus on those areas of empirical facts where social becoming will manifest itself most conspicuously. In other words, we have to find what Merton calls

An earlier and different version of this chapter appeared as 'Social movements: structures in *statu nascendi*' in *The Polish Sociological Bulletin*, No. 2, 1987, pp. 5–26.

'strategic research materials' and defines as 'the empirical material that exhibits the phenomena to be explained or interpreted to such advantage and in such accessible form that it enables the fruitful investigation of previously stubborn problems and the discovery of new problems for further inquiry' (1987: 10–11).

In this, final part of the book I shall pick out two specific varieties of the comprehensive process of social becoming and subject them to more detailed scrutiny.

First I shall focus on social movements as particularly important initiators and carriers of social becoming. Merton's observation from the seventies is still more relevant today: 'In our time, vastly evident social change is being initiated and funneled through a variety of social movements' (1973b: 101). They enter the front pages of newspapers, appear in every television newsreel. We read about them, listen about them, observe them practically every day. Some of us personally experience the excitement of their victories and the agony of their failures: the labour movement, the peace movement, the ecological movement, the human rights movement, the gay movement, the students' movement, the feminist movement, the anti-abortion (or pro-abortion) movements, the political movements, the youth movements, the countercultural movements, the alternative movements etc. Their names themselves signify some of the most disturbing social problems, the focal points of human misery and the vistas of human strivings. In them and through them people regain at least a feeling of mastery over their social world, and from time to time some actual mastery too. No wonder that theories of social movements have become one of the flourishing fields of contemporary sociology. In 1985 Morris and Herring referred to 'an explosion of theoretical and empirical writings on social movements and collective action within the last decade' (p. 1). The authors of a more recent trend report fully confirm it: 'the field has experienced a renaissance in the last decade and a half' (McAdam et al. 1988: 695). We shall try to show how some insights from the voluminous literature on social movements can be rephrased in terms of SB, manifesting their new, hidden heuristic potential.

As the second focus of our interest we select a particularly salient and spectacular form in which the phenomenon of social becoming manifests itself in history. Revolutions are seen as the peak of social becoming, the cases where it occurs in its most condensed, intensive, rapid and consequential form. Because of their unusual character, they have been the subject of human curiosity from time immemorial: 'Written observations on revolution thus stretch back more than 4000 years, extending through Plato and Aristotle to Machiavelli, de Tocqueville and Marx' (Goldstone 1982: 187). For a long time, however, the study of revolutions has been quite marginal for sociology as a scientific discipline.[1] It is only recently that a 'new wave' of sociological theories of revolution has appeared, especially in the wake of the 'burgeoning of interest in political violence and revolutions which took place in the United States during the 1960s and early 1970s' (Taylor 1984: 6). But of course, it is not only an American experience. The world of the twentieth century has witnessed innumerable revolutions, great and small, violent and peaceful, radical and 'self-limiting', 'silent' and salient, progressive and regressive, successful and failed. Sociology tries to account for them, producing an array of conceptual models and explanations. We shall see how some of the ideas spelled out within this new body of theories, may be rooted in SB, as its straightforward interpretations or implementations.

To repeat, in this part of the book I shall focus on two significant modes of social becoming: first, 'double morphogenesis', as the effecting of structural changes by social movements which mobilize and structure themselves in the very process; and second, revolution, as the condensed eruption of social becoming in a particularly conspicuous form. The present chapter is devoted to the first of these modes.

Strategic research area

There is one domain of sociological inquiry where social becoming is particularly visible, the study of social movements. First of all, social movements embody the characteristic two-sidedness of social reality, the dialectics of individuals and social wholes, which has been taken as the foundational premise of SB. Anthony Oberschall believes that the processes occurring in social movements are 'providing a link between the micro-and macroaspects of [sociological] theory' (1973: 21). Zurcher and Snow aptly point out: 'Nowhere is the reciprocity between the individual and social structure more conceptually and empirically obvious than in the operation of social movements.' Hence: 'the social movement milieu is an excellent stage upon which to observe how social factors influence and are influenced by actors' (1981: 447, 475). Thus, social movements represent an intermediate form in the anatomy of social reality.

In the second place, social movements represent also an intermediate stage in the dynamic emergence of the social fabric. Thus they allow us to grasp social reality as it comes into being, reflecting the central focus of SB. This intermediate quality of social movements means, on the one hand, that they participate in the shaping, constructing and reforming of external society. They are some of the most important agents of structural change and structure-building. As Alain Touraine puts it: 'social movements belong to the processes by which a society produces its organization on the basis of its system of historical action and via class conflicts and political transactions' (1977: 298). This role is growing in modern society through extended opportunities – economic, political and ideological – for the mobilization and functioning of movements. In most developed societies they may become crucial agents of change. Adamson and Borgos make a relevant observation with respect to American society: 'mass-based movements and the conflict they generate are the primary agents of social change' (1984: 12). In sum, studying social movements allows us to grasp wider social structures in the process of their emergence or transformation.

Social movements have an intermediate quality also in another sense; in their internal constitution they are something in between mere congeries of acting individuals and fully-fledged, crystallized social wholes: 'movements are neither fully collective behavior nor incipient interest groups . . . Rather, they contain essential elements of both' (Freeman 1973: 793). They 'last longer and are more integrated than mobs, masses and crowds, and yet are not organized like political clubs and other associations' (Banks 1972: 8). Thus, studying social movements allows us to grasp the intermediate phase of internal structure-building, to see how the internal structures of the movement emerge and change. Killian sums up this point almost in the language of SB: 'the study of social movements is not the study of stable groups or established institutions, but of groups and institutions in the process of becoming' (1964: 427).

Bringing those observations together, we shall notice that social movements are very peculiar objects indeed; they participate as crucial agents in the building of structures external to themselves, and at the same time they build up their own internal structure; they structure themselves for the sake of structuring (or restructuring) the wider society. This crucial property is identified in Claus Offe's discussion of the so-called 'new social movements' and their characteristic mode of operation: 'This typically involves two aspects: the mode by which individuals act together in order to constitute a collectivity ("internal mode of action") and the methods by which they confront the external world and their political opponents ("external mode of action")' (1985: 829). Similarly, Banks refers to social movements as 'socially creative', but at the same time 'self-creative' collectivities (1972: 16). One may call this process specific for social movements a 'double morphogenesis'.[2] Taking part in a double morphogenesis, social movements appear as agents of structure-building *par excellence*, shaping both internal and external structures in mutually interlinked, concurrent processes.

My focus in this chapter will be on the processes of structure-building *by* the movements and *in* the movements; and particularly on the mutual interactions of these two processes – external morphogenesis and internal morphogenesis. The analysis will proceed in our usual way – through a series of successive approximations. Several models will be presented, from the simplest and most abstract to the most complex and restrictive, gradually approaching the concreteness of actual social events.

External morphogenesis

As a start, we shall abstract from internal structure-building, the self-cystallization of the social movement, treating it as a black box, and focusing entirely on its impress on the external structures of wider society. Look at some typical definitions of social movements: 'collective enterprises to establish a new order of life' (Blumer 1951: 199), 'collective enterprises to effect changes in the social order' (Lang and Lang 1961: 507), 'collective efforts to modify norms and values' (Smelser 1962: 3), 'collectivity acting with some continuity to promote or resist change in the society or group of which it is a part' (Turner and Killian 1972: 246), 'collective efforts to control change, or to alter the direction of change' (Lauer 1976: xiv), 'organized efforts by groups of people to bring about social change' (Luhman 1982: 460).

From these definitions, a basic model can be derived: the social movement effects or at least attempts to effect changes in the external structures of the society to which it belongs. The crucial property of the movement is its effectiveness in introducing such structural transformations. This may be called its morphogenetic potential. Such potential may manifest itself in the disruptive (destructive) and creative (constructive) modes. Normally, in order to introduce structural innovations, the movement has to break down or at least weaken existing structures. Only later can the constructive attempts start. Some movements stop short of the truly creative potential, exercising only the disruptive, destabilizing influence. Movements devoid of creative potential are in a sense crippled; a fully-fledged movement has to exhibit both potentials, destructive and constructive, to be historically consequential.

Morphogenetic potential, both destructive and constructive, may take various forms depending on the aspect (level, dimension) of social structure at which it is aimed. Recalling our fourfold INIO scheme of social structure,[3] we may distinguish four forms of morphogenetic potential. The ideological potential of the movement may be conceived as the measure of its impact on the ideal structure, the degree to which the movement's creed, *Weltanschauung*, vision of the present, image of the future, definitions of enemies and allies etc. spread out in a society. For example, the significant ideological role of the Civil Rights movement in the US is stressed by Coser: 'the shock of recognition, the jolt to conscience, occurred only when the Negroes, through by-and-large non-violent action in the South and through increasingly violent demonstrations and even riots in the North, brought the problem forcibly to the attention of white public opinion and the white power structure' (Coser 1967: 86). In the case of Poland, the Solidarity movement, suppressed and outlawed by martial law in 1981, developed extensive underground publishing and educational activities, revealing to the masses various 'white-spots' of Polish history, the true dimensions of Stalinist crimes, abuses of state bureaucracy, the irrationality of economic policies etc. This prepared the ground for its eventual electoral victory and the demise of communist government in June 1989.

The reform potential of the movement will mean the measure of its impact on the normative structure, expressed in the introduction of new values, ways of life, rules of conduct and role-models among the wider population. Movements able to do that achieve what Burns and Buckley have called the 'meta-power' or 'relational control' (1976: 215); they institute a new framework of rules for the social game. This ability is rightly considered to be most essential: 'Major struggles in human history and contemporary society revolve around the formation and reformation of major rule systems, the core institutions of society' (Burns et al. 1985: v).

Then, there is the reorganizational potential, understood as the measure of impact on the patterns and channels of social interaction (social organization); the establishing of new social ties, the formation of new groups, creating communication networks, forming inter-group coalitions etc. This process is clearly visible in the transition from the monolithic, centralized, autocratic systems of Eastern Europe to pluralistic, democratic, market-oriented societies. During the 'autumn of nations' in 1989, we witnessed the mushrooming of innumerable associations, voluntary groups, political parties, unions, filling out the 'sociological vacuum' so characteristic of totalitarian regimes.[4]

Finally, one may distinguish the redistributional potential, as the measure of the movement's impact on the opportunity structure; the extent to which the movement is able to raise benefits, privileges, gratifications for its members, followers, adherents or sympathizers, and by the same token to take them away from the its opponents or enemies. The disbanding of the 'nomenklatura' system in post-communist societies of Eastern Europe is a telling example. The redistribution of 'life chances' among the population is the final effect of the movement's structure-building activity, and access to power proves especially crucial for preserving the benefits achieved and controlling the distribution of resources and goods in the future. As Tarrow remarks: 'In the absence of changes in the structure of political power, the advantages gained and legitimate access accorded during cycles of protest are always reversible' (1985: 53). This explains why the issue of power is so central for all reform-oriented or revolutionary movements attempting the redistribution on the largest scale.

Only if all four domains of social structure are effectively attacked does the social movement exhibit its full dynamic potential. I would reserve the term 'revolutionary' for this extreme case. In actual reality, movements are often crippled, one-sidedly focusing on single areas of structural change. For example, some succeed solely in spreading myths, utopias, wishful thinking and empty ideologies – with no counterpart in other dimensions of the social structure. Speaking of peasant rebellions Wolf stresses that this is far from sufficient for success: 'such a myth often can and does move peasants to action, but it provides only a common vision, not an organizational framework of action. Such myths unite peasants, they do not organize them' (1969: 108). Other movements may focus on spreading new patterns of interaction, new ways of life, which in itself is also not enough for significant and lasting structural change. The examples of Beatniks, Hippies, Punks, Skins and similar counter-cultural movements easily come to mind.

If we turn to revolutionary movements – many-sided in the character of their targets and most comprehensive in the scope of their structural impact – two typical, alternative sequences of external morphogenesis may be observed. One originates 'from below'; it starts with a new ideology, from which new norms and values are gradually derived, whose implementation produces actual new patterns of interaction and organization, and those finally entail new networks of vested interests. This is the spontaneous morphogenetic process. An alternative sequence proceeds in the reverse order. It starts with the redistribution of resources, opportunities, life-chances 'from above', by decree of the movement which seized power; then the exercise of new opportunities leads to new patterns of interaction via facts rather than via rules. It is only their gradual crystallization and patterning which results in new norms and values. Finally new ideas, beliefs and creeds emerge as justifications or rationalizations of new structural arrangements in other spheres. This is the cycle of enacted morphogenetic process.

Judging the effectiveness of the movement in introducing structural changes, multiple relativization is necessary. The success (or failure) of the movement may be treated in instrumental terms, measured by its impact on external structures, but also in autonomous terms, as the extent of preservation or continuation of the movement itself. Its impress on external structures may be further evaluated in relation to the movement's proclaimed goals, or in comparison to concrete, objective historical chances. Piven and Cloward succintly remind us: 'What was won must be judged by what was possible' (1979: xiii). Similarly, the manifest effects of the movement of which its members are fully aware must be distinguished from possible latent functions (unintended and unrecognized side-effects). Finally short-range effects must be distinguished from long-range effects which will manifest themselves only in the future.

Thus, the balance of consequences of the social movement is always complex and ambivalent. What is a success in terms of one relativization, may well prove to be failure in terms of another – and vice versa. For example, the defeated, crushed, destroyed movement of the oppositional type may leave lasting structural effects, preparing the way for its ultimate victory. As Oberschall puts it: 'A movement may be ruthlessly suppressed and yet many of the changes it had sought might still be brought about at a later time, for confrontation is a warning signal to the ruling groups that they had better change course or else face even more explosive upheavals in the future' (1973: 344). For example, it may be shown that in spite of the initial demise of the Solidarity movement with the imposition of martial law, it succeeded in infusing the system with the 'logic of reform', enlarged the scope of participation in political life, transformed the balance of forces in political elites, and left a strong imprint on the collective consciousness (Sztompka 1988 [1984]). That prepared the victory of Solidarity eight years later. On the other hand, the movement apparently realizing all of its proclaimed goals may prove to be a failure in relation to the pool of abandoned historical possibilities, to what was objectively attainable under given circumstances. Here it is usually many years later that such earlier possibilities are unravelled. Further, the effects considered to be a movement's successes may entail unintended and unrecognized (latent) costs outweighing the benefits. Finally, immediate gains may well be lost in the course of long-range developments.

A cause or a carrier of change?

So far, we have been talking of a social movement as if it were an ultimate cause of structural change. There may be an opposite perspective, where social movements are treated as epiphenomena (symptoms, side-effects) of ongoing social transformations. Both approaches are wrong. A more adequate model gives the movement a sort of mediating location, between the pre-existent structure, out of which the movement itself emerges, and the later structure, modified under its impact. Here the movement acquires the status of a mediator, transmitter, vehicle, carrier of structural change, rather than its ultimate originator or indicator. It does not arise in a vacuum, but at the same time it actively reshapes received structural conditions.

In general, the pre-existent structure may be said to constitute a pool of resources and facilities for the movement. Keeping in mind that the pre-existent structure may also be analysed in terms of our fourfold INIO scheme, one may distinguish various more specific influences exerted by such structures on the social movement. Thus the ideal pre-existent structure normally serves as a treasury of ideas from which the movement shapes its creed, ideology, definition of goals, identification of enemies and allies, and its vision of the future. Those are never pure inventions. Rather, the ideological horizon of a given society, cultural area or historical epoch is always pre-established. The movement articulates those encountered, traditional views, selects from them, changes emphases, arranges them into coherent systems, and of course on this basis adds innovations, but never produces its ideological system from scratch. Apparent novelty is never absolute; at most it is partial. This was already observed long ago with respect to revolutionary movements, which were found to borrow rather than invent their slogans and battle-cries as wells as their images of the better world. For example, some hints in this direction given by Marx were later developed into a whole 'theory of revolutionary retrospection' by a Polish Marxist of the early period K. Kelles-Krauz: 'The ideals with which the whole reformist movement wishes to replace the existing social norms are always similar to norms from the more or less distant past. . . . The source of the ideal of the future, like the source of any idea, has to be in the past – in a certain social form that becomes antiquated' (1962 [1896]). For instance, if we look at the whole symbolic and ideological sphere of the Solidarity movement in Poland, it could not be comprehended without reference to the long tradition of Polish Catholicism.[5]

Turning to the next area of pre-existent structure, the normative structure, it is found to play a different role. It often serves as a target for the movement. The norms, values, institutions and roles of the established normative order are rejected, criticized, ridiculed and challenged. Some movements focus on norms, treating them as inefficient, inadequate or improper means to otherwise accepted ends. Other challenge values as well, as unjust, wrong or misconceived. As a rule, a certain sequence seems to obtain; Smelser argues that it is only when 'norm-oriented movements' are strongly opposed by countermovements, blocked by authorities, suppressed or endangered, that the escalation of goals and qualitative change of demands occurs, leading to the appearance of 'value-oriented movements' (1962: 330–5). Again, the Solidarity movement in Poland, like other liberating movements in

Eastern Europe, provides perfect illustrations of this effect, when the constant radicalization of demands could be observed largely as a result of the stubborn resistance of the entrenched political elites. The most violent, bloody and tragic revolutionary outburst came precisely in the country, where tyranny, repression and governmental control were most rigid – in Romania.

The pre-existent interactive (organizational) structure has other functions. It produces the field of constraints as well as facilitations for the movement. The communication networks established among members of a society or some segment of the population prior to the beginning of the movement, play a crucial role in the process of recruitment and mobilization. Freeman discusses 'the key role of pre-existing communication networks as the fertile soil in which new movements can sprout' (1973, 1983b). She illustrates it with the case of the Women's Liberation Movement. Similarly, the networks of interlinked associations or communities based on common religious or ethnic loyalties (clubs, churches, ethnic groups, patriotic societies etc.) are helpful for speeding up mobilization and recruitment to social movements once the occasion arises. In the case of the Civil Rights movement in the US, it is often observed that 'among Blacks – the dense network of segregated colleges, women's clubs, newspapers, union locals, and small businesses, provided the organizational infrastructure of the movement. The black church provided many of its organizers, its music and rhetoric, and much of its resilient spirit' (Adamson and Borgos 1984: 129). A similar role on the part of the Catholic Church, as well as in earlier informal circles and associations of oppositional character (e.g. the Committee for the Defence of Workers (KOR)), was clearly visible during the beginnings of the Solidarity movement in Poland in the eighties. An equally important role is played by existing channels of political expression, or, as it is sometimes called, the 'political opportunity structure' (available associations, self-governing bodies, local administrative centres, cooptable political elites etc.). As Zald and Useem point out, 'political structures vary in the extent to which they provide movement opportunities' (1982: 15).

Finally, we come to the last area – the pre-existent opportunity structures in the strict sense of the term – the established hierarchies of inequality. Here, the pre-existent economic and power inequalities with resulting contradictions and conflicts among segments of the population (classes, strata, interest groups etc.) are often taken to be the prime motivating factor for the mobilization of movements. The hierarchical differentiation of vested interests is seen to produce tensions and strains, grievances and deprivations in the population, motivating people to join the movements of protest or reform. Those deprived of opportunities, life-chances and access to valued goods and resources provide a ready clientele for social movements, and are easily recruited and mobilized to action aimed at the structural redistribution of privileges and gratifications (Dahrendorf 1959; Oberschall 1973).[6]

Between the pre-existent structure (of whatever form), the movement itself and the later structure it actively shapes there are various feedback loops. Our next approximation recognizes that the social movement is significantly co-determined, as it evolves, by the reflexive impact of its own effects on the external structure. This may be represented by means of a simple scheme (figure 7.1).

Both the success and the failure of the movement in the instrumental sense – the attainment or non-attainment of changes in the external structure – influence the fate and 'career' of the movement. Direct feedback operates mainly via the awareness of its members and followers through an amplifying, positive impact of success, and a negative impact of failure. In case of success (even when only temporary or partial) it normally results in raised mobilization, strengthened secondary recruitment ('bandwagon effect'), escalation of hope etc. In case of failure, it

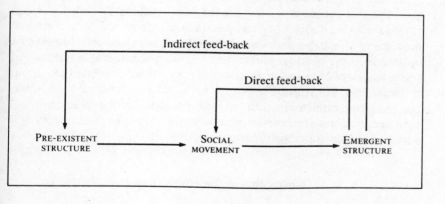

Figure 7.1

easily produces demobilization, dispersion of members, desertion of followers, general disenchantment and apathy. Of course, other empirical possibilities are open under specific conditions not precisely known. Sometimes the complete success of the movement may, so to speak, pre-empt its goals and lead to its quick dissolution. This is what some movement leaders refer to as 'a crisis of victory' (Adamson and Borgos 1984: 4). In other cases failure may help the leaders to distinguish and define weaknesses in earlier efforts, identify the truly committed supporters, eliminate the opportunists, regroup their forces, put the enemy in the spotlight, and in effect allow them to reshape the movement's tactics and bring about its revival in new forms. This is what happened with the suppressed Solidarity movement in Poland in the late eighties, and led to its ultimate victory in 1989.

Another feedback loop is more indirect and works through the reshaping of the wider structural context in which the movement continues to operate. As Lauer puts it: 'Any change that results from a movement will react in some way back upon the movement' (1976: xxvi). Thus, the new structural arrangements introduced under the movement's own impact may be conducive to further development of the movement. Etzioni discusses this under the heading of 'mutual reinforcing process': 'Mobilization uses whatever options the structure allows for changing it and changing the structure can expand these options' (1968a: 417). This is an amplifying loop. For example, such an effect can be expected o movements enhancing widespread attitudes of activism, creativeness and optimism in the ideal structure, while leaving considerable margins o tolerance, permissiveness and allowance for nonconformity in the norma tive structure. They produce extensive and attractive networks of inter personal communication and group-formation in the organizationa structure, and stimulate democratic, just and consistent criteria of differ entiation in the opportunity structures.

Movements in the wider context

The next model abandons the assumption that a social movemen operates in isolation, and locates it in the context of other socia movements present in a society at the same time. There is always complex and heterogeneous network of social movements, rather than single movement. Borrowing the idea from the 'resource-mobilizatio perspective', one may distinguish first of all movements and counte movements linked in a 'loosely coupled conflict' (Zald and Useem 1982: of mutually stimulating and reinforcing quality. To be more exact: 'mov ments of any visibility and impact create conditions for the mobili ation of countermovements. By advocating change, by attacking the established interests, by mobilizing symbols and raising costs to others, they create grievances and provide opportunities for organizational entrepreneurs to define countermovement goals and issues', (p. 1). The countermovement develops a peculiar, distorted mirror-image of the movement it opposes: 'the countermovement gains its impetus and grows from showing the harmful effects of the movement . . . It chooses its tactics in response to the structure and tactics of the movement' (p. 2). The appearance of strong countermovements usually leads to the dogmatization of the movement's ideal structure, rigidity and inflexibility in its normative structure, strongly enforced loyalties and tight integration in the organizational structure,[7] and the oligarchization and strict lines of authority (bureaucratization) in the opportunity structure.

McCarthy and Zald speak of 'social movement industries' as the more inclusive systems covering movements of similar or identical goals, defending the common set of preferences (1976: 1219). Garner and Zald define the most inclusive entity as the 'social movement sector': 'it is the configuration of social movements, the structure of antagonistic, competing and cooperating movements which in turn is part of a larger structure of action (political action, in a very broad sense) that may include parties, state bureaucracies, the media, pressure groups, churches, and a variety of other organizational factors in a society' (1981: 1–2). It represents the totality of social movement activity present in a given society at a given historical moment, significantly influencing each of the separate movements operating within it.

A whole gamut of new phenomena is heuristically suggested by such an enriched model. One may conceive of a synthetic measure of societal activism and passivism related to the scope and vitality of the whole social movement sector.[8] A society which wants to take a full advantage of its own creative potential, which wishes to form and reform itself for the benefit of its members, has to allow and even to encourage the free operation of social movements, resulting in a rich and varied social movement sector. This is the 'active society' (Etzioni 1968a). On the other hand, societies which suppress, block or eliminate social movements destroy their own mechanism of self-improvement and self-transcendence. With a narrow or non-existent social movement sector, they become the 'passive societies' of ignorant, indifferent and impotent people, who are given no chance to care for the fate of their society and therefore stop caring altogether. Their only historical prospect is stagnation and decay.

The fifth model locates the whole social movement sector, and the processes of structure-building its generates, in the wider flow of social processes proceeding independently, while exerting their influence on

161

every movement within the sector. Even though we attach so much importance to social movements as agents of morphogenesis, it cannot be forgotten that they are by no means the sole agents. Social becoming cannot be reduced to the operation of social movements. There are numerous processes of structure-building which go on in a society quite independently of any social movements, brought about by other agents or by the immanent unfolding of existing structures. All those processes make up a dynamic milieu for the functioning and development of each single social movement. For example, I have in mind such master processes as modernization, urbanization, demographic booms, economic cycles, civilizational, technological or scientific progress, environmental destruction, global crises etc. Such wide processes may influence social movements in various ways, through at least three points of entry.

They may directly stimulate or paralyse the whole social movement sector, infusing it with a mood of activism or passivism, the ethos of progress or decay, the thrust toward change or toward the preservation of the status quo. Then, they may reshape pre-existent structural conditions in ways either conducive or detrimental to the movements, their incipience or continuous operation. Finally they may result in structural changes which are either parallel, supplementary or contradictory to those sought or produced by the movements. In this way, as the Langs put it: 'the social movement, while itself a collective enterprise to effect changes in the social order, is also a response to changes in the social conditions that have occurred independently of its efforts' (Lang and Lang 1961: 507). This peculiar dialectic of the movements and the surrounding flow of changes caused by other agents or other non-agential factors is also well grasped by Lauer: 'Social change both generates social movements and also results from social movements.' Therefore 'to study a social movement in the context of the larger society . . . is to study motion within motion' (1976: xiv).

Internal morphogenesis

Moving to the sixth model we make a crucial step, abandoning the assumption of a black box. So far social movements have been viewed only from the perspective of external processes, structures and contexts. The internal dynamic of their development has not been considered. Now, the time has come to unravel the processes of self-crystallization of the movement itself, the building and evolving of its structure from an aggregate of mobilized individuals to a fully-fledged organization. This internal, emergent quality of social movements was emphasized by the classic of the field, Herbert Blumer: 'a movement has to be

162

constructed and has to carve out a career in what is practically always an opposed, resistant or at least indifferent world' (1957: 147).

Our fourfold typology of the social structure (INIO scheme) applies also to the internal structure of the movement, and therefore we can distinguish four dimensions of internal structure and four sub-processes of internal morphogenesis. To begin with, one may observe the gradual emergence (articulation) of new ideas, beliefs, creeds, 'a common vocabulary of hope and protest' (Rudé 1964: 75). Then, there is the emergence (institutionalization) of new norms and values, regulating the internal functioning of the movement and providing criteria for the critique of external conditions on which the movement targets itself. This is the focus of Turner's theory of the 'emergent norm' (Turner and Killian 1972). It is worth noticing that the internal norms and values of the movement may refer to its internal operation, its behaviour toward co-members, bonds of loyalty or comradeship etc.; they may also specify certain ways of dealing with opponents and of carrying out external structural changes. The latter make up the 'repertoires of contention' (Tilly 1978) or tactics of struggle which define what is permitted, preferred, prescribed or proscribed in dealings with the movement's opponents and enemies. In the internal normative structure of the movement, one may thus distinguish 'the ethos of solidarity' and 'the ethos of struggle'.

The next sub-process is the emergence (patterning) of new internal organizational structures: novel interactions, relationships, bonds, ties, loyalties, commitments among members. What Zurcher and Snow say of commitment may be applied *mutatis mutandis* to any of the other interpersonal links obtaining in the movement: 'it is an emergent and interactional phenomenon that must be developed by the movement itself' (1981: 463). The ultimate effect of internal structure-building in this area is the appearance of a fully formed 'social movement organization' defined as 'a complex, or formal organization which identifies its goals with the preferences of a social movement or a countermovement and attempts to implement those goals' (McCarthy and Zald 1976: 1218). For example, the Civil Rights movement in the US comprised several organizational forms: the Congress of Racial Equality, the National Association for the Advancement of Colored People, Southern Christian Leadership Conference, the Student Non-Violent Coordinating Committee etc. Similarly, the movement known under the name of Solidarity, includes the Citizens' Committees, Fighting Solidarity, Independent Association of Students, Rural Solidarity etc. Finally, as the last of the sub-processes, there is the emergence (crystallization) of new opportunity structures, new hierarchies of dependence, domination, leadership, influence and power, within the movement. The movement's membership base is always internally stratified; there are various levels of participation, commitment, responsibility. The optimum effect is certainly 'the allignment of individual interests and movement goals' (Zurcher and Snow 1981: 472), when participation in the movement satisfies members' needs and aspirations while at the same time contributing to the social changes sought by the movement.

Two typical sequences of these morphogenetic processes can be singled out, depending on the movement's origins. When the movement arises in a 'volcanic', spontaneous fashion ('from below') as a sort of eruption of long-accumulated grievances and discontents, it normally begins at the interactive level. Common participation in outbursts of collective action (riots, manifestations, crowds, etc.) breeds bonds, loyalties, commitments, and in effect produces some rudimentary organizational structure. Then comes ideology, sometimes infused into the movement from without, sometimes borrowed from earlier doctrine, sometimes articulated by charismatic leaders. Next the normative system slowly evolves when the ethos of solidarity and the ethos of struggle emerge. Finally the internal divisions of leaders, followers, rank-and-file, sympathizers, 'fellow travellers' and 'free riders' become crystallized in the opportunity structure.

The alternative sequence is to be observed when the movement arises as a result of manipulation, conspiracy or organizational entrepreneurship ('from above'). In such a situation its beginning is normally marked by indoctrination disseminating a suggestive vision of the future as well as a radical critique of the present, and indicating persons or groups blocking the way to the movement's goal. Then comes the institutionalization of the new normative order entailed by the ideology. This is enacted by the movement's organizers and backed by the sanctions they administer. On this basis, new actual patterns of interaction and more permanent relationships slowly appear among the movement's members. Finally the differentiation of opportunities within the movement (variable access to various resources controlled by the movement) becomes crystallized, with clear-cut divisions between leadership elite and rank-and-file, members and the public, participants and sympathizers.

Of course, in concrete empirical situations both sequences may overlap, and the processes may mutually reinforce each other. For example, in the case of the class-based, grass-roots movements of social protest in the US, 'The glue which cemented the ranks of these movements was a commitment to certain programmatic goals [ideal and normative structure in terms of the INIO scheme], and equally important, an engagement in mass action – in boycotts, cooperatives, sit-ins, strikes' (Adamson and Borgos 1984: 14).

Various sub-processes or phases in the internal morphogenesis of the movement do not necessarily proceed harmoniously. Often one may observe the overgrowth of some at the expense of others, giving rise to various forms of pathology and producing internally crippled movements. Thus too strong an emphasis on the articulation of the ideal structure produces utopianism and various brands of dogmatism or fundamentalism. Too much concern with the institutionalization of the normative structure leads to overregulation, and paradoxically often breeds anomie. A heavy stress on the personal bonds, private loyalties, intimate and intense interactions among a movement's members easily degenerates into factionalism, nepotism and particularistic criteria of acceptance to higher positions. Differentiation of opportunities, vested interests, life-chances among members often leads to oligarchization and displacement of goals, when the leadership puts the preservation of the movement itself above the realization of the movement's initial pro-gramme. McCarthy and Zald see this danger clearly: 'SMO's [social movement organizations] operate much like any other organization, and consequently, once formed they operate as though organizational survival were the primary goal. Only if survival is assumed can other goals be pursued' (1976: 1226). Needless to add, any of the pathological developments described above seriously impair the external effectiveness of the movement in producing change and cripple it in yet another way. On the other hand, harmonious internal morphogenesis raises the structure-building potential: 'As mobilization advances, as the unit com-mands more resources, and as more of the available total resources are used jointly rather than individually, the unit increases its ability to act collectively' (Etzioni 1968b: 243).

To enrich our analysis of internal morphogenesis we must now allow for internal feedbacks operating between the various phases of structure-building. In the seventh model both positive (amplifying) and negative (compensatory) feedback loops are recognized. Through its amplifying loops the movement gains internal momentum, a self-propelling dynamic. For example, in the 'volcanic' sequence, the appearance of ideology adds strength to the already existing interactive networks (of collective outbursts). The same effect is due to the emergence of norms and values (a movement's ethos, which becomes a strong integrative force). Finally, in the later phase the crystallization of leadership helps to articulate ideology better, by means of more systematic and explicit images of the future, critiques of the present and ascriptions of blame, spread through indoctrination. The same mechanism operates with respect to the normative tactics of the movement, with the ethos of solidarity and the ethos of struggle imposed and sanctioned by the leaders. In a similar way, in the 'manipulated' sequence of internal morphogenesis, the appearance of a tight, cohesive collectivity and strong internal organization gives a stamp of viability to the initially proposed ideological programme; the appearance of strong leadership and the setting of a large social distance between leaders and followers, allow regulation and sanctioning of the conduct of members within the movement in a rigorous and coordinated manner. As Oberschall puts it: 'if the movement can successfully build up a centralized organizational structure accepted by all, the choice of leaders and collective decision-making can become regularized and the resources of the members fully exploited for the pursuit of the movement's goals' (1973: 144).

Negative feedback loops, operating in the opposite direction, paralysing a movement, arresting its momentum and leading to its gradual demise, emerge together with the discordances among the phases of internal morphogenesis and consequent pathological developments. For example, oligarchization and bureaucratization often erode a movement's ideology, moving the emphasis toward purely pragmatic considerations (consider what is happening to communist ideology in so-called communist movements and parties all over the world). The displacement of goals toward sheer self-preservation of the movement undermines the normative structure rooted in the external goals and ideas and produces demoralization of the members. All this works toward the weakening of bonds and loyalties among them, displaces their commitment to its programme and results in atomization, hostility and egoistic, self-centred and competitive attitudes.

So much for internal feedbacks. Our enriched model of internal morphogenesis allows us also indirectly to specify the operation of external feedbacks, the results of a movement's success or failure on its internal functioning. For example, the amplifying impact of success will now be found to operate as a sort of validating loop affecting mainly the ideal structure. Success proves the vision and programme to be viable and endows it with greater justification. It also adds more legitimacy to the norms and values professed by the movement. Similarly success strengthens the ties and bonds among the movement's members. Finally it stabilizes or even solidifies a leadership proved effective in practice. The negative impact of failure would work in the reverse manner, putting the ideological premises in doubt, shaking optimistic visions of the future, undermining norms and values, breeding interpersonal hostilities, antagonisms, resentments and mutual accusations, and finally shaking the stability of a leadership patently shown to be ineffective.

Of course, we are dealing here only with the most typical developments. As was indicated before, the impact of success and failure may sometimes become less straightforward, with success leading paradoxically to the movement's demise, and failure to increased mobilization for further struggle.

Social movements: double morphogenesis

Toward a truly dynamic model

This brings me to the final, most complex model, the eighth. Throughout our discussion there has been an implicit assumption that the internal morphogenesis (emergence of the movement's internal structure) precedes in time the external morphogenesis (emergence or transformation of wider social structures under the impact of the movement). It has looked as if, the movement first crystallized itself in order to acquire morphogenetic potential, and only later was able to employ it in structural reform. This assumption of the linear time-sequence must now be discarded and the categories of 'before' and 'after' abandoned.

A social movement produces or influences changes in a society not only when it is completely, finally structured itself, but rather all the time from its origin, during its own internal morphogenesis. Similarly the changes in a society going on outside the movement itself, feedback on its development not only when they are completed, but all the time during their development, constantly modifying the movement's career, its momentum, speed and direction. As Lauer aptly observes: 'When we deal with a social movement, we are dealing with two processes that intersect and interact with each other – the process of the movement itself and the processes of the larger society within which the movement is operative' (1976: xiv). Two interrelated processes of structural emergence – internal and external – proceed concurrently. The becoming of the movement and the becoming of new social structures are mutually and intimately interlinked, stimulating or arresting each other. There is a constant mutual interplay of partial internal morphogenesis with partial external morphogenesis.

This gives a particularly dynamic character to the phenomenon of social becoming via social movements. Perhaps it is not an exaggeration to claim with G. T.Marx and J. L.Wood that 'social movements are more dynamic than most other social forms' (1975: 394). This is probably the source of difficulty in joining the processes occurring *within* social movements and those in society *due to* social movements in neat cause-and-effect terms or linear sequences. But only a recognition of such a complex, circular, interlinked and truly dynamic quality in social movements and their creative impact on social change will bring us closer to empirical reality and give our models some measure of historical adequacy.

Incidentally, it is this complexity and circularity which makes the study of social movements particularly challenging and also particularly promising. Such a study may throw much light on the most fundamental processes of social becoming, the making of society by society.

8

Revolutions: the peak of social becoming

The idea of revolution: myth and theory

The history of the idea of revolution is long and convoluted (Taylor 1984). But it is clear that the concept acquires particular salience in the nineteenth and twentieth centuries. The 'rebellious century' is the name given by some historians to the period from 1830 to 1930 (Tilly and Tilly 1975), and several sociologists refer to our own times as the 'era of revolutions' (Banks 1972). Perhaps together with 'progress' and 'science', 'revolution' makes up a trio of concepts embracing the meaning of our era.

Like most social concepts, 'revolution' lives a double life, appearing in two guises. First, it belongs to societal discourse, pervading common sense thinking. Here it evolves into a complex image, strongly imbued with valuations and emotional commitments, which may be called the myth of revolution. Second, it belongs to sociological discourse, appearing in scientific reasoning. Here it evolves into a complex theoretical construct, engendering explanatory hypotheses. It is normally called a theory of revolution (Goldstone 1982).

Both levels of discourse – societal as well as sociological – are components of social consciousness. As such they enter a two-sided dialectical relationship with social life: they reflect actual conditions, human actions, forms of social organizations and institutions; and they also reflexively feed back on social life. The myth and the theory of revolution are therefore both 'the mental reconstructions' of our time

An earlier and different version of this chapter first appeared as 'Agency and revolution' in: *International Sociology*, No. 2, 1990, pp. 129–144.

(Alexander 1990: 1) and the significant causal influences of their own.

They are mutually interdependent, too, and the second dialectical relationship operates not so much between two levels, but this time within the level of social consciousness, between societal and sociological discourse. As we know all too well sociological theory is often little more than sophisticated common sense. The theory of revolution draws heavily on the myth of revolution; with some inevitable time-lag it explicates and systematizes what common people think about revolutions. But it also acquires some autonomy, goes beyond common sense. This is possible because theory, inspired as it is by common sense, may develop its own momentum, start to live its own life and follow its own logic of elaboration. A single theory is not isolated but links with other theories, falls under the impact of a wider 'theoretical movement' and reflects the premises of a dominant theoretical approach or orientation. Going beyond common sense, the theory of revolution may then feed back reflexively on the myth of revolution, become an important factor in reshaping the widespread image of revolution, and hence, indirectly, influence the probabilities and forms of revolutionary action.

I shall claim that this is precisely the case with the discourse on revolutions at the end of the twentieth century. The demise of the myth is accompanied, paradoxically, by the rise of a new, significant wave of theory focusing on the active side of historical processes and the creative and constructive capacities of the members of society, the theory of agency and historical sociology. Parting with the premises of the old, popular image of revolution, the new theory may feed back on that image, help to produce a new, or at least a revised myth, and so influence actual revolutionary practice.

To substantiate this claim I have first to sketch the changing fates of both the myth and the theory of revolution for the last century and a half. The idea of revolution – in both forms – seems to reach its peak in the nineteenth century. The era of triumphant modernity finds its intellectual rationale in developmentalist thinking. Society is seen as undergoing necessary directional change, guided by reason, or history, and moving toward progress. Revolutions are inevitable, crucial thresholds on this road, marking the irreversible sequence of epochs; they are the moments of galvanizing and accelerating rational and beneficent processes.

This ideological monolith starts to crumble and break down in the twentieth century, the era of decaying modernity. Progress gives way to crisis as the leitmotif of the epoch. The myth of revolution is undermined by the convoluted and tragic experience of actual revolutions. Two questions cannot but arise in the common consciousness. First, why is it that revolutions never end in what was dreamt of by the revolutionaries?

169

In fact, by some irony of history, they often end in its opposite, resulting in more injustice, inequality, exploitation, oppression and repression. Second, why is reason so often replaced by violence, sheer coercion, thoughtless destruction? Why are the Promethean revolutionaries typically displaced by an aggressive, irrational and terrorist mob? Revolution is still perceived as a fundamental break in social continuity, brought about by human masses in a violent and sudden manner, but it is no longer seen as an embodiment of some wider logic of history, nor as necessarily progressive, nor as ultimately reasonable. The metaphors of volcanic eruption, prairie fire or earthquake suggest that revolutions are viewed as catastrophes or disasters, rather than the redemption or salvation of mankind. Most people no longer dream of revolutions, they are afraid of them. In effect, the original core-meaning splits, and two somewhat crippled notions of revolution become indiscriminately applied to a wide range of phenomena: one identifies it with all outbursts of mass violence, even those which do not engender change; the other, with all basic, fundamental change, whatever its source. This signifies the dissolution of the idea and the myth.[1]

At the level of theory, the changes inevitably follow suit, but with a considerable lag. Inertia and the partial autonomy of theoretical thought clearly manifest themselves. For a large stretch of the twentieth century the developmentalist approach still reigned in the study of revolutions. In fact it is only in the seventies and the eighties that postdevelopmentalism has become the creed of the day. The focus moves from the overall pattern, the necessary direction and ultimate outcomes toward the causal agents, the mechanism and alternative scenarios of social processes. Revolution begins to be seen as the strongest manifestation of human agency, operating by means of collective action at critical junctures of the historical process.

As an illustration of this major paradigmatic shift in dealing with the phenomenon of revolution, consider the orthodox version of historical materialism in comparison with the modern theory of social movements. On the face of it, the difference lies only in the kind of social collectivities picked out for consideration. But in fact it runs much deeper. In the earlier theory, revolutions are brought about by social classes. But social classes are just demiurges of history, the vehicles or carriers of necessary developmental tendencies. They are inevitably evoked by universal historical patterns, emerge at predetermined moments to fulfil their revolutionary mission and then leave the social stage. In modern theory, social movements rather than classes, become the true causal agents of revolution, and are seen not merely as the emanations of some autonomous historical process. They produce, construct and create revolutions, and do not merely execute them. They self-consciously write the script of history, rather than playing out prescribed roles. Therefore they do not automatically appear when needed, but have to be actively recruited and mobilized. They fight not for some preordained, final end of history but for specific causes. They want to change something, not necessarily to save mankind. It is a striking shift of emphasis indeed.

Thus, as the twentieth century draws to a close we have a clear view of the fundamental transformation of the idea of revolution, both in its common-sense and in its scientific meaning. Theories of revolution finally leave the domain of historiosophy and become truly sociological. Let us trace some recent tendencies in the new postdevelopmentalist thinking about revolutions.

The theory of revolution: new directions

Behind most sociological theories of revolution there is a dualistic image, where the dimension of totalities or social wholes of various scale (social formations, social systems, social organizations, social groups etc. and their operation) is counterpoised to the dimension of individualities (actors and their action). Depending on the focus chosen by a given author, two contrasting models of revolution are to be found, each with significant varieties. The first model emphasizes the mobilization of actors: revolution erupts from below, when the volume of grievances, discontents and frustrations felt by human populations exceeds a certain threshold (Gurr 1970). One variety of this model carries a sort of volcanic image (Aya 1979): revolution is seen as a spontaneous outburst of collective behaviour, which only later acquires leadership, organization and ideology. (Here, revolutions just happen.) Another variety carries an entrepeneurial or conspiratorial image: revolution is treated as a purposeful collective action, recruited, mobilized and controlled by leaders and ideologues (conspirators, 'movement entrepreneurs' etc.) in an attempt to reach specific goal. (Here, revolutions are made) (Tilly 1978).

The second, opposite model emphasizes the structural context: revolution breaks out when conditions, circumstances, situations are conducive. One variety of this model is rooted in the metaphor of the safety-lid: revolutionary potential (present in some measure in every society, and treated as constant) is released from above, when the constraints, blocks and controls at the level of totalities are weakened (Skockpol 1979). Another variety emphasizes access to resources: revolutions are evoked by the opening of new means and opportunities, facilitating revolutionary action (McCarthy and Zald 1976; Jenkins 1983). Most often the character of the political system and particularly the scope of the 'political opportunity structures' (Tarrow 1984) – in the sense both of constraints and of facilitations – are indicated as the core, decisive factor, and hence this brand of theories is sometimes labelled as political theories of revolution.

The focus on human agency, typical for recent sociological theory, results in the demise of mechanistic images, where revolutions miraculously happen, break out, erupt; it is replaced by a growing emphasis on activist images, where revolutions are made, constructed, produced by self-conscious, knowledgeable human actors. Revolution as the accomplishment of people rather than the emanation of structures – such is the current view. In terms of the first model, it means that the entrepreneurial (or conspiratorial) version is favoured over the volcanic version. In terms of the second model it means that the resource-emergence version is favoured over safety-lid version.

But there is also another tendency in modern sociological theory which leaves a strong impress on modern theories of revolution. It refers to a certain style of theorizing; irrespective of substantive content it rejects dogmatism and opts for pluralism and multi-dimensionality.[2] Let me illustrate this tendency by four telling examples from the sociology of social movements, the area which is becoming central for current research on revolutions.

Bert Klandermans argues that the strong structural (organizational) bias of the fashionable resource-mobilization theory of social movements leads to the neglect of the individual, social-psychological dimension. This, he believes, has to be redressed by combining new, modified social-psychological theory (stressing rational action, mobilization of consensus and mobilization for action) with a properly curbed resource-mobilization approach. The author proclaims: 'The theory formulated in this paper aims at a break with both the traditional social-psychological approaches to social movements and the neglect of social-psychological analyses by resource mobilization theory' (1984: 596–7).

Myra Ferree and Frederick Miller make a similar attempt to enrich the resource-mobilization perspective by elaborating the missing subjective level. They focus on two psychological processes crucial to reform-oriented or revolutionary movements. One is system attribution (in most cases – politicization), i.e. directing discontent and putting the blame on institutional structures rather than on persons (rulers). Another is evoking the commitment of participants, i.e. shaping the motivations conducive to recruitment and action. In their view, an improved psychological perspective has to be restored to structural-organizational theories to make them more adequate. 'Incorporating cognitive social psychological assumptions in place of incentive terminology in the resource mobilization framework should help clarify both the relationship between movements and the wider society and the processes of development and growth movement

172

organizations undergo' (Ferree and Miller 1985: 55).

Even more striking is the attempt to 'bridge the gap between collective behavior and resource mobilization' proposed recently by one of the leading exponents of the collective behaviour approach, Ralph Turner. He recognizes the cognitive gains reached within the resource-mobilization perspective and argues against treating it as an unreconcilable alternative to the more traditional approach of Park, Blumer, Smelser and himself. He admits that resource-mobilization theory adds crucial insights to three questions unresolved within the orthodox theory of collective behaviour. One is the question of 'extrainstitutionality': why people depart from established institutional ways. Another is 'translating feelings into action': why people convert extrainstitutional dispositions into actions. The third is the puzzle of 'acting collectively': why people get together to express their feelings and drives. Thus, both schools of theory 'can be articulated, to produce a more complete and balanced theory of social movements incorporating the most essential contributions from each' (1988: 1).

The effort at compromise comes also from the opposite side of the theoretical divide. The very founders of the resource-mobilization perspective, Doug McAdam, John McCarthy and Mayer Zald, reviewing the field of social movements in the monumental *Handbook of Sociology*, have hardly started on their way before they issue a manifesto of reconciliation: 'Only by combining the broad conceptual foci of the newer and older approaches can we hope to produce a full understanding of movement dynamics' (1988: 695). Their thrust is concentrated on rejecting one-sided explanations, whether 'from above', invoking structures, or 'from below', invoking actions. They aim to explicate the links between macro-structural conditions (political, economic, organizational) and the micro-dynamics of evolving movements. 'The point is [they claim] we can no more build social movements from the individual up than down from some broad societal process. We believe the real action takes place at a third level, intermediate between the individual and the broad macro contexts in which they are embedded' (p. 709).

This trend is right and proper. Sociological wisdom is not the preserve of one theory or school. The tremendous complexity of the phenomenon of revolution demands multiple sources of enlightenment and can be adequately explained only by a plurality of theories, or ultimately by a multidimensional theory. But, granting this, one must be aware of the danger of mere eclecticism, putting side by side disparate components of various theories in a purely additive fashion, rather than linking them together into a systematic theoretical edifice. It seems to me that most recent attempts at synthesis have not been able to avoid this peril. One wonders why is this so.

The applications

The answer is to be found in some pervasive methodological traits of the received theories of revolution. Their first trouble is that they are often written by traditional historians, or by sympathizers with the traditional historical method. In effect, they are usually *inductive, ex post facto* generalizations drawn from selected cases. They are built from below, starting from the consideration of concrete historical revolutions, and trying to discover their common characteristics or patterns. This is obviously the case with the so-called 'natural histories of revolution' by Brinton (1965 [1938]) or Edwards (1927), and also, to some extent, with quite modern efforts by Skockpol (1979), Tilly (1978), Baszkiewicz (1981). The second trouble is that revolutions are treated as *exceptional*, unique, totally unusual events. And among revolutions, the so-called Great Revolutions (British, French, American, Russian) are seen as special cases and sometimes given exclusive attention. Hence their explanations are constructed in isolation from wider theories of social change or social processes, as if they constituted an independent domain, a fully specific subject matter not related to other, more mundane social phenomena.[3]

This strategy of theory construction must be rejected as inadequate. The theory of revolution should be built from above, in a *hypothetico-deductive* fashion, and it should start from the general image of social change and social processes. The explanation of revolutions should follow from the abstract account of social dynamics, as its particularly interesting but by no means unique variety. This is the only way to resist the temptation of eclecticism.

More than a decade ago Robert Merton, recognizing the indispensable pluralism of sociological theories, issued a call for 'disciplined eclecticism' (1976: 142). For me, this means precisely 'disciplining' the chaos of lower-level theories by a more general, common theoretical framework.[4] To be more specific, it involves integrating and synthesizing a variety of theories by means of a common set of assumptions, fundamental premises or conceptual frameworks. The received models, underlying most sociological theories of revolution and founded on the traditional opposition of totalities (wholes) and individualities (actors), seem to engender at most the 'undisciplined' eclectic combination of components from various theories (e.g. adding psychological insights to organizational theory, or supplementing the theory of motivation with availability of resources, or enriching the study of micro-dynamics with some consideration of macro-constraints). To reach a true synthesis, the integrating framework must be improved. The model of social becoming, with its synthesizing *leitmotif* - founded on the attempt to overcome one-sided points of view - seems particularly well suited for this goal.

Revolution as a mode of social becoming

I shall consider revolution as the strongest mode of production of society by society, the strongest expression of social becoming. In other words, it is the peak manifestation of human agency, the most significant manifestation of the social potentiality for self-transcendence in its attempt to attain the actuality of social change.

The theory of revolution, treated as a form of social becoming, must focus on two crucial areas of variables: first, the factors determining or conditioning the appearance of certain specific potentialities in the social fabric, the emergence of an agency of a particular kind, which may be called *revolutionary agency*; second, all varieties of filtering mechanisms, the factors blocking or stimulating, constraining or facilitating the actualization of revolutionary agency, when it turns into *revolutionary praxis*. In the remaining part of this chapter, I shall attempt to draw a tentative list of variables which must be taken into account in the explanation of the emergence of revolutionary agency, and of its actualization in revolutionary praxis.

What are the determinants of revolutionary agency? One set of variables refers to existing structures. Revolutionary consciousness is a fragment of the ideal structure, including such components as belief in the changeable nature of the world, in human capacity to influence these changes, in the effectiveness of mass action and in the feasibility of certain 'repertoires of contention'. It is nourished by the visions of past revolutions (e.g. the myths of the Great Revolutions), and the images of possible better worlds (e.g. utopias).[5] If we think of any historical example of revolutions – major or minor – such antecedent shapes of social consciousness are clearly to be seen. In the French Revolution, the significance of the *'philosophes'*, the *'Encyclopédistes'* and the whole intellectual climate of the Enlightenment in the decades preceding the outbreak is widely accepted. In the Soviet Revolution, agitation and the indoctrination of the working class with ideology (adequate 'class consciousness') by intellectuals and professional revolutionaries was one of the core preoccupations of Lenin. In the Polish 'self-limiting revolution' of the Solidarity movement, the underground cultural and educational programmes, publications and artistic campaigns aimed at changing the perceptions, definitions and imagination of the masses clearly prepared the ground for the mobilization of 1980, and then again became crucial to the revival of Solidarity in 1989 and its amazing electoral victory.

The revolutionary ethos is a subset of the normative structure including such values as justice, equality, solidarity, loyalty and commitment, such norms as activism, mobilization and organization, such roles as leaders, fighters and ideologues, and such institutions as parties, movements etc. Most theories of revolution emphasize the importance of revolutionary ideology, a purposefully articulated and systematized pool of categorcial and normative beliefs (revolutionary consciousness and revolutionary ethos together). If we think again of historical instances, the character and quality of a given revolution seem to depend quite significantly on the accepted 'ethos of struggle': compare non-violent revolutions in the style of Gandhi, Martin Luther King, or Solidarity's Lech Wałesa, with the bloody violence of, say, the Jacobins, the Iranian revolutionaries, or the Palestinian *intifada*.

The importance of the pre-existing interactional channels or communication settings for the chances of revolutionary mobilization has always been stressed by theories of revolution. It was noticed by Marx in his emphasis on urbanization and industrialization, bringing together masses of people in close proximity and generating intense interactions. Then the theme runs through the theories of mass society, the study of church and school networks as crucial to the American Civil Rights Movement, identifying university campuses as milieux of student movements (Freeman 1983a and 1983b), pointing to religious communities and church organization as a base for the Polish Solidarity movement etc.

Finally revolutionary opportunities make up the subset of wider opportunity structure. They consist of contradictions, tensions, strains and cleavages generated by the distribution of all generally valued resources: wealth, power, prestige and education. But they also depend on the distribution of resources specifically relevant to revolutionary activity: money, access to the mass media, and the discretionary time and enargy of potential followers. This level of social structure has always been treated as central by conflict theories of revolution, from Marx to Oberschall (1973, 1978), as well as by the proponents of the resource-mobilization theory, McCarthy and Zald (1976), Tilly (1978) and others. In the earlier theoretical tradition, the focus is on the social inequalities, injustice, exploitation producing widespread grievances, deprivations, discontent and frustrations, i.e. a ready, easily mobilizable human potential for revolutionary outbreak. In the latter, it is emphasized how the phenomenon of multiple 'new social movements' is born by the releasing of a rich pool of discretionary resources (free time, money etc.) in affluent modern societies.

The structures conducive to revolution, as described above, make a real impact on the emergence of revolutionary agency only if they are sufficiently widespread in a society. The crucial factor is the relative scope of such structures: they may be prevailing or only marginal. The prevalence of revolutionary consciousness and revolutionary ethos brings about a conducive revolutionary 'atmosphere' in the domain of human thinking. The prevalence of revolutionary networks and revolutionary opportunities couples this with real, objective chances for revolutionary action. Together they make a revolutionary situation.

The emergence of a revolutionary situation need not occur uniformly across a whole social structure. The historical evidence shows that there are usually some core, strategic areas where revolutionary agency is born, spreading out afterwards, by a process akin to diffusion, to other segments of society. To put it otherwise, there are some groups which become the bearers of the revolutionary ideology, have greater access to interactional networks, are victims of deeper injustices, and have command of larger opportunities for action. The urban bourgeoisie in the French Revolution; the proletariat and peasant masses in socialist revolutions; Western-educated intellectual and administrative elites in the Third World countries; highly skilled, better educated and relatively young segments of the working class in the Solidarity movement – these are some examples of those collectivities which under specific historical conditions, because of their conducive structural location, become the central forces, the carriers of revolutionary agency.

The existence of structures conducive to revolution is an objective fact, influencing the agency 'from above'. But to shape revolutionary agency it must coincide with another determining influence working 'from below'. It must fall on the 'fertile soil' of competent, ready and willing actors. The objective structural conditions must turn into subjective knowledge, motivations, commitments and attitudes of human individuals. The real causal, agential significance of revolutionary ideas starts only when people entertain them; of revolutionary ethos, when people internalize it; of revolutionary networks, when people are aware of them; of revolutionary opportunities, when people experience them as deprivations, injustices, humiliations. In sum, the decisive factor is the emergence of the *revolutionary mind*.

In the wider perspective of making history, revolutionary structures – ideology, ethos, organizations, hierarchies – are of course the outcomes, products, remnants of earlier praxis. But at a given moment, from the perspective of a single cycle of social becoming they must be treated as given, encountered. Hence, internalization of those structures by the actors, creating the revolutionary mind – in short, socialization for revolution – appears as the crucial mediating process in shaping the revolutionary agency. In part its results are determined by the relative pervasiveness (domination) of revolutionary structures which impose themselves on individual minds, in part by the receptiveness of actors (e.g. their level of education, intellectual and emotional maturity, readiness and openness to information, perceptiveness, imagination), and the relative prevalence (hegemony) of change-oriented agents in the population.

The existence of revolutionary agency is only a precondition, a necessary but certainly not a sufficient requirement for the outbreak of revolution. This is only a latent potentiality, which turns into the manifest actuality of revolutionary praxis only under specific conditions. Several mediating variables or filtering mechanisms may be tentatively indicated.[6] Again, as an analytic device we may look at revolutionary structures and the revolutionary mind separately. The actualization of structures means in effect spreading them widely, acquiring domination for them. Here, the filtering factor is power in its various guises. Claims for the legitimacy of the revolutionary ethos and ideas may be met by counterclaims, which, if backed by sufficient ideological power, will keep revolutionary ideology in its latent status. Claims for access to networks and resources may also be met by counterclaims, which, if backed by sufficient coercive power will limit revolutionary opportunities to the latent form. In brief, at the level of structures, the decisive factor is the balance of revolutionary and counterrevolutionary (conservative) structures (Tilly 1970). The observation of many students of historical revolutions, from Tocqueville to Davies, that their outbreak is usually preceded by a period of liberalization, democratization, relaxing of rigid, restrictive regimes, loses its paradoxical flavour when we remember that it is a precondition for the freer circulation of revolutionary ideologies, more effective revolutionary socialization and more successful organizing for future struggle.

The actualization of the revolutionary mind and revolutionary opportunities means in effect the active recruitment, mobilization and organization of actors for revolutionary action. Here, the filtering factor is again power. The clash of challengers and defenders of the status quo, like the clash of proponents and opponents of revolutionary means of action within the former group, may end in various outcomes, depending on the relative influence and coercive capacity of the parties or factions. Recruitment may be prevented, solidarities and loyalties among revolutionaries undermined, revolutionary organizations broken, countermobilization encouraged (Etzioni 1968b). In such a case, revolutionary mind will remain in its latent form, and revolutionary opportunities will remain unused. In brief, at the level of actors, the decisive factor is the opposition and struggle of revolutionaries and counterrevolutionaries (defenders of the status quo), and the resulting hegemony of one or the other party. It is not by accident that revolutions usually break out when the existing power structure is notably weakened – be it by wars, economic crises or factional struggles. The Bolsheviks won in Russia at the moment when Tsarist regime collapsed under the burden of the First

World War; the Solidarity movement won in Poland, when the Communist Party was no longer able to contain the huge economic crisis. These are just two illustrations of an almost universal regularity.

Synthesizing these observations at the mediating level of agency and praxis allows us to see how social becoming is always the contingent product of complex contradictions and conflicts in different segments of society. Even with the presence of revolutionary agency, actual revolution is at most a contingent possibility. Its occurrence depends on the intricate and shifting balance of power among social forces (structures, groups, classes and movements).[7]

The promise of agential and historical theory

I have presented a case for developing the theory of revolution within the framework of the theory of social becoming; liberated from the traditional assumptions of fatalism, finalism and utopianism, devoid of mechanistic overtones, brought down from the historiosophical heights to the level of sociological discourse. Outlining a tentative framework for such an agential theory of revolutions by means of a certainly incomplete sample of hypothetical variables, I have tried to show its potential for elaboration and empirical testing. I have also argued that it may serve an important integrating function, replacing one-sided points of view, and bringing together in a synthetic fusion various strands and directions of thinking about revolutions.

But there may be an extra bonus, an additional reason for its plausability. It was observed in chapter 4 that social ideas are not only *about* society but *in* society; they become a significant part of the reality they account for, they enter the social causal nexus as important factors *per se* by changing the conditions of human action, the knowledge and preferences of actors. In one apt formulation 'among the ideas which move people are the ideas about what moves them' (Hollis 1987: 13).

Ideas, concepts, theories of revolution are not exempt from this reflexive mechanism. They may acquire a self-fulfilling or a self-defeating quality. The theory of revolution as the mode of social becoming may reflexively influence the myth of revolution, and indirectly the forms of revolutionary action. On the one hand it may finally kill the myth in its traditional quasi-religious, providential form. On the other, it may help to revive it in a this-worldly, realistic shape, as the recognition of a powerful means of improving human society, transcending its limitations, overcoming its barriers and extending its frontiers. It may also serve as a reminder that the human condition requires us constantly to hope, strive and struggle for those lines of future development which seem the better. The proposed theory of revolution may become in its own right a mobilizing influence on human awareness and activism, and hence not only interpret but also contribute to the crucial phenomenon of social becoming.

Notes

Chapter 1 Toward a theoretical reorientation

1 At least from Alvin W. Gouldner's prophecy in *The Coming Crisis of Western Sociology* (1970).

2 What has always been constitutive of sociological tradition was missing here. 'Sociologists are sociologists because they believe there are patterns to society, structures somehow separate from the actors who compose it' (Alexander 1988b: 84).

3 This synthetic, integrative thrust in recent theorizing is noticed by several commentators. Alexander sees it as the core feature of the 'new theoretical movement', and the focus of such theory is 'a new synthetic model of the interrelation between action and structure' (p. 78). Ritzer observes: 'The most general similarity in the work in the United States and Europe is the shared desire for integration and synthesis' (1989: 19). And he specifies the focus of these efforts: 'In the United States, a widespread agreement seemed to surface in the 1980's that the issue of micro – macro linkage is crucial while in Europe a similar consensus appeared to be reached on the centrality of the agency – structure synthesis' (ibid.: 1). Describing the fall of structuralism and the 'return of the actor and the subject' to the fore of French sociology, Chazel indicates that 'the present trends are in the direction of a model of sociology which is pluralist, open' (1988: 199). From the British perspective Archer contends that 'The problem of structure and agency has rightly come to be seen as the basic issue in modern social theory' (1988: x).

4 Misleading because it sounds like a separate subdiscipline of sociology, whereas in fact it is a specific way of looking at society, a particular

181

theoretical and methodological orientation (see: Sztompka 1986b). A parallel ambiguity attaches to the term 'sociology of knowledge', again obviously not a subdiscipline, but a distinct point of view or theoretical approach.

5 Of course I am not the first to use this concept. Several commentators have discovered its occasional use already in Marx. Erich Fromm observes that 'Marx like Hegel – looks at an object in its movement, in its becoming, and not as a static "object" which can be explained by discovering the physical "cause" of it' (1968: 11). Richard Bernstein claims that Marx sees a human individual as someone who 'does not seek to remain something formed by the past, but is in the absolute movement of becoming' (1972: 64). Gyorgy Lukács treats the notion as defining the ontology of the social domain: 'This reality is not, it becomes' (1971: 203), and consequently as the epistemological imperative: 'Man must be able to comprehend the present as a becoming. He can do this by seeing in it the tendencies out of whose dialectical opposition he can make the future' (ibid.: 204). Similar ideas may be found in the work of Antonio Gramsci (1971, 1972). The concept of becoming appears also in other theoretical traditions. In a sophisticated version of structuralism it is put forward by Jean Piaget: 'the being of structures consists in their coming to be, that is, their being "under construction"' (1971: 140). Modern historical sociologists find in the concept of becoming a tool for synthesizing the 'two sociologies': 'The sociology of becoming is for the sociologist the best way of discovering the real relationship of structure and action' (Abrams 1982: 7).

6 By taking history seriously I mean utilizing concrete historical research rather than applying preconceived historiosophical schemes. 'Historical sociology' is sociology (theory of society) derived from history, rather than sociology (patterns, forms, logic) imposed upon history. In the modern sense of the term, Comte, Spencer, Durkheim (or Hegel for that matter, as well as the deterministic, finalistic Marx) must be treated as ahistorical, and therefore in no way as predecessors of 'historical sociology' (Sztompka 1986b).

7 Even though there are a growing number of contributions focusing on the Marxian image of an individual and his account of action. This is true both of 'Western Marxism' and of some recent reorientations in Eastern (or Soviet) Marxism. Two representative appraisals can be quoted: 'Marx's theory of alienation places the acting and acted-upon individual in the center of his account . . . Man continues, of necessity, to occupy a central position in Marx's theories' (Ollman 1975: ix, xii); 'Sociological and philosophical understanding of the essence of man and of the historical development of his nature is a component of Marxism which is not accidentally attached, but rather constitutes the core of the Marxian system' (Kieszelawa 1977: 12).

8 It is to the *naïveté* of youth that I must attribute my own belief of

seventeen years ago that deductive-nomological (C. G. Hempel's) models of explanation are immediately applicable to the social domain, and that sociological theory can be produced in an axiomatic form (Sztompka 1973). Since those days I have come to my senses.

Chapter 2   The evolving focus on agency

1   An interesting variant of this theme is to be found in modern structural-functionalism when the responsibility for the change of society (as opposed to changes in society) is ascribed to deviants. But deviance 'occurs for socio-logically – and that means structurally – unknown and unknowable reasons. It is the bacillus that attacks the system from the dark depths of individual psyche or the nebulous reaches of the outside world' (Dahrendorf 1968: 116).

2   It is closely related to another opposition: consensus versus conflict. Society with reigning consensus, harmony and equilibrium has no conceivable internal cause for change; whereas society permeated with dissensus, conflict and disequilibrium is naturally prone to transform itself. That is why some authors (e.g. Dahrendorf 1968, Rex 1961) link those dimensions and subsume what we call static and dynamic models under more comprehensive categories of consensus models versus conflict models.

3   From within the functionalist camp, the revisionist attempt to incorporate conflict and change was made by Robert Merton, resulting in his innovative 'dynamic functionalism' (Sztompka 1986a, ch. 5).

4   In fact offering the utopian image *par excellence* (the vision of the homogeneous, unified, stable, harmonious social world based on liberal-democratic consensus) as the criticism of utopias as such (with their progressive and future-oriented message).

5   A less episodic and more fundamental diagnosis of the essence of postmodern society is suggested by Zygmunt Bauman, who draws a picture of a consumer society, replacing labour-oriented society. In the present phase of capitalism, he believes, 'consumer conduct (consumer freedom geared to consumer market) moves steadily into the position of, simultaneously, the cognitive and moral focus of life, integrative bond of society, and the focus of systemic management' (Bauman 1989: 137). This new social system must be grasped by means of a new sociological theory, the sociology of postmodernity.

6   In 1979 I outlined the programme of such a synthesis at the meta-theoretical level, indicating the ways to overcome six basic 'sociological dilemmas' haunting sociological theory from the early nineteenth century to the current debates (Sztompka 1979). In 1982–3 the monumental effort to reread the sociological classics undertaken by Jeffrey Alexander was subordinated to the search for 'multidimensional theory' (Alexander 1982–3).

7   I discuss them more extensively in my intellectual biography of R. K. Merton identifying irony and paradox as basic themes of his sociology (Sztompka 1986a).

8   Which I describe in detail elsewhere (Sztompka 1986b).

Chapter 3   On the shoulders of Marx

1   Gerhard Lenski observes that 'The power of Marxian theory is not merely a function of the political strength of the Marxian movement, as some imagine. It is capable of commanding respect in its own right, as evidenced by the large number of scholars and intellectuals who have borrowed from it in greater or lesser degree despite their lack of sympathy for the political movements which act in Marx's name' (Lenski 1966: 12).

2   Ten years ago I wrote: 'There is much more to Marxism than some of the most outspoken Marxists have ever dreamt about. I shall focus exclusively on this primary, and strangely neglected, intellectual aspect. In the course of this analysis Marxism will be seen first as a scientific approach, rather than as a political program, and second as a theoretical and methodological orientation, rather than as a full-fledged, close and final dogmatic system' (Sztompka 1979: 36).

3   Not to be mixed up with 'historism' which, as we have already seen, is a completely different story.

4   Of course Alexander is aware of various passages where Marx refers to human nature, individual creativeness, choice etc. But he argues that they are residual, marginal themes. One strategy of argumentation relegates such considerations to the ideological, moralistic, 'prophetic' level of Marx's work – inconsistent with his theoretical, 'scientific' contribution. 'Recent critics have too often conflated Marx's ideological commitment to human emancipation with his presuppositions about action and order, arguing that if Marx wanted to create a voluntaristic and normatively ordered society, he must also have embraced this perspective in his sociological theory of contemporary society' (Alexander 1982a: 66). Another strategy treats Marx's discussion of the indeterminist, voluntarist and contingent side of human society, as 'exceptionalist' and marginal, referring to the vaguely perceived future society devoid of alienation, whereas the capitalist society he actually studied, pervaded with alienation and reification, led to 'collectivist instrumental' assumptions at the level of theory.

5   Contrary to Alexander, Tucker also claims that Marxian ideology, politics, morality and 'prophetism' are fully congruent with his theory. He ascribes to Marx the individualist ethics, matching his individualist ontology of the social world and his individualist methodological orientation (1980: 57ff).

6   For my purposes it is not decisive whether this interpretational hypothesis is actually true, whether Marx 'really meant it'. Let us assume that he did, because it is heuristically much more fruitful than the opposite hypothesis. The 'hostile interpretation' closes the matter in a destructive fashion, and does not open any new prospects for going beyond Marx. The 'sympathetic interpretation' turns our attention to the search for bridges, links between seemingly opposite aspects or dimensions of society. It demands the specification of what the concept of 'dialectics' may mean in terms of concrete social mechanisms and processes. And that is a direction in which contemporary systematic theory must proceed. Whether Marx really anticipated that is

important for the appraisal of his stature in the history of sociology. Whether his theory may be used today to generate this kind of synthetic search is crucial for systematic theorizing. And for this task it is to some extent irrelevant whether Marx was himself fully aware of the multidimensional nature of social reality, or whether he felt it intuitively, or whether he hit upon it by sheer accident, or whether it is the artefact of reading him with contemporary eyes.

7 E.g. the term is used widely by a leading Polish historian, Jerzy Topolski (1968, 1974, 1978, 1983), though with a slightly different meaning.

8 Sometimes this level is misleadingly referred to as 'subjective', suggesting a focus akin to psychology. As I shall argue later, the consideration of human individuals need not be psychological. In fact Marx almost completely neglected the psychological aspects of men and women (motivations, intentions, emotions etc.) and took a quite different approach, abstracting their properties as acting agents and participants in social structures. I shall call such an approach 'sociological'.

9 This level is sometimes misleadingly referred to as 'objective'. But of course it includes also such patterned, structured 'subjective' phenomena as ideology, law, morality, religion, art, science, or what Marx calls succinctly 'the forms of social consciousness'. It is not the 'subjective' or 'objective' character of phenomena which is significant, but rather the fact that they make up emergent, super-individual wholes.

10 Notice that the concept of dynamics (or diachrony) is not treated naïvely as synonymous with change. It is reserved for the 'changes of' an entity (be it society or an individual), rather than 'changes in' an entity. Changes obviously occur all the time, but only some of them transform the society, others simply express its everyday 'life', its constant, repeatable functioning. Changes of the latter sort, which do not produce transformations, are embraced by the concept of statics (or synchrony).

11 Notice that in this discussion I am concerned exclusively with Marx's theoretical discourse rather than with his ideological or moral pronouncements. The distinction between potentialities and actualities refers to the area of 'what is': what a certain existing potentiality is, and how it is actualized. It should not be mixed up with the area of 'what should be'. Here the images of the preferred rather than the real world enter. Marxism abounds in those, but they are not of interest to me, at least not in the context of this book.

12 It is noteworthy how strongly Marx opposes reification of social reality, in all forms it may take. When he deals with such reified wholes, he almost without exception treats them as the emanations of social consciousness, images which are prone to appear in specific social conditions (of class societies, alienation, commodity production etc.) and present a distorted view of reality. They make up the core of 'false consciousness'.

13 One can interpret Marx's term 'social relations' as referring not only to interpersonal relations, but also to human relations to nature.

14 See particularly the Preface to *Capital* (Marx 1954, vol. 1).

15 This strategy of analysis is also advocated by contemporary theorists: 'An

analysis of social action might start with a model and then ask what sort of actors are needed for it' (Hollis 1987).

16 See detailed accounts of the Marxian theory of alienation in Schaff (1970); Schacht (1970); Ollman (1971); Israel (1972); Kieszelawa (1977).

17 In an early article (1924) Gramsci already says that Marxism 'is a theory of action, the theorisation of human doing, of praxis' (Paggi 1979: 125).

18 'Hegel had indeed been right – Lukács claims – to re-locate the subject-object problem within a historical setting; for only within a consistently historical perspective does it become possible to find a subject which is at one and the same time producer and product' (Connerton 1974: 170).

19 As a modern commentator explains: 'The auto-genesis of man implies that, in satisfying his biological needs through his contact with nature, man also develops new material wants as well as the possibilities of their fulfillment. Human needs are thus historical, not naturalistic, and the never-ending pursuit of their creation and satisfaction underlies historical development' (Femia 1987: 114).

Chapter 4   Ontology of the constructed world

1 I use the same strategy in a book of this title (Sztompka 1979), and the discussion in this chapter follows some ideas from Part IV of that volume, pp. 241–344.

2 It is an interesting question how this perception itself evolves from some early, relatively stable or stagnant 'societies without history' to modern societies pervaded with 'historicity' (Giddens 1984: 203). But it was certainly well developed when sociology entered the stage in the early nineteenth century. In fact sociology may be treated, at least in part, as an intellectual response to this spreading perception.

3 It is closely akin to narrow empiricism and presentism – two attitudes reigning in sociological research for the best part of the twentieth century.

4 I give an extensive account of the various meta-theoretical formulations, and theoretical applications of both standpoints elsewhere (1979, ch. 7).

5 I emphasize 'ontological', because the standpoints are very often phrased in a methodological mode. Then the real issue is not 'existence' but the possibility of 'reduction', whether the concepts and propositions about social wholes can or cannot be derived (by definitional or deductive means) from concepts and propositions about individuals and their actions. Here I am not concerned with this methodological variety of the dispute (I discuss it extensively in my earlier book (1979, ch. 3).

6 This change of perspective is already clearly visible in various branches of science in the fifties and sixties. The properties and regularities of the objects studied are found to originate not so much in the inherent character of the materials out of which those objects are built, but rather in the arrangement or organization of their components. Conversely, the properties and regularities of components are derived from their position within wider, more comprehensive networks of relationships – the external structure. Wittgenstein

(1953) advised scientists to pay attention to the network, the geometry of arrangement, rather than to the immanent characteristics of the things that the network encompasses. Von Bertalanffy put forward a similar directive: 'In the last resort we must think in terms of elements in mutual interaction' (1968: 45).

7 By way of illustration, the social structure is defined by various authors as: 'organized set of social relationships in which members of the society or group are variously implicated' (Merton 1957 [1949]: 216), 'organization of relationships' (Giddens 1971: 67), 'definable articulation, an ordered arrangement of parts' (Nadel 1969: 7), 'pattern, i.e. observable uniformity of action or operation' (Levy 1952: 57), 'the patterned arrangements of role-sets, status-sets and status-sequences' (Merton 1957 [1949]: 370), 'essential, deep, underlying conditions' (Allen 1975: 194), 'the arrangement of the parts which controls much of the variance in the phenomena' (Goode 1975: 74), 'relations among groups and individuals that find expression in their behavior' (Blau 1974: 1).

8 'Organicism' of a less critical variety, claiming that society is an organism, and human individuals its cells, would be the best embodiment of this assumption.

9 It is akin to Hegel's vision of history, as ontologically distinct from the arena of actual human conduct.

10 This is a paraphrase of the famous statement by Gellner concerning history: 'History is *about* chaps. It does not follow that its explanations are always in terms of chaps. Societies are what people do, but social scientists are not biographers *en grande série*' (Gellner 1968 [1956]: 268).

11 Notice that it is independent of any specific theoretical orientation, and particularly is not limited to those 'schools' which introduced the term 'actor' itself, like structural functionalism, or the theory of action. I claim that all sociological approaches have to treat the individual as an actor, whether they adopt the term or not, and whether or not they treat action as their central concern.

12 The reader may find it in my earlier book (1979, ch. 6).

13 Normally written with a capital 'H'.

14 For more detailed discussion of these two modes of freedom see, for example, Nagel 1966, Berlin 1980, Suchting 1972, Addis 1968.

15 The fact that they can considerably enlarge their capacities by the 'prosthesis' of technology does not change the essence of this natural limitation.

16 Notice that the normative delimitation of the field of possibilities always works in this fashion. There is only a certain, quite variable likelihood that people will obey the laws, morals or customs. All of them disobey at least sometimes, and some – known as deviants – most of the time. People can always say 'no', even to strongly sanctioned rules, and they can always 'act otherwise' than normatively expected.

17 I address some of these 'epistemological dilemmas' elsewhere (1979, chs 4 and 5). Probably the most pointed description of the riddle is given by Hollis, who compares the situation to 'weather forecasting in a world where forecasts affect the weather' (Hollis 1987: 99).

18 Other terms used to describe this dilemma are 'materialism' and 'idealism'. They have a long philosophical tradition, and may carry connotations

irrelevant in the present context. Therefore we choose a more neutral pair: 'objectivism' and 'subjectivism'.

19 Or in other words: 'Information on what is going to happen puts a future-oriented animal such as man into a different choice situation' (Stinchcombe 1975: 21).

Chapter 5 The model of social becoming

1 Here we follow closely the suggestion of Marx and 'activist Marxism' as interpreted in ch. 3.

2 If, for a moment, we think of agents as individual people (remembering that in our definition this category comprises concrete groups and collectivities as well), this means that the army is more than soldiers, a corporation more than all those employed, and Poland more than all Poles.

3 Again, if for the sake of simplicity we think of agents as human individuals, this is grasped well by the observation that humans are never fully and completely socialized; they can deviate, innovate, rebel, evade structural constraints etc. (see Wrong 1961).

4 In schematic form: If actions of type 'A' prevail, then future actions are also apt to belong to type 'A'.

5 Schematically: If stage 'A' is reached, then stage 'B' is likely to follow.

6 The mechanism of self-amplification is often operative in such cases (see: Maruyama 1963).

7 To put it schematically: If 'A' occurs, 'C' cannot follow immediately, but must be preceded by 'B'.

8 In the final analysis the dynamics of structures are always derivative from the actions people take, but it is an aggregated effect going beyond the meaning, purposes, intentions and expectations of the actors.

9 There is a close parallel to this in the famous body–mind problem in philosophy and psychology. There are no human bodies without mind, and there are no free-floating minds not anchored in bodies. At the same time one does not reduce to the other; mind is something more than a bodily trait, and bodies have a corporeal nature not dissolving in mind.

10 Following our analogy, a similar solution may be offered to the mind–body problem: mind and body are completely fused in each person and in actions undertaken by human individuals. Human, individual reality consists of personal events (actions) in which various admixtures of those inseparable ingredients manifest themselves.

11 It does not mean that, for analytical purposes, one or another aspect cannot be 'bracketed' and the remaining one studied in abstraction from the complexity. In fact we shall follow this heuristic strategy in the discussion that follows, but with a full recognition that it is merely a heuristic method to approach the integral, multidimensional social fabric, both agential and structural, in any of its real manifestations.

12 Of course I have in mind *social events*, as opposed to natural events, occurring without any human intervention, even though sometimes relevant for human

populations (rainfalls, hurricanes, earthquakes, floods, volcanic eruptions, climatic changes etc.).

13 Compare three statements: 'Czechoslovakia has awoken to the struggle for freedom and democracy'; 'Czechs have developed pro-democratic commitments and demonstrate in Wenceslas Square in Prague; the Popular Front is calling for a change of government'; 'There are insurmountable tensions and contradictions in the structure of the Czechoslovakian economy and polity, producing stagnation.' The first statement is about agency and praxis; it summarizes the partial accounts about agents (given in the second statement) and structures (given in the third statement). Agents (Czechs and their organizations) in the structural conditions (of stagnant economy and polity) produce overal social potentiality (agency) for certain praxis (readiness to fight for democracy, turning into actual struggle). It is only when we combine the two, that an adequate account of what happened in Czechoslovakia in the autumn of 1989 appears. Each of the actual social events is understandable only in this double, merged context: of agents' actions and structural conditions.

14 I have referred to this process in a more concrete context as 'double morphogenesis' (Sztompka 1987). Archer calls it the 'morphogenesis of the agency' (1989).

15 There may be a suspicion that it requires teleological thinking in terms of some mechanism of self-regulation or directive organization (Sztompka 1974a), but this is not the case. We shall show later that a normal causal interpretation will do provided that the historical extension of social becoming is allowed.

16 Marion Levy makes a similar distinction by opposing 'human heredity' to 'nonhuman environment' (1952: 155).

17 In the ironic formulation of Harre and Secord, the model of man should at least be 'anthropomorphic' (Harre and Secord 1972).

18 The limits put on the field by nature are hard, material. The limits imposed by consciousness may be treated as soft, ideological. This does not mean that the latter cannot exert extremely strong constraints on the agency. The history of totalitarian regimes, dogmatic despotisms, religious fundamentalisms etc. shows to what extent people may be enslaved by ruling doctrines and ideologies. The phenomenon variously described as 'captive mind' (Milosz 1953), 'thought control' (Koestler 1941) or 'third-dimensional power' (Lukes 1978) clearly refers to this kind of constraint.

19 It occurs in all kinds of praxis, including everyday conduct, but there are some domains of praxis directly oriented to this task. In modern society it is of course science.

20 It is not static only in the most trivial sense that it recognizes some movement within social reality. This is not seriously doubted by any student of society, irrespective of theoretical orientation. The acknowledgement of movement does not make the model dynamic. Something more is required.

21 Therefore a fruitful procedure for the science of history is a variant of 'counterfactual method', namely the search for abandoned historical opportunities: what could have happened if other decisions and choices had been taken at crucial junctures of the historical process by strategically located agents?

22 To drive difficult points home organic analogies have always proved useful

189

for sociologists. Let us think of a dog. Social functioning is comparable to his breathing, social change to his waking up and jumping on my couch, historical change to his growth from a little puppy to a huge beast. The change we are considering now is comparable to evolutionary mutation, when my dog's ancestors reportedly emerged from fish.

23 Even the advocates of planning speak of the necessity to 'plan for spontaneity', to anticipate randomness and to predict the possibility of the unpredictable (Himmelstrand 1981).

24 We introduced this assumption in ch. 4 under the name INDIVIDUALISM₁ and treated it is as a core component of the standpoint of 'structuralism'.

25 I am drawing from many sources, but mostly from the tradition of humanism, and its modern expression in the work of the young Marx and the activist Marxism of Gramsci and Lukács.

26 To those who have any doubts concerning inherent human creativeness, I would recommend a tour of the Louvre, Prado, Ermitage, Vatican or the British Museum. In places like these I have always been overwhelmed by the incredible richness of human creation, the traces of that universal and compulsive drive toward creative expression.

27 Is it not indicative that the idea of self-transcendence – overcoming barriers, fighting obstacles, breaking through limitations – is such a pervasive cultural theme appearing time and again in various formulations such as 'achievement motivation', 'reaching toward new frontiers', 'Faustian quest', 'conquest of space', 'striving for fulfilment', 'unended quest' (Popper 1982) etc.? It is grasped in all its paradoxical ambivalence in the definition of unhappiness attributed to G. B. Shaw: 'not to have one's heart's desire and to have it'.

28 I borrow this term from Cohen, who uses it in a similar sense in his account of Marxian theory: 'we predicate a perennial tendency to productive progress, arising out of rationality and intelligence in the context of the inclemency of nature' (1978: 155).

29 The idea of 'secondary needs' as arising when 'primary needs' are fulfilled has a long history, and seems to be an area of consensus between philosophers (Marx (see Fromm 1966)), social anthropologists (Malinowski 1960 [1944]) and psychologists (Maslow 1954).

Chapter 6 Active and passive society

1 The history of ancient Egypt is a particularly instructive example. In almost 3000 years of its existence 'it is the stability and conservative power of Egyptian civilization which is the most striking thing about it' (Roberts 1980: 83).

2 I proposed it as the elaboration of some aspects of R. K. Merton's theory in Sztompka 1986a, ch. 6, and then refined it in subsequent publications (1987, 1989).

3 For example, this has been the experience of Poland since the birth of the Solidarity movement, and of the rest of Eastern Europe in the incredible autumn of 1989.

4   For example the ban on forming associations and public manifestations, censorship etc.
5   Here the infamous system of 'nomenklatura', reserving certain privileged, managerial positions exclusively for members of the Communist Party, may be an excellent example.
6   Compare the modern institution of citizenship, which embraces all members of society in a common interactive framework, with the ancient Roman concept, excluding the majority of inhabitants (not only slaves, but also large segments of the free people), and also with all other versions of elitism, ethnic or racial discrimination etc.
7   The breaking of pluralistic ignorance is one of the crucial preconditions for active society. Will quotes T. Garton Ash as saying that 'the puncturing of the Berlin wall did for Germany what the pope's 1979 visit did for Poland: it caused an epiphany, a sudden comprehension by the people that they all felt and thought the same way. They quickly understood that they could be, collectively, a body politic, strong when acting in concert. The result in both cases was solidarity. In Poland a trade union midwifed the rebirth of a nation. In Germany the result soon will be reunification' (Will 1989: 4).
8   The famous phenomenon of 'groupthink' (Janis 1972) is the extreme example of the latter situation.

Chapter 7   Social movements: double morphogenesis

1   As opposed to history or political science, for which it has always been a central topic.
2   This idea is elaborated further by Archer (1989).
3   Presented in detail in ch. 6, and earlier in Sztompka 1986a, 1987 and 1989.
4   This concept was introduced in 1979 by Stefan Nowak in his reflections on Polish society: 'We can thus see that a kind of sociological vacuum exists between the level of the primary group and the level of national society. If we wanted to draw a gigantic "sociogram" based on human feelings about group links and identifications, then the social structure of our country would appear as a federation of primary groups, families and groups based on friendship, united in a national community which has very weak links of other types between the two levels' (1981 [1979]: 17). Another way to describe it is the atrophy of 'civil society', which normally mediates between a citizen and the state.
5   For foreign observers, the pictures of the workers receiving Holy Communion during an occupational strike, the portraits of Lech Wałesa with the image of the Virgin Mary in his lapel, and the prime minister, Tadeusz Mazowiecki, kneeling in church seem quite surprising and even incongruent. They are entirely natural in the context of Polish culture.
6   Of course, there are numerous psychological variables intervening in this process of a movement's incipience, but these fall beyond the scope of the present discussion. They are most extensively treated within so-called 'relative deprivation theories of social movements' (Davies 1962 and 1971; Gurr 1970).

7 The famous 'Simmel–Coser law' seems to operate here: 'Conflict with another group leads to the mobilization of energies of group members and hence to increased cohesion of the group' (Coser 1964, p. 95).

8 This idea has already been alluded to in ch. 6, where we were considering possible empirical indicators for the agential capacity of a whole society.

Chapter 8 Revolutions: the peak of social becoming

1 Of course we should not fall into the ethnocentric trap. The demise of the myth of revolution is neither universal nor uniform in all parts of the world. My observations are intended to fit the experience of Western culture and highly developed societies. In large areas of the Third World, some socialist societies, several underdeveloped societies etc. the myth of revolution is still very much alive. In fact, its link with strong religious or nationalist fundamentalism gives it a particularly vicious flavour. In our contemporary globalized world, the 'demonstration effect' of some recent revolutions – Libyan, Philippine, Nicaraguan, Iranian – seen so clearly on our television screens in all their tragedy and barbarism, and also in their pathos, may lead to the renewal of the myth in perverse forms (e.g. terrorism, 'action directe' etc.).

2 A particularly resonant argument for the multidimensionality of theories is given by J. Alexander (1982a).

3 This is similar to the predicament of the traditional theories of deviance, which considered crime or delinquency as totally distinct from 'normal' social behaviour and tried to construct for this area *special* theories, unrelated to general theories of human action. The breakthrough came with the realization that deviance is brought about by the same social and psychological mechanisms as the most exemplary conduct. This lesson should be carefully studied by the students of revolution.

4 This need not mean the return of the fallacy of a single 'grand theory'. The integrating job may well be done by Merton's 'theories of the middle range', not *most* general, but simply *more* general than specific concrete accounts of historical cases.

5 This is a particular segment of the Popperian Third World. Ideas and beliefs once discovered, once formulated and articulated by somebody, sometime, somewhere, remain there in a latent form, ready to be drawn upon by human actors.

6 As we remember, in the theory of social becoming it is assumed that there exists an inherent natural tendency of human societies toward self-transcendence, which derives from the 'natural' human capacity and disposition to creativity. Hence only those variables are truly problematic which relate to factors which block or suppress the revolutionary agency.

7 This is perhaps the reason why revolutions have never been predicted, and in principle seem unpredictable. Were they predictable, they would be preventable, mobilizing opponents of revolution to stop it in its tracks. Any sufficiently widespread and publicized prediction of revolution has to end as a self-defeating prophecy. The theory of revolution has to abandon predictive ambitions, or risk refutation by the reflexive logic of counteraction.

Bibliography

Abel, Theodore 1970: *The Foundation of Sociological Theory*. New York: Random House

Abrams, Philip 1982: *Historical Sociology*. Ithaca: Cornell University Press

Adamson, M. and Borgos, S. 1984: *This Mighty Dream: Social Protest Movements in the United States*. Boston: Routledge & Kegan Paul

Addis, Laird 1968: 'Historicism and historical laws of development', in: *Inquiry*, vol. 11, pp. 155-74

Addis, Laird 1969: 'The individual and the Marxist philosophy of history', in: M. Brodbeck (ed.) *Readings in the Philosophy of the Social Sciences*. New York: Macmillan, pp. 317-35

Agassi, J. 1973: 'Methodological individualism', in: J. O'Neill (ed.), *Modes of Individualism and Collectivism*. London: Heinemann, pp. 185-212

Alexander, Jeffrey C. 1982a: *Positivism, Presuppositions and Current Controversies* (vol. 1 of *Theoretical Logic in Sociology*). London: Routledge & Kegan Paul

Alexander, Jeffrey C. 1982b: *The Antinomies of Classical Thought: Marx and Durkheim* (vol. 2 of *Theoretical Logic in Sociology*). Berkeley: University of California Press

Alexander, Jeffrey C. 1983a: *The Classical Attempt at Theoretical Synthesis: M. Weber,* (vol. 3 of *Theoretical Logic in Sociology*). Berkeley: University of California Press

Alexander, Jeffrey C. 1983b: *The Modern Reconstruction of Classical Thought: Talcott Parsons* (vol. 4 of *Theoretical Logic in Sociology*). Berkeley: University of California Press

Alexander, Jeffrey C. (ed.) 1985: *Neo-functionalism*. London: Sage

Alexander, Jeffrey C. 1988a: *Action and Its Environments*. New York: Columbia University Press

Bibliography

Alexander, Jeffrey C. 1988b: 'The new theoretical movement', in: Neil J. Smelser (ed.), *Handbook of Sociology*. Newbury Park: Sage, pp. 77–102

Alexander, Jeffrey C. 1990: 'Between progress and apocalypse: social theory and the dream of reason in the twentieth century', in: J. Alexander and P. Sztompka (eds), *Rethinking Progress*, London: Unwin & Hyman, pp. 15–38

Allen, V. L. 1975: *Social Analysis: A Marxist Critique and Alternative*. London: Longman

Archer, Margaret S. 1985: 'Structuration versus morphogenesis', in: S. N. Eisenstadt and H. J. Helle (eds), *Macro-Sociological Theory*, vol. 1. London: Sage, pp. 55–88

Archer, Margaret S. 1986: 'Taking time to link structure and agency'. New Delhi: Eleventh World Congress of Sociology (mimeographed)

Archer, Margaret S. 1988: *Culture and Agency*. Cambridge: Cambridge University Press

Archer, Margaret S. 1989: 'The morphogenesis of social Agency'. Uppsala: SCASSS (Swedish Collegium for Advanced Studies in the Social Sciences) (mimeographed)

Aya, Rod 1979: 'Theories of revolution reconsidered', in: *Theory and Society*, vol. 8, no. 1, pp. 39–99

Banks, Joseph A. 1972: *The Sociology of Social Movements*. London: Macmillan

Baszkiewicz, Jan 1981: *Wolność, Równość, Własność* (Freedom, Equality, Ownership). Warsaw: Czytelnik

Bauman, Zygmunt 1989: 'Sociological responses to postmodernity', in: C. Mongardini and M. L. Maniscalco (eds), *Moderno e Postmoderno*. Rome: Bulzoni, pp. 127–52

Baumgartner, Tom, Buckley, W., Burns, T. R. and Schuster, P. 1976: 'Meta-power and the structuring of social hierarchies', in: T. R. Burns and W. Buckley (eds), *Power and Control*. Beverly Hills: Sage, pp. 215–88

Bell, Wendell and Mau, J. A. 1970: 'Images of the future: theory and research strategies', in: J. C. McKinney and E. A. Tiryakian (eds), *Theoretical Sociology*. New York: Appleton-Century-Crofts, pp. 205–34

Bell, Wendell and Mau, James A. 1971: 'Images of the future: theory and research strategies', in: W. Bell and J. A. Mau, *The Sociology of the Future*. New York: Russell Sage Foundation, pp. 6–44

Berlin, Isaiah 1980: *Concepts & Categories*. Oxford: Oxford University Press

Bernstein, Richard J. 1972: *Praxis and Action*. London: Duckworth

Bertalanffy, Ludwig von 1968: *General System Theory*. New York: George Braziller

Bhaskar, Roy 1986: *Scientific Realism & Human Emancipation*. London: Verso

Bierstedt, Robert 1981: *American Sociological Theory: A Critical History*. New York: Academic Press

Blau, Peter M. 1964: *Exchange and Power in Social Life*. New York: Wiley

Blau, Peter M. 1974: 'Focus on social structure', in: American Sociological Association, Programme of the ASA Meetings, Montreal: ASA, pp. 1–2

Blumer, Herbert 1951: 'Collective behavior', in: A. McClung Lee (ed.), *Principles of Sociology*. New York: Random House, pp. 166–222

Bibliography

Blumer, Herbert 1957: 'Collective behavior', in: J. B. Gittler, *Review of Sociology: Analysis of a Decade*. New York: Wiley

Bock, K. 1979: 'Theories of progress, development and evolution', in: T. Bottomore and R. Nisbet (eds), *A History of Sociological Analysis*. New York: Basic Books, pp. 39–80

Boulding, Kenneth E. 1964: 'The place of the image in the dynamics of society', in: G. K. Zollschan and W. Hirsch (eds), *Explorations in Social Change*. Boston: Houghton Mifflin, pp. 55–16

Brinton, Crane 1965 [1938]: *Anatomy of Revolution*. New York: Vintage Books

Buck, R. C. 1963: 'Reflexive predictions', in: *Philosophy of Science*, no. 4, pp. 359–74

Buckley, Walter 1967: *Sociology and Modern Systems Theory*. Englewood Cliffs: Prentice Hall

Burke, P. 1980: *Sociology and History*. London: Allen and Unwin

Burns, Tom 1976: *The Dialectics of Social Systems*. Olso: University of Oslo Working Papers (mimeographed)

Burns, T., Baumgartner, T. and Deville, P. 1985: *Man, Decisions, Society: The Theory of Actor-System Dynamics for Social Scientists*. New York: Gordon and Breach

Burns, Tom and Buckley, W. 1976: *Power and Control*. London: Sage

Burns, Tom R. and Flam, H. 1987: *The Shaping of Social Organization*. Beverly Hills: Sage

Chazel, François 1988: 'Sociology: from structuralist determinism to methodological individualism', in: J. Howorth, and G. Ross (eds), *Contemporary France: A Review of Interdisciplinary Studies*, vol. 2. London: Pinter Publishers, pp. 187–202

Chodak, Szymon 1973: *Societal Development*. New York: Oxford University Press

Cohen, G. A. 1978: *Karl Marx's Theory of History: A Defence*. Oxford: Clarendon Press

Collins, Randall 1981: 'On the micro-foundations of macro-sociology', in: *American Journal of Sociology*, vol. 86, pp. 984–1014

Collins, Randall 1986: 'Is 1980's sociology in the doldrums?' in: *American Journal of Sociology*, vol. 91, pp. 1336–55

Connerton, Paul 1974: 'The collective historical subject', in: *The British Journal of Sociology*, vol. 25, pp. 162–78

Cooley, Charles H. 1962 *Social Organization*. New York: Schocken Books

Cooley, Charles H. 1964 *Human Nature and the Social Order*. New York: Schocken Books

Coser, Lewis A. 1964: *The Functions of Social Conflict*. New York: Free Press

Coser, Lewis A. 1967: *Continuities in the Study of Social Conflict*. New York: Free Press

Coser, Lewis A. 1975a: 'Merton's Uses of European Sociological Tradition', in: L. A. Coser (ed.), *The Idea of Social Structure: Papers in Honor of Robert K. Merton* New York: Harcourt Brace Jovanovich, pp. 85–100

Coser, Lewis A. 1975b: 'Structure and conflict', in: P. Blau (ed.), *Approaches to the Study of Social Structure*. New York: Free Press, pp. 210–19

Bibliography

Crozier, Michel and Friedberg, Erhard 1982: *Człowiek i system: ograniczenia działania zespółowego* (Man and System: The Limits of Collective Action). Warsaw: Państwowe Wydawnictwo Ekonomiczne

Dahrendorf, Ralf 1959: *Class and Class Conflict in Industrial Society*. Stanford: Stanford University Press

Dahrendorf, Ralf 1968: *Essays in the Theory of Society*. Stanford: Stanford University Press

Dahrendorf, Ralf 1979: *Life Chances*. Chicago: University of Chicago Press

Dahrendorf, Ralf 1980: 'On representative activities', in: T. F. Gieryn (ed.), *Science and Social Structure: A Festschrift for Robert K. Merton*. New York: New York Academy of Sciences, pp. 15–27

Davies, James C. 1962: 'Toward a theory of revolution', in: *American Sociological Review*, vol. 27, pp. 5–19

Davies, James C. 1971: *When Men Revolt and Why*. New York: Free Press

Dawe, Alan 1970: 'The two sociologies', in: *The British Journal of Sociology*, vol. 21, no. 2, pp. 207–18

Dawe, Alan 1978: 'Theories of social action', in: T. B. Bottomore and R. Nisbet (eds), *A History of Sociological Analysis*. New York: Basic Books, pp. 362–417

Desroche, Henri 1979: *The Sociology of Hope*. London: Routledge & Kegan Paul

Durkheim, Emile 1972: *Selected Writings* (ed. A. Giddens). Cambridge: Cambridge University Press

Eder, Klaus 1990: 'The cultural code of modernity and the problem of nature', in: J. Alexander and P. Sztompka (eds), *Rethinking Progress*. London: Unwin & Hyman, pp. 67–88

Edwards, L. P. 1927: *The Natural History of Revolution*. Chicago: University of Chicago Press

Elias, Norbert 1978: *What is Sociology?* London: Hutchinson

Elias, Norbert 1982: *The Civilizing Process*, vols 1 and 2. Oxford: Basil Blackwell

Elias, Norbert 1987: 'The retreat of sociologists into the present', in: *Theory, Culture & Society*, vol. 4, no. 2–3, pp. 223–48

Erikson, K. T. 1971: 'Sociology and the historical perspective', in: W. Bell and J. A. Mau (eds), *The Sociology of the Future*. New York: Russell Sage

Etzioni, Amitai 1968a: *Active Society*. New York: Free Press

Etzioni, Amitai 1968b: 'Mobilization as a macrosociological conception', in: *The British Journal of Sociology*, vol. 19, no. 3, pp. 243–53

Femia, J. 1987 [1981]: *Gramsci's Political Thought*. Oxford: Clarendon Press

Ferree, Myra M. and Miller, Frederick D. 1985: 'Mobilization and meaning: toward an integration of social, psychological and resource perspectives on social movements', in: *Sociological Inquiry*, vol. 1, pp. 38–59

Fletcher, Ronald 1971: *The Making of Sociology*, vols 1–3. New York: Charles Scribner's

Freeman, Jo 1973: 'The origins of the women's liberation movement', in: *American Journal of Sociology*, vol. 78, no. 4, pp. 792–811

Freeman, Jo 1983a: 'A model for analyzing the strategic options of social movement organizations', in: J. Freeman (ed.), *Social Movements in the*

Sixties and Seventies. New York: Longman, pp. 193–210

Freeman, Jo 1983b: 'On the origins of social movements', in: J. Freeman (ed.), *Social Movements of the Sixties and Seventies*. New York: Longman, pp. 8–30

Friedrichs, Robert W. 1972: 'Dialectic sociology: toward a resolution of the current "crisis" in Western sociology', in: *British Journal of Sociology*, vol. 23, pp. 263–74

Fromm, Erich 1941: *Escape from Freedom*. New York: Holt, Rinehart and Winston

Fromm, Erich 1963 [1956]: *The Sane Society*. London: Routledge & Kegan Paul

Fromm, Erich 1966 [1951]: *Marx's Concept of Man*. New York: Ungar

Fukuyama, Francis 1989: 'The end of history?' in: *The National Interest*, Summer 1989, pp. 3–18

Garner, Roberta and Zald, M. N. 1981: '*Social movement sectors and systemic constraint: toward a structural analysis of social movements*'. Ann Arbor: Center for Research on Social Organization (Working Paper no. 238) (mimeographed)

Gellner, Ernest 1968: 'Holism versus individualism', in: M. Brodbeck (ed.), *Readings in the Philosophy of the Social Sciences*. New York: Macmillan, pp. 254–68

Gewirth, Allan 1969: 'Can men change laws of social science?' in: L. I. Krimerman (ed.), *The Nature and Scope of Social Science: A Critical Anthology*. New York: Appleton, pp. 217–27

Giddens, Anthony 1971: *Capitalism and Modern Social Theory*. Cambridge: Cambridge University Press

Giddens, Anthony 1977: *Studies in Social and Political Theory*. London: Hutchinson

Giddens, Anthony 1979: *Central Problems in Social Theory*. London: Macmillan

Giddens, Anthony 1981: *A Contemporary Critique of Historical Materialism*. London: Macmillan

Giddens, Anthony 1984: *The Constitution of Society*. Cambridge: Polity Press

Giddens, Anthony 1987: *Social Theory and Modern Sociology*. Cambridge: Polity Press

Giddens, Anthony 1989: *Sociology*. Cambridge: Polity Press

Goffman, Erving 1963: *Behavior in Public Places*. New York: Free Press

Goffman, Erving 1967: *Interaction Ritual*. Garden City: Doubleday (Anchor Books)

Goffman, Erving 1971: *Relations in Public*. New York: Harper & Row

Goldstone, Jack A. 1982: 'The comparative and historical study of revolutions', in: *Annual Review of Sociology*, vol. 8, pp. 187–207

Goode, William J. 1973: *Explorations in Social Theory*. New York: Oxford University Press

Goode, William J. 1975: 'Homans's and Merton's structural approach', in: P. M. Blau (ed.), *Approaches to the Study of Social Structure*. New York: Free Press, pp. 66–75

Gouldner, Alvin W. 1970: *The Coming Crisis of Western Sociology*. London: Heinemann

Bibliography

Gouldner, Alvin W. 1972: 'Two Marxisms'. Caracas: International Institute of Sociology (mimeographed)

Gouldner, Alvin W. 1974: 'Marxism and social theory', in: *Theory and Society*, no. 1, pp. 17-35.

Gramsci, Antonio 1971: *Selections From the Prison Notebooks*. New York: International Publishers

Gramsci, Antonio 1972: *The Modern Prince and Other Writings*. New York: International Publishers

Gurr, Ted 1970: *Why Men Rebel*. Princeton: Princeton University Press

Harre, R. and Secord, P. F. 1972: *The Explanation of Social Behaviour*. Oxford: Basil Blackwell

Himmelstrand, Ulf (ed.) 1981: *Spontaneity and Planning in Social Development*. Beverly Hills: Sage

Hollis, Martin 1977: *The Models of Man*. Cambridge: Cambridge University Press

Hollis, Martin 1987: *The Cunning of Reason*. Cambridge: Cambridge University Press

Homans, Geoge C. 1971: 'Bringing men back in', in: H. Turk and R. L. Simpson, (eds), *Institutions and Social Exchange*. Indianapolis: Bobbs-Merrill, pp. 102-16

Homans, George C. 1974: *Social Behavior: Its Elementary Forms*. New York: Harcourt Brace Jovanovich

Hook, Sidney 1955 [1943]: *The Hero in History*. Boston: Beacon Press

Israel, Joachim 1971: *Alienation*. Boston: Allyn and Bacon

Israel, Joachim 1972: 'The principle of methodological individualism and Marxian epistemology', in *Acta Sociologica*, no. 14, pp. 145-50

Janis, Irving L. 1972: *Victims of Groupthink*. Boston: Houghton-Mifflin

Jarvie, I. C. 1972: *Concepts and Society*. London: Routledge & Kegan Paul

Jenkins, J. Craig 1983: 'Resource mobilization theory and the study of social movements', in: *Annual Review of Sociology*, vol. 9, pp. 527-53

Johnson, Allan G. 1986: *Human Arrangements*. New York: Harcourt Brace Jovanovich

Johnson, Harry M. 1960: *Sociology*. New York: Harcourt Brace Jovanovich

Jones, Gareth S. 1977: 'The Marxism of the Early Lukács', in: New Left Review Editions, *Western Marxism: A Critical Reader*. London: NLB, pp. 11-60

Kelles-Krauz, Kazimierz 1962: *Pisma Wybrane* (Collected Works). Warsaw: Książka i Wiedza

Kieszelawa, Warłam W. 1977: *Humanizm rzeczywisty i pozorny* (Humanism: real and spurious). Warsaw: Kśiążka i Wiedza

Killian, L. M. 1964: 'Social movements', in: R. E. L. Faris (ed.), *Handbook of Modern Sociology*. Chicago: Rand McNally

Klandermans, Bert 1984: 'Mobilization and participation: social-psychological expansions of resource mobilization theory', in: *American Sociological Review*, vol. 49, pp. 583-600

Koestler, Arthur 1940: *Darkness at Noon*, translated by Daphne Hardy, 1975 [1941] New York: Bantam Books.

Kołakowski, Leszek 1976: *Główne nurty marksizmu, tom I* (Main Trends of Marxism, Paris: Institut Littéraire

Bibliography

Kołakowski, Leszek 1978: *Main Currents of Marxism*, vols 1–3. Oxford: Clarendon Press

Kuhn, Thomas S. 1970: *The Structure of Scientific Revolutions*. Chicago: University of Chicago Press

Lang, K. and Lang, G. 1961: *Collective Dynamics*. New York: Crowell

Lauer, Robert H. (ed.) 1976: *Social Movements and Social Change*. Carbondale: Southern Illinois University Press

Lenski, Gerhard E. 1966: *Power and Privilege*. New York: McGraw-Hill

Levy, Marion 1952: *The Structure of Society*. Princeton: Princeton University Press

Lichtman, Richard 1967: 'Indeterminacy in the social sciences', in: *Inquiry*, vol. 10, pp. 139–50

Lloyd, Christopher 1988 [1986]: *Explanation in Social History*. Oxford: Basil Blackwell

Loomis, C. P. and Loomis, Z. K. 1961: *Modern Social Theories*. Princeton: Van Nostrand

Luhman, R. 1982: *The Sociological Outlook*. Belmont: Wadsworth

Lukács, Gyorgy 1971: *History and Class Consciousness*. Cambridge, Mass.: MIT Press

Lukács, Gyorgy 1982–5: *Wprowadzenie do ontologii bytu społecznego* (Introduction to the Ontology of the Social Object), vols 1–5. Warsaw: PWN (Polish Scientific Publishers)

Lukes, Steven 1974: *Power: A Radical View*. London: Macmillan

Lukes, Steven 1978: 'Power and authority', in: T. B. Bottomore and R. Nisbet (eds), *A History of Sociological Analysis*. New York: Basiç Books, pp. 663–76

Lukes, Steven 1985: *Marxism and Morality*. Oxford: Clarendon Press

McAdam, Doug, McCarthy, J. D. and Zald, M. N. 1988: 'Social movements', in: Neil J. Smelser (ed.), *Handbook of Sociology*. Newbury Park: Sage, pp. 695–738

McCarthy, John D. and Zald, Mayer N. 1976: 'Resource mobilization and social movements: a partial theory', in: *American Journal of Sociology*, vol. 82, no. 6, pp. 1212–41

McEwen, William P. 1963: *The Problem of Social-Scientific Knowledge*. Totowa: Bedminster Press

McLellan, David 1971: *The Thought of Karl Marx*. New York: Harper & Row

McMurtry, J. 1978: *The Structure of Marx's World-View*. Princeton: Princeton University Press

McRae, Donald G. 1974: *Max Weber*. New York: Viking Press

Malinowski, Bronisław 1960 [1944]: *A Scientific Theory of Culture*. London: Oxford University Press

Mandelbaum, Maurice 1948: 'A critique of philosophies of history', in *Journal of Philosophy*, vol. 45, pp. 365–78

Mandelbaum, Maurice 1966: 'Societal laws', in: W. H. Dray (ed.), *Philosophical Analysis and History*. New York: Harper & Row, pp. 330–46

Mandelbaum, Maurice 1969a: 'Societal laws', in: L. I. Krimerman (ed.),

Bibliography

The Nature and Scope of Social Science: A Critical Anthology. New York: Appleton-Century-Crofts, pp. 642–50

Mandelbaum, Maurice 1969b: 'Societal facts', in: L. I. Krimerman (ed.), *The Nature and Scope of Social Science.* New York: Appleton Century Crofts, pp. 632–41

Mann, Michael 1986: *The Sources of Social Power.* Cambridge: Cambridge University Press

Martindale, Don 1964: 'The roles of humanism and scientism in the evolution of sociology', in: G. K. Zollschan and W. Hirsch (eds), *Explorations in Social Change.* Boston: Houghton Mifflin, pp. 452–90

Maruyama, Mogoroh 1963: 'The second cybernetics: deviation-amplifying mutual causal processes', in: *General Systems*, vol. 8, pp. 233–41

Marx, Gary T. and Wood, James L. 1975: 'Strands of theory and research in collective behavior', in: *Annual Review of Sociology*, vol. 1, pp. 363–428

Marx, Karl 1953: *Grundrisse der Kritik der politischen Oekonomie* (Outlines of the Critique of Political Economy). Berlin: Akademie Verlag

Marx, Karl 1964: *Selected Writings in Sociology and Social Philosophy.* New York: McGraw-Hill

Marx, Karl 1971: *The Grundrisse* (edited and translated by D. McLellan). New York: Harper & Row

Marx, Karl 1975: *Early Writings* (translated by Rodney Livingstone and Gregor Benton, introduced by Lucio Colletti). London: Penguin Books

Marx, K. and Engels, F. 1960: *Dzieła* (Works). Warsaw: Książka i Wiedza

Marx, K. and Engels, F. 1962: *Selected Works.* Moscow: Foreign Languages Publishing House

Marx, Karl and Engels, F. 1968: *Selected Works.* Moscow: Progress Publishers

Marx, K. and Engels, F. 1975: *O materializmie historycznym* (On Historical Materialism). Warsaw: Książka i Wiedza

Marx, K. and Engels, F. 1985 [1848]: *The Communist Manifesto.* New York: Pathfinder Press

Maslow, Abraham 1954: *Motivation and Personality.* New York: Harper & Row

Merrington, John 1977: 'Theory and Practice in Gramsci's Marxism', in: New Left Review Editions, *Western Marxism: A Critical Reader.* London: NLB, pp. 140–75

Merton, Robert K. 1957: *Social Theory and Social Structure.* Glencoe: Free Press

Merton, Robert K. 1964: 'Anomie, anomia, and social interaction: contexts of deviant behavior', in: M. Clinard (ed.), *Anomie and Deviant Behavior: Discussion and Critique.* New York: Free Press, pp. 213–42

Merton, Robert K. 1967: *On Theoretical Sociology.* New York: Free Press

Merton, Robert K. 1968: *Social Theory and Social Structure.* New York: Free Press

Merton, Robert K. 1973a: 'The Matthew Effect in Science', in: R. K. Merton (ed. N. Storer), *The Sociology of Science: Theoretical and Empirical Investigations.* Chicago: University of Chicago Press, pp. 439–59

Merton, Robert K. 1973b: 'The perspectives of insiders and outsiders', in Merton 1973a, pp. 99–136

Merton, Robert K. 1976: 'The unanticipated consequences of social action', in: R. K. Merton, *Sociological Ambivalence.* New York: Free Press, pp. 145–55

Bibliography

Merton, Robert K. 1979: 'Foreword', in: E. Garfield, *Citation Indexing: Its Theory and Application in Science, Technology and Humanities*. New York: John Wiley, pp. vii–ix

Merton, Robert K. 1982: *Social Research and the Practicing Professions*. Cambridge, Mass.: Abt Books

Merton, Robert K. 1984: 'Socially expected durations: a case study of concept formation in sociology', in: W. W. Powell and R. Robbins (eds), *Conflict and Consensus: A Festschrift for Lewis Coser*. New York: Free Press, pp. 262–83

Merton, Robert K. 1987: 'Three fragments from a sociologist's notebooks', in *Annual Review of Sociology*, vol. 13, pp. 1–28

Merton, Robert K. and Kendall, P. 1944: 'The Boomerang Response', in: *Channels (BBC)*, vol. 21, no. 7, pp. 1–7

Mills, C. Wright 1959: *Sociological Imagination*. New York: Oxford University Press

Milosz, Czesław 1953: *The Captive Mind*. New York: Alfred Knopf

Mongardini, Carlo 1990: 'The decadence of modernity: the delusions of progress and the search for historical consciousness', in: J. Alexander and P. Sztompka (eds), *Rethinking Progress*. London: Unwin & Hyman, pp. 53–66

Moore, Barrington 1966: *Social Origins of Dictatorship and Democracy*. Boston: Beacon Press

Moore, Wilbert E. 1963: *Social Change*. Englewood Cliffs: Prentice Hall

Morris, Aldon and Herring, C. 1985: 'Theory and Research in Social Movements: A Critical Review'. Ann Arbor: University of Ann Arbor (mimeographed)

Mouffe, Chantal 1979: 'Hegemony and Ideology in Gramsci', in: C. Mouffe (ed.), *Gramsci and Marxist Theory*. London: Routledge & Kegan Paul, pp. 168–204

Nadel, S. F. 1969: *The Theory of Social Structure*. London: Routledge & Kegan Paul

Nagel, Ernest 1966: 'Determinism in history', in W. H. Dray (ed.) *Philosophical Analysis and History*. New York: Harper & Row, pp. 347–82

Nisbet, Robert 1969: *Social Change and History*. New York: Oxford University Press

Nisbet, Robert A. 1970: 'Developmentalism: a critical analysis', in: J. C. McKinney and E. A. Tiryakian (eds), *Theoretical Sociology*. New York: Appleton-Century-Crofts, pp. 167–204

Nisbet, Robert 1974: *The Sociology of Emile Durkheim*. New York: Oxford University Press

Nowak, Stefan 1981 [1979]: 'A Polish self-portrait', in: *Polish Perspectives*, vol. 7, pp. 13–29

Oberschall, Anthony 1973: *Social Conflict and Social Movements*. Englewood Cliffs: Prentice Hall

Oberschall, Anthony 1978: 'Theories of social conflict', in: *Annual Review of Sociology*, vol. 4, pp. 291–315

Offe, Claus 1985: 'New social movements: challenging the boundaries of

Bibliography

institutional politics', in: *Social Research*, vol. 52, no. 4, pp. 817–68

Ollman, Bertell 1975: *Alienation: Marx's Conception of Man in Capitalist Society*. Cambridge: Cambridge University Press

Ossowski, Stanisław 1957: *Struktura klasowa w społecznèj świadomości* (Class Structure in Social Consciousness). Łódź: Ossolineum

Ossowski, Stanisław 1962: *O osobliwościach nauk społecznych* (On the Peculiarities of the Social Sciences). Warsaw: PWN (Polish Scientific Publishers)

Paggi, Leonardo 1979: 'Gramsci's general theory of Marxism', in: C. Mouffe (ed.), *Gramsci and Marxist Theory*. London: Routledge & Kegan Paul, pp. 113–67

Piaget, Jean 1971: *Structuralism*. New York: Harper & Row

Piven, F. F. and Cloward, R. A. 1979: *Poor People's Movements*. New York: Vintage Books

Plamenatz, John 1975: *Karl Marx's Philosophy of Man*. Oxford: Clarendon Press

Polak, Frederik L. 1961: *The Image of the Future*, vols 1 and 2. New York: Oceana Publications

Popper, Karl R. 1964 [1957]: *The Poverty of Historicism*. New York: Harper & Row

Popper, Karl R. 1966 [1945]: *The Open Society and Its Enemies*, vol. 2: *Hegel and Marx*. London: Routledge & Kegan Paul

Popper, Karl R. 1982 [1974]: *Unended Quest. An Intellectual Autobiography*. London: Fontana/Collins

Rex, John 1969: *Key Issues in Sociological Theory*. London: Routledge & Kegan Paul

Ridgeway, Cecilia L. 1983: *The Dynamics of Small Groups*. New York: St Martin's Press

Ritzer, George 1989: 'Agency-structure and micro–macro syntheses: consensus in contemporary theorizing?' Uppsala: SCASSS (Swedish Collegium for Advanced Studies in the Social Sciences) (mimeographed)

Roberts, J. M. 1980: *The Pelican History of the World*. Harmondsworth: Penguin Books

Rubinstein, David 1981: *Marx and Wittgenstein*. London: Routledge & Kegan Paul

Rudé G. 1964: *The Crowd in History*. New York: Wiley

Rybicki, Paweł 1979: *Struktura społecznego świata* (The Structure of the Social World). Warsaw: Państwowe Wydawnictwo Naukowe

Schacht, Richard 1970: *Alienation*. Garden City: Doubleday-Anchor

Schaff, Adam 1970: *Marxism and the Human Individual*. New York: McGraw-Hill

Schneider, Louis 1971: 'Dialectic in sociology', in: *American Sociological Review*, vol. 36, pp. 667–78

Segerstedt, Torgny T. 1966: *The Nature of Social Reality*. Stockholm: Svenska Bokforlaget

Shils, Edward 1981: *Tradition*. Chicago: University of Chicago Press

Skidmore, W. L. 1975: *Sociology's Models of Man*. New York: Gordon & Breach

Bibliography

Skockpol, Theda 1979: *States and Social Revolutions*. Cambridge: Cambridge University Press

Skockpol, Theda (ed.) 1984: *Vision and Method in Historical Sociology*. Cambridge: Cambridge University Press

Smelser, Neil J. 1962: *Theory of Collective Behavior*. New York: Free Press

Stinchcombe, Arthur L. 1975: 'Merton's theory of social structure', in: L. A. Coser (ed.), *The Idea of Social Structure: Papers in Honor of Robert K. Merton*. New York: Harcourt Brace Jovanovich, pp. 11–34

Suchting, W. A. 1972: 'Marx, Popper, and "historicism"', in: *Inquiry*, vol. 15, pp. 235–66

Swingewood, Allan 1975: *Marx and Modern Social Theory*. London: Macmillan Press

Szacki, Jerzy 1980: *Spotkania z Utopią* (Encounters with Utopia). Warsaw: Iskry

Sztompka, Piotr 1973: *Teoria i wyjaśnienie* (Theory and Explanation). Warsaw: PWN (Polish Scientific Publishers)

Sztompka, Piotr 1974a: *System and Function*. New York: Academic Press

Sztompka, Piotr 1974b: *'The logic of sociological laws'* Toronto: ISA World Congress of Sociology (also printed in Polish in *Studia Socjologiczne*, no. 3, pp. 51–86)

Sztompka, Piotr 1979: *Sociological Dilemmas*. New York: Academic Press

Sztompka, Piotr 1982: 'Dynamika ruchu odnowy w świetle teorii zachowania zbiorowego' ('The dynamics of social renewal in the light of collective behavior theory'), in: *Studia Socjologiczne*, no. 3–4, pp. 69–93

Sztompka, Piotr 1983a: 'Social development: the dialectics of theory and action', in: *Reports on Philosophy*, vol. 7, pp. 79–98

Sztompka, Piotr 1983b: 'Zmiana strukturalna społeczeństwa: szkic teorii' ('The structural change of society: a theoretical sketch'), in: *Studia Socjologiczne*, no. 2, pp. 125–51

Sztompka, Piotr 1984a: 'On the change of social laws', in: *Reports on Philosophy*, vol. 8, pp. 33–40

Sztompka, Piotr 1984b: 'The global crisis and the reflexiveness of the social system', in: *International Journal of Comparative Sociology*, vol. 25, no. 1–2, pp. 45–58

Sztompka, Piotr 1986a: *Robert K. Merton: An Intellectual Profile*. London: Macmillan

Sztompka, Piotr 1986b: 'The renaissance of historical orientation in sociology', in: *International Sociology*, vol. 1, no. 3, pp. 321–37

Sztompka, Piotr 1987: 'Social movements: structures in *statu nascendi*', in: *Polish Sociological Bulletin*, no. 2, pp. 5–26

Sztompka, Piotr 1988 [1984]: 'The social functions of defeat', in: L. Kriesberg and B. Misztal (eds), *Research in Social Movements, Conflicts and Change*, vol. 10. Greenwich, Conn.: JAI Press, pp. 183–92

Sztompka, Piotr 1989: 'Pojęcie struktury społecznej: próba generalizacji' ('The concept of social structure: tentative generalization'), in: *Studia Socjologiczna*, no. 3, pp. 51–66

Tarrow, Sidney 1984: *Struggling to Reform: Social Movements and Policy Change During Cycles of Protest*. Ithaca: Cornell University Center for

Bibliography

International Studies (Occasional Paper no. 15)

Taylor, Stan 1984: *Social Science and Revolutions*. London: Macmillan

Tilly, Charles 1970: 'The analysis of a counter-revolution', in: Joseph R. Gusfield (ed.), *Protest, Reform, and Revolt*. New York: John Wiley, pp. 47–67

Tilly, Charles 1978: *From Mobilization to Revolution*. Reading, Mass.: Addison-Wesley

Tilly, Charles 1981: *As Sociology Meets History*. New York: Academic Press

Tilly, Charles 1984: *Big Structures, Large Processes, Huge Comparisons*. New York: Russell Sage Foundation

Tilly, Charles, Tilly, L. and Tilly, R. 1975: *The Rebellious Century* (1830–1930). Cambridge, Mass.: Harvard University Press

Tocqueville, Alexis de 1955 [1856]: *The Old Regime and the French Revolution*. New York: Doubleday Anchor

Topolski, Jerzy 1968: *Metodologia historii* (Methodology of History). Warsaw: PWN (Polish Scientific Publishers)

Topolski, Jerzy 1974: 'Aktywistyczna koncepcja procesu dziejowego' ('Activist conception of the historical process'), in: J. Kmita (ed.), *Metodologiczne implikacje epistemologii marksistowskiej* (Methodological Implications of Marxian Epistemology). Warsaw: PWN (Polish Scientific Publishers)

Topolski, Jerzy 1978: *Rozumienie historii* (Understanding History). Warsaw: PIW (Polish Editorial Institute)

Topolski, Jerzy 1983: *Teoria wiedzy historycznej* (Theory of Historical Knowledge). Poznań: Wydawnictwo Poznańskie (Poznań Publishers)

Touraine, Alain 1977: *The Self-Production of Society*. Chicago: University of Chicago Press

Touraine, Alain 1985: 'Social movements and social change', in: Orlando Fals Borda (ed.), *The Challenge of Social Change*. London: Sage, pp. 77–92

Tucker, D. B. F. 1980: *Marxism and Individualism*. Oxford: Basil Blackwell

Turner, Ralph H. 1988: 'Social movement theory: bridging the gap between collective behavior and resource mobilization'. Los Angeles: UCLA (mimeographed)

Turner, R. and Killian, L. M. 1972 [1957]: *Collective Behavior*. Englewood Cliffs: Prentice Hall

Will, George F. 1989: 'The quadrille of nations', in: *Newsweek*, 18 December 1989, p. 4

Wittgenstein, Ludwig 1953: *Philosophical Investigations*. New York: Macmillan

Wolf, E. R. 1969: *Peasant Wars of the Twentieth Century*. New York: Harper & Row

Wrong, Dennis 1961: 'The oversocialized conception of man in modern sociology', in: *American Sociological Review*, no. 2, pp. 183–93

Zald, M. and Useem, B. 1982: 'Movements and countermovements: loosely coupled conflict'. Ann Arbor: CRSO Working Paper no. 276 (mimeographed)

Zeitlin, Irving M. 1981: 'Karl Marx: aspects of his social thought and their contemporary relevance', in: B. Rhea (ed.), *The Future of the Sociological Classics*. London: Allen & Unwin, pp. 1–15

Bibliography

Znaniecki, Florian 1971: *Nauki o kulturze* (The Sciences of Culture). Warsaw: PWN (Polish Scientific Publishers)

Zurcher, L. A. and Snow, D. A. 1981: 'Collective behavior: social movements', in: M. Rosenberg and R. H. Turner (eds), *Social Psychology: Sociological Perspectives*. New York: Basic Books, pp. 447–82

205

Index

HM 101 .S989 1991
Sztompka, Piotr.
Society in action